Ron Biela

The Music
of Emotion

ISBN 978-1-7325463-1-8

Published January 2023

CONTENTS

Prelude: A Different Approach to Emotion

EMOTION has been talked, written and thought about so much, we think we know what it is. I think we've been wrong.

I'm not sure why it's so hard for us to change our ideas about emotion as some-thing that's separate from thinking or rationality, that comes over us in named states, that is more often than not a problem. I'm not sure why it isn't obvious that emotion is more like a flow of experience than a state, a process that infuses our perceptions and interpretations, that resounds through us as the soundtrack of the meanings of each moment we live. I hope to allow you a different way to relate to what's known as emotion, that connects you to its sensations as the music of the songs, musical theater or opera you live.

I've practiced psychotherapy or, my preferred term, counseling, for 25 years, dealing with a wide range of people's emotional lives. I'm not sure how long it took me to realize that emotions aren't what the mental health professions say they are. In fact, most practitioners I've talked to don't have a clear idea of what human emotion is. They'll repeat jargon like "depression," "affect regulation," or symptoms of "mood disorders," or, if they've read or heard of parts of the brain, they'll mention the limbic system, dopamine, serotonin and other flavors. It's amazing that the caring professions don't get beyond the labels and words and symptoms. Most commonly, psychiatrists, therapists and counselors depict human emotion as labeled states that, with the right techniques (or pills) can be manipulated, alleviated and managed. You won't hear them talk about living with passion, facing adversity, how each moment can be experienced in subtle, vibrant, deeply meaningful and beautiful ways, while each moment is affected by one's past, one's culture and by the creative presence of nature naturing.

If you're seeing a mental health practitioner for professional services or otherwise know one, simply ask what he or she means by "emotion." If the professional repeats some vague phrases or jargon about the brain, as noted above, please ask whether there's ever a moment that isn't experienced as an ever-shifting flow of energy connected to your meanings in life, whether and how the flow moves beyond the labeled categories of anxiety, depression, etc., whether emotion is all in the brain. Ask how emotion can move you to joyous committed action or demoralized despair. This can prepare you for what'll be discussed in this book. Questions I've considered most important are: Can I be present with the flow of emotion without limiting it to names? Can I realize emotion's presence in every thought, how it interfuses meaning every moment?

How does the quality of my experience and life relate to the quality of emotion playing in me? How do I create that quality? I would suggest to the professional and anyone else that emotion is playing the vibrant or sluggish meaning of every moment on the instrument of the mind and body, just as music is played according to composed or improvised notes and chords.

The flow of emotion can't be captured by what professionally and popularly are labeled as words for certain states. I describe this flow with the metaphor of music, not to capture it or manipulate it, but to realize this living process can be played in an almost infinite range of qualitative tones, rhythms, pitches, intensities and bodily equilibria that connect with our thinking and creativity to yield meanings that are felt differently by each individual at each moment. We can play this music with the discipline and skill to be virtuosos in the art of living.

This book isn't meant to set up yet another theory of emotion. The explanations and theories can never fully contain or tame the reality of emotional experience, which has inexhaustible forms, like music. I consciously employ metaphors to evoke the reader's imaginative associations rather than illusions of certainty. Metaphors are commonly considered merely literary and not direct knowledge. In the next section, I go into a bit more detail about metaphorical concepts and conceptual blending. Scholarly investigations have given insights into how all of our concepts, even the most scientific, are metaphorical in nature.

How metaphorical concepts tell us about reality

The method I'll use to explore emotion as music is based on "metaphorical concepts" or "conceptual metaphors." The terms are used in this book interchangeably, as they both mean "the understanding of one idea, or conceptual domain, in terms of another" (from the Wikipedia entry, "Conceptual Metaphor"). Although the method is, for me, more poetic than conventionally scientific, it's based on work developed by cognitive scientists, linguists, psychologists, philosophers and literary scholars over the last few decades.

In their landmark book, *Metaphors We Live By*, the cognitive linguist George Lakoff and philosopher Mark Johnson showed how all knowledge is based on metaphorical concepts. Even knowledge articulated in what appears to be purely objective, abstract or scientific terms is constructed with metaphors, as human thinking is formed in metaphors—a cognitive framing of reality influenced by being embodied. All thinking, all reasoning involves perceiving through our fundamental physical connection to reality. As Lakoff puts it, "Our brains take their input from the rest of our bodies. What our bodies are like and how they function in the world thus structures the very concepts we can use to think. We cannot think just anything—only what our embodied brains permit."[1]

Related to the scholarly work on metaphorical concepts or conceptual metaphors is that on conceptual blending, primarily established by the cognitive linguists Gilles Fauconnier and Mark Turner. They examined how we can form ideas—including scientific and social concepts—through a blending of different

[1]   https://www.edge.org/3rd_culture/lakoff/lakoff_p1.html

concepts from different "mental spaces" in different neuronal groups of the mind's complex networks. Blending concepts from different groups of neural connections can produce a new emergent idea. The idea I present in this book is such an emergent concept. Emotion as music is the blend of the mind-body's energies with qualities of music. I experience energies, flowing through my body, infusing my mind's perceptions and interpretation of each moment, not as notes heard or as neurochemistry, but as rhythms and pitches of sensations, themes of meaning flowing like melodies, chords, concertos.

One could object that this approach to emotion isn't objective. Lakoff wrote about the "objectivist paradigm," which presents reality according to "set-theoretical models"—i.e., as objects and properties, independent of human experience, grouped in sets. He showed how the objectivist neatly categorizes phenomena: "the world consists of

entities

the properties of those entities

the relations holding among those entities."[2]

This "God's Eye View" is often the favored perspective of writers who explain just about anything. The objectivist paradigm follows from our most fundamental, flawed way of (metaphorically) perceiving the world: as a container of objects mechanically related. Lakoff shows how the objectivist instinct to categorize fails to render an accurate or adequate account of reality. For instance, modern biology recognizes the complexity of life beyond the earlier science, upsetting rigidly formed categories with the dynamic processes of "variation

---

[2]   *Women, Fire and Dangerous Things: What categories reveal about the mind* (Chicago: University of Chicago Press, 1987), p. 159

within species, adaptation to the environment, gene pools, etc."[3] The usual descriptions of emotion are objectivist, separating emotions into properties (depressed, sad, anxiety, etc.) But this follows a metaphorical model—i.e., emotions and moods are states, discretely categorized, distinctly grouped in a contained set (of feelings), contained in other boxes (the nervous system). Treating emotion as a set of objects or states misrepresents the way emotion is continually shifting in dynamically occurring variations, arising from diverse sources that aren't in separate containers. Defining emotion with labels gives the illusion of separate states, ignoring how feelings continually flow and fluctuate in qualities that may be subtle or intense, connected with and influenced by flows of the physical, cultural and social environment. Rather than being bounded in a state, we are responding to phenomena with qualities that we can affect if we're aware of the flows around and from us and how we can improvise and compose with styles, movements, harmony or dissonance that can be most engaging and meaningful.

Lakoff and Johnson's work has shown how communicating about reality isn't simply about categorizing and fitting words to the categories, but "is a matter of imagination and a matter of constructing coherence."[4] That is my aim in using the metaphor of music: to open up a way of relating to emotional experience without the objectivist illusions of neatly distinct categories and smug conclusions. I suggest a way people can coherently relate to their energies of emotion, with all its dynamism and

---

[3]   Id. p. 195

[4]   George Lakoff and Mark Johnson, *Metaphors We Live By* (Chicago: University of Chicago Press, 1980), p. 227

potential, through the metaphor of a live music played by each person's instrument of body and mind.

Playing with the metaphor

The metaphorical concepts[5] I present are not meant to be truths superior to other truths, which would be a form of objectivism. This book on the music of emotion is offered to show an alternative to the ways of turning emotions and persons into objects, mechanisms and categories, which I've found to be pervasive in current teachings and practices of the mental health professions. My hope is that each individual discovers her or his own ways of allowing feeling and passion as wondrous connections to everyday living. The metaphor of music may allow greater ability to open to what is continually changing and meaningful in felt experience and may allow the energies to carry one into fulfillment of her or his potential, as part of a symphony of the whole of the social and natural world. As Laura Quinney puts it: "Subjectivity is illuminated; the subject begins to experience his or her own subjectivity differently, sees the possibility of a new way of existing as a subject, and strives for it."[6]

I invite you to consider emotion as musical qualities of reality, rather than a defined state of mind. I'm not after some superior theory but hope you can experiment with the metaphor to open to emotion's mystery and potential. Consider how, when a loved one dies, emotion plays in you in so many

---

[5] As mentioned above, the term, metaphorical concept, always includes what's meant by the cognitive linguists' term, "conceptual metaphors."

[6] Laura Quinney, *William Blake on Self and Soul*, (Cambridge: Harvard University Press, 2010), p. 45

tones and textures, from music composed by memories, your own vulnerabilities, harmonies, dissonances and transcendent inspirations. The music may arise from sources in you that are painful, scary, loving. The music may play as requiems, songs or hymns.

I wouldn't be so arrogant or foolish as to try to do without the term "emotion" or words for feelings like anger, fear, etc. I will use the terms because they're inseparable from common thinking about our experience. But I hope to avoid any connotations that the qualities of emotion we experience are distinct categories or simply equal to identified brain chemistry. Though I'll of course use words, I hope they'll point beyond words alone. I wish to add meaning to the words we've used by opening a new relation to the music of the experience we call emotion.

I believe the best knowledge of the physical processes and origins of reality has come from science. But the experience of emotion isn't to be confused with scientific explanations of its physical sources. Those sources in the brain and body are important, and I rely on science to guide my understanding of how our physical and neural systems are part of the instrument of the music. This book focuses on lived experience, which is distorted when a scientist or psychiatrist imposes the metaphor of measurement. Scientific observation and measurement work by (metaphorically) stepping away from the experience, abstracting from it, usually counting it. Prescribers of psychiatric meds, considered the most scientifically oriented clinical professionals, paid to dispense chemicals that affect molecules in the nervous system, typically apply measures. I've seen how prescribing and diagnosing alone can mishandle people whose music of emotion, played in multiple situations of life, cries out for attunement and expression.

Though this isn't a book on science, nothing in it is meant to deny or contradict any of the valid, updated neuroscience of emotion. What I write about here is an overlay on that science, concerned with the quality of subjective experience, with how individuals can relate to and create their styles of playing the music of emotion without knowing exactly how their neurons are firing together. I have experimented with and refined this metaphorical concept over many years as a counselor.

My focus is limited to adult emotional experience. The music of infants, children and adolescents can be endearing, heart-warming and bewildering, but kids' instruments of body and mind are being formed and influenced in wild leaps and bounds, until mature adulthood. It's hard to say much about their music because it changes so much so fast. But I will tell of how the kid stays in us. Patterns created in early experiences influence the emotional music we play throughout our lives.

Another word about words. Much has been written, especially on theories of emotions, to distinguish "feelings" from "emotions." Emotions are thought to have particular themes (e.g., sadness) while feelings are meant by many writers to refer only to the physical sense of them. I dispense with such distinctions and will use the terms interchangeably. That's what we ordinarily do in talking about our emotions. When I use pronouns such as "we", "you" and "I" it's almost always for ease of expression rather than to apply what I say to everyone universally or to reveal myself autobiographically or to make presumptions about the reader.

This book isn't meant to be any kind of authoritative explanation or systematic theory. I suggest you read it as an unfolding of possibilities to provoke your own ideas, inspirations and experiments about experiencing. Rather than trying to convince you of what I say, I hope to invite you to free associate from what I write, see what you may discover, regardless of whether you think or feel I'm right or wrong about anything here.

CHAPTER 1: CONCEPTUALLY BLENDING
MUSIC AND EMOTION

—⊶ⅉⅉ⑂﹙⑂ⅉ⑂⊷—

DRIVING rhythms of fully engaged thinking and acting. Droning, repetitive notes of boredom or obsession or numbness. Exuberant flows of feeling like Vivaldi playing through and around you. Chaotic creativity pulsating like techno or contorting in free jazz. Desperate passions of the blues. The sublime silences of the stars in the night, the blazing star in the day.

In this book, I'll propose a new way to talk about the human experience and potential of what we call emotion. I'll suggest that we can have a better relationship to emotion by considering it as music played in complex processes of the body and mind responding to everyday situations we encounter in the mystery of this vibrant universe. The music I mean isn't that which we listen to. It is our entire body and mind attuning and responding to all of reality as vibrant, rhythmic energies in everyday living.

I've been especially compelled to find a new way to talk about and relate to emotion because the education offered in clinical psychology (studied by all clinical professionals who engage in what's called mental health services, including social work and nursing, especially the practices of psychiatry and psychotherapy) has a particular perspective that is deaf and blind to emotion as *continual attunement and response to the natural and social worlds in which we live.* Clinical psychology theorizes emotion in abstract, mechanical terms, treats emotion as something measurable that can cause problems and can be fixed, something that comes from the limbic system of the brain. There is no adequate conception of how that soaring hawk in the sky stirs my heart. The living connection is ignored in favor of a model of you as nothing more than mechanically operating parts. Psychology refuses to recognize the alive world that calls to us. As a result, clinicians can hold their clients back from realizing ways of experiencing and enacting their greatest potential. As a practitioner of counseling in mental health clinic settings for 25 years, I learned from a wide range of psychological texts, from the psychoanalytic to the behaviorist. The profession offered no critique or alternatives to the mechanistic models, nothing from centuries of wisdom about the passions, excellence and nobility of human beings. I've had to find, on my own, guides to ways of counseling that draw from the most current neuroscience to wise teachings outside the textbooks. I've had to discover new metaphorical concepts that incorporated the best scientific knowledge and aesthetic perspectives to practice in the reality of the wondrous aliveness of emotion. I allowed people to open to emotion, not as a state or thing, but as music which can open up imaginative and creative energy to get unstuck in episodes or patterns of thinking, feeling and acting, and to continually expand ideas and ways of living.

Music is a very different experience than words, formulas and explanations. Rather than tagging words or categories onto what we feel or should feel, we can relate to what's called sensations, moods and feelings as qualities of how we're uniquely participating in a world in which we're vibrantly charged by rhythms, tones and dynamically ordered systems of the body and mind, uniquely alive to respond to each day with choices of values by which to live and die.

The metaphorical concept of human emotion as music isn't an arbitrary, idiosyncratic theory, but is offered as a means to feel and be energized by emotion rather than to be its victims, to welcome emotion as indivisible from thinking and acting, as a source of living in love, beauty and continually generative creativity. Every day, we have times of getting stuck in confusion, self-criticism and other negative movements which are usually labelled with single words, like stress, anxiety, anger, depression. Emotion is usually considered the problem. Considering emotion as music is a very different experience than words, formulas and explanations. Rather than tagging words or categories onto what we feel, we can become aware of the dynamically flowing qualities and structures of every moment of the body and mind in the world, playing in harmonious, discordant, droning, disorganized, etc., ways of playing the music of emotion.

Relating emotion to music is accomplished in the same way any concept can be formed and talked about—the process of conceptual blending. The process is described by its theoretical father, Gilles Fauconnier:

> Conceptual blending is a basic mental operation that leads to new meaning, global insight, and conceptual compressions useful for memory and manipulation of otherwise diffuse ranges of meaning. It plays a fundamental role in the construction of meaning in everyday life, in the arts and sciences, and especially in the social and behavioral sciences. The essence of the operation is to construct a partial match between two inputs, to project selectively from those inputs into a novel 'blended' mental space, which then dynamically develops emergent structure.[1]

The one input, Emotion (the physiological, neural and cognitive system traditionally identified in psychology and ordinary usage with the term "emotion") is blended with the input of Music (as a physically and cognitively received aesthetic experience). This blend of Emotion—Music can be projected as a meaning that generates an emergent structure for an individual to understand, feel and enact emotion according to: one's individual, evolving meaning or purpose in living (which I'll discuss as Personal Myth); blockages and limits to meaning; the felt and perceived qualities of experience. The blended metaphorical concept of Emotion—Music isn't merely for the sake of a concept. It's a guide to allowing feeling to be experienced and directed by an individual to live meaningfully.

---

[1] Entry for *The Encyclopedia of the Social and Behavioral Sciences* (Gilles Fauconnier)

My emotional experience is a non-verbal, physically charging quality of my uniquely composed and performed meanings, flowing through body and mind. The patterns of my feelings and behavior can be felt as musical movements and themes, as contributions to a larger symphony I'm part of. When I know emotion as essential to my performance of meaning, my various experiences—e.g., dullness, withdrawal, vanity, exceptional creativity—can be known as being played by me, with others, in a culture, ecosystem, relationship. The potentially infinite permutations, combinations and layers of my music of emotion far exceed the available words used for emotion. Rather than fixed states, tagged with words and measurements, I can sense my emotion as a melody of the ever changing felt experience of reality.

The blending of the concept of Music with that of Emotion doesn't produce a new mix of a single state or mood. The flow of emotion is a dynamic event, a happening, not a rule-based, constructed, fixed meaning. It happens differently at different times and is continually in a performance of this life, right now. We may think emotion isn't happening if it's not noticed as high or low energy, painful or pleasurable, or otherwise of a certain intensity. We're taught that being soberly rational is not emotional. However, the music of emotion is always playing, sometimes so calm or subtle, it doesn't have a name. And the best neuroscience tells us there is no separation of rationality and cognition from emotion in the brain and nervous system. When we accept that being alive is always in a flow of qualities of emotion, we may learn different ways to compose and improvise. Though I'll sometimes use musical terms for the experience, such as tones, rhythms, notes, ensemble, I'm analogizing for the sake of a sensing of what is being created and sustained in us every moment, uniquely experienced by each individual.

Using analogies and metaphors may seem a dodge of the rigors of science. Though this is not a book of science, I rely on science throughout for the best knowledge we have. Simply by forming concepts and communicating, science uses metaphors and analogies. The cognitive science on this issue is way too lengthy to go into here. The work of George Lakoff, Mark Johnson, Gilles Fauconnier and Mark Turner have made much of the science available to the public. There is an illusion that there are "objectivist models" that describe reality without the possible distortions or inaccuracies of metaphors and analogies. Lakoff and Johnson showed that "objectivist philosophy is empirically incorrect in that it makes false predictions about language, truth, understanding and the human conceptual system. ... Formal scientific theories are attempts to consistently extend a set of ontological and structural metaphors."[2] The conceptual blending of Music and Emotion is based on the cognitive operations of metaphor and analogy. Analogy has faced a similar challenge to validity from those who prefer a model of the world as distinct entities with fixed formal definitions of the entities. Gilles Fauconnier and Mark Turner described the resistance to analogical thinking:

> Analogy has been viewed as a powerful engine of discovery, for the scientist, the mathematician, the artist, and the child. In the age of form, however, it fell into disrepute. Analogy seemed to have none of

---

[2] George Lakoff and Mark Johnson, *Metaphors We Live By* (Chicago: The University of Chicago Press, 1980), pp. 218, 220

the precision, found in axiomatic systems, rule-based production systems, or algorithmic systems. When these new and powerful systems came to be viewed as the incarnation of scientific thinking, analogy was contemptuously reduced to the status of fuzzy thinking and mere intuition.[3]

I've heard a psychiatrist describe a patient strictly in terms of molecules in the brain. He firmly believed and firmly dictated to his patients that the right molecular changes from the right medication is pretty much all the patient needs. I wonder whether this doctor would insist that music is nothing but frequencies of sound. His patient, unfortunately, did not improve under the regimen prescribed and the mechanical metaphor. I have heard psychotherapy trainers teach similar reductions of people to rules of thinking and behavior. I have challenged such limitations in meetings and trainings at which we were taught that people are entities of mechanically operated parts and therapists have the operating manuals. I had gone through many years of experiencing the limitations and degradations this model imposed on people I was seeing. In counseling sessions, I've allowed people to realize their imaginative resources, learn to play their music of emotion. People choose ways of thinking and acting to develop repertoires of acting in the world, although they often don't realize they're forming such patterns. Being aware of one's creative potential through such metaphorical concepts as the music of emotion

---

[3] Gilles Fauconnier and Mark Turner, *The Way We Think: Conceptual Blending and the Mind's Hidden Complexities* (New York: Basic Books, 2002), p. 14. This is the foundational text, explaining to the general public the details of how conceptual blending works.

allows conscious responsibility and flexibility in choosing what to play in situations. Realizing that living is an art involving the complex conducting of one's own neural concerto and the dance of daily activities allows individuals to enact uplifting, complex, imaginative music from the mind-body, amid the music of reality.

There have been voices in psychology in the past that would allow a broader, more imaginative approach to human emotional experience. James Hillman was one such thinker: "Here I am suggesting both a *poetic basis of mind* and a psychology that starts neither in the physiology of the brain, the structure of language, the organization of society, nor the analysis of behavior, but in the process of imagination."[4] Such voices have been so marginalized in current academic and professional institutions as to now be effectively silenced. Psychology may develop beyond the objectivist ways of modeling and communicating about the body and mind without losing its valuable knowledge and research. In clinical theory, there are practical and societal needs for non-reductive, imaginative, aesthetic understandings of how we think and feel. In this book, I offer a way to be aware of and responsible for how emotion is the individual's live playing of the music of meanings one enacts.

I will not be strictly correlating emotion with aural music but offering ways individuals can utilize the metaphor and analogy of music to relate to feelings, sensations and moods as a range of physically energized, behaviorally enacted expressions of meaning. Such music can give rise to images, words, visions,

---

[4]   *Blue Fire: Selected Writings* by James Hillman, edited by Thomas Moore (New York: Harper and Rowe, 1989), p. 22

ideas and actions, just as performed aural music has inspired audiences or listeners. What's been curiously untouched by psychology is recognition of the aesthetic dimension. I'll be exploring this always present, active human dimension, available to us for assessing and creating qualities of ideas, experiences and acts of ourselves and others.

Emotion shouldn't be understood as a private phenomenon contained within the nervous system or the body. The music of emotion plays within human contexts of relationships, cultures, natural and artificial environments. We can't help being influenced by concepts about emotion that are promulgated by psychology and psychiatry, which are accepted by the culture. Therefore, I'll examine the model and metaphorical concepts of emotion from those professions' teachings and practices, which have dominated our cultural beliefs. As will be analyzed in detail in this book, how we feel is indivisible from concepts continually formed by neural processes. Our concepts are affected by influences of our culture and social relations. Therefore, it's necessary to be aware of how those influences may limit or liberate the potential of one's music of emotion and how alternatives to the dominant models and teachings can open the way to greater freedom, creativity and meaning for individuals.

"Everybody Knows Psychology Is Not a Real Science"[5]

This is the title of an article published in the leading journal of professional psychology. It summarizes the many reasons

---

[5] Title of article by Ferguson, Christopher J. Ferguson in *American Psychologist*, Vol 70(6), Sep 2015, 527-542

why psychology, which certainly tries to give the impression it's a "real science," fails to meet the standards of science. The issue is important in examining the authoritative teachings of psychology, which create models and language about emotion commonly accepted in the culture. In the cited article, Ferguson tries to save the profession's credential, but summarizes many of its problems: publicized studies are not replicated by subsequent scientific studies to validate the findings; research that would invalidate prior studies are suppressed and usually not even attempted; statistics are manipulated to favor findings; "there often exists a gulf between psychological science's explanation for human behavior, which tends to be narrowly focused, mechanistic, and rigid, and the lives people actually live"; "how psychology is 'sold' to the general public."

From twenty-five years of working as a therapist in outpatient mental health clinics dominated by psychologists and psychiatrists, with ongoing research projects involving the patients, I speak from direct experience of how the "clinical trials" of clinical psychology wouldn't hold water in "real" sciences like biology and physics. Studies are conducted to gain the label of "evidence-based practice" for certain therapies to be credentialed for professional practice. Cases I supervised were required to follow "protocols" in which the counselor must follow a manual, which doesn't allow her or him to say or do much outside the required scripts and questionnaires. This ignores the vast number of variables of human experience that occur in the counseling session and in the person's life. I was cautioned to select participant-patients for clinical studies with a consideration for their amenability to the "treatment"—i.e., cherry-picking participants to support success of the treatment.

Drop-outs from "clinical trials" weren't analyzed for why the therapy didn't work for them. The claims for being "evidence based" are used for marketing therapies and to conform to the wishes of insurance companies and other funders, which have shaped brands, like Cognitive Behavior Therapy (CBT), for "mental health." As Robert L. Woolfolk has written, "[An alternative] perspective holds that we have learned less in recent years than the contemporary research journals or the pharmaceutical industries claim and that people of the future may look back on the practice of today's mental health professionals and regard them the way we currently evaluate 'scientific breakthroughs' of the past such as mesmerism, phrenology and lobotomy."[6]

In training and clinic meetings, I raised questions and objections about the rigid, limited models of the "evidence-based therapies" (EBTs) we were supposed to follow, how they weren't serving the people we were seeing and departed from wise practices of the past. To no avail. As I let everyone know, I'd continue to be a heretic for the sake of the people I was seeing. The main institution governing therapy, the American Psychological Association (APA), dominates clinical graduate programs as well as mental health clinics funded by governments and insurance companies. Therapists and counselors, including clinical social workers and nurses, are usually required to stick with the EBTs, which purport to be science-based techniques and remedies to repair or expand the mind according to the institutionally fostered model of human functioning. Not only is the "science" a deceptive imitation of real science, the

---

[6] Robert L. Woolfolk, *The Value of Psychotherapy: The Talking Cure in an Age of Clinical Science* (New York: The Guilford Press, 2015), p. 16

norms for the practice are tied to socially decided purposes. The perspective that dominates psychology for clinical practice interprets the mind and the person as a *mechanically operated unit* whose proper functioning is to behave in accordance with this culture's norms for productive work and social relations.

Prior to the controlling influence of insurers and its system of "managed care" adopted in most mental health clinics, much more prominence was given to the practice of therapy or counseling as an art of engaging with another human being who was experiencing crises in life purpose, meaning and values. What was known as "humanistic psychology" flourished in therapy and counseling. Its original voices included Abraham Maslow, Carl Rogers and Erich Fromm. Woolfolk notes how the humanistic approaches generally emphasized "a celebration of the passions, a cultivation of sensitivity to experience, and the development of spontaneity and emotionality."[7] Such an approach to practicing therapy and counseling today would be prohibited by the dominant institutions and employers governing clinical practice. Lots of people have turned to practitioners who don't rely on insurance or institutional funding, as well as certain life coaches, for help when EBTs prove to be unhelpful.

Dominant Mythologies and the Personal Myth

I still find it incredible that psychology's teachings and cultural influences keep emotion locked within the individual's skull and nervous system. What its clientele and trusting public will miss from that perspective is how emotion is about meaning

---

[7]   Robert L. Woolfolk, *The Cure of Souls: Science, Values and Psychotherapy* (San Francisco: Jossey-Bass Publishers, 1998), p. 63

enacted outside one's skull: how each person's body and mind are inspirited with emotion's music playing live for daily actions and motivations in contexts of relationships, work, society, world and universe. Perhaps the profession has decided that meaning is too complicated to bother with, better to leave those issues alone, don't burden psychology with having to understand and take stands on issues by which an individual and a culture are guided. It's easier and less controversial to stick with telling people that emotion begins and ends in the brain, that therapists and psychiatrists have the operating manual for how it works and how to make you feel better. By accepting this model of "mental health," people are unlikely to seriously sort out values and meanings they're living by, those which their culture may require. The dominant model now tries to convince us that we only need to alter our behavior and brain chemistry by prescribed chemicals and/or techniques to adapt to the society we live in and even feel happy.

The alternative I propose opens to the felt sense of the meanings of what we are doing in our lives, including how we're affected by and motivated for our relationships, work, parenting, creativity, sense of beauty, political and moral stands, and relation to nature. How we interpret our actions within daily contexts and personal potential, the histories of ourselves and our culture are all affected by values and norms of our culture. How the dominant cultural values affect complex felt meanings of individuals' everyday roles and actions isn't seriously considered in professionally diagnosed emotional disorders.

The perspective of clinical psychology in defining and intervening in human emotion is shaped by the dominant mythology of our culture. By the metaphor *Mythology* I mean a culture's primary model of how its people should live, including the pervasive meanings, values, beliefs, narratives and roles for living. A society's Mythology isn't in some book of myths, such as religious texts or *Quotations from Chairman Mao Tse-tung* (aka the Little Red Book). The Mythology is enacted in people's daily ways of living, manifested in common beliefs such as "the land of opportunity," structures of work and leisure activities, including practices in parenting and family life, education, social events, artistic productions. The Mythology is shown in what's actually practiced in daily living, even if there's a discrepancy between those practices and proclaimed beliefs about values. As will be discussed later, the culture's Mythology is introduced into consciousness from infancy, but, upon development toward adulthood, individuals may depart from it as part of the process of forming their Personal Myths.

Why will I be focusing on concepts of Mythology and Personal Myths in presenting a new approach to emotion? As will be discussed in greater detail in the chapter on the neuroscience of emotion, the neural concert of the mind depends upon concepts forming indivisibly from the felt energies and qualities of emotion. Good science shows you can't consider emotion simply in terms of brain regions and neurochemistry independently of neural formations of concepts. Concepts are continually forming in neural processes and are integral to emotion. How we feel and are motivated are guided by the concepts forming in the mind every moment. It's comparable to motifs of music to be performed. We compose each moment of emotion with concepts guiding the energies of the mind and body to make sense of and respond to reality. Myths are the traditional ways in which meaning and values of a society and a person are expressed. Therefore, I'll consider the unity of one's conceptual formations with one's felt energies, sensations and moods to understand emotion as music playing from the Mythology of the culture and in the individual's Personal Myth.

Notwithstanding self-help gurus, a Personal Myth doesn't consist of formulas for success, power or fulfillment. It is how you form meanings from the challenges, failures, defeats and generosities on your life path, how you enact what you stand for, what you learn from life experiences, what you are being called to do to participate in the world. Your Personal Myth will be affected by the fitness of your mind and body, the life purposes and styles you choose, the risks you take, and the results of your adventures of living. The metaphor of the Personal Myth has been written about by various theorists. I do not restrict the concept to a story that's told or imagined about one's life. I mean it as the whole of one's actual day to day living, including patterns of thinking, acting and aspiring. D. Stephenson Bond's concept in his book, *Living Myth*, is much closer to what I mean by the Personal Myth:

> … *what we experience as our own individual life as well as what we experience as universally human can only be expressed—which is to say, can only become a meaning—through a Personal Myth. Because in a very real way general and outward facts fail to do justice to experience-as-lived precisely insofar as one cannot live a life generally, but only subjectively.* … Our problem is thus not so much to preserve the meanings we inherit, as to participate in the process of meaning unfolding.[8]

---

[8]   D. Stephenson Bond, *Living Myth: Personal Meaning as a Way of Life* (Boston: Shambhala Publications, Inc. 1993), pp. 58-59 (emphasis in original)

Our choices and actions as characters in a living culture, including the settings and plots we live in, are subject to complex influences. The roles we play change. Living a Personal Myth is like how an actor inhabits a role or how a character lives in a novel. The difference is that your Myth isn't just what you say it is, to others and to yourself. Your Myth is lived in a body which is cared for or not, in norms of how you behave, especially in relationships with others and with the wider society and ecosystem. You can choose whether your life will conform to the cultural mainstream or veer toward dissident or experimental responses to the dominant Mythology. You can examine and step out of the patterns the culture's Mythology encourages or requires. The story of you in this life doesn't flow as in conventional realistic novels. You can be bewildered and pause, interrupt and change the story. You keep much of your thinking and fantasies to yourself. It's hard to see any of reality, including yourself, without the bias, limits and distortions of a self-oriented perspective on needs and desires. Once you can be honest with yourself about your beliefs and behaviors, bracketing as much of the ego's dominance as you can, you may understand what isn't right for you about your Myth, what you should do to make changes, what discipline can correct some bad habits. You may choose not to follow the plots and norms laid out by the dominant culture, economic system or religion. Bond tells us that "the Personal Myth is the form that potential takes in an individual—someone who is forced to become an individual. ... The Personal Myth is even the vehicle through which such a person becomes an individual. The myth opens up a way of life through which the potential can be lived."[9]

9   Id. p. 72

He also makes it clear that the Personal Myth isn't a single or perpetual story. There are different Myths that rise and fall within a life. No Personal Myth should be clung to as infallible truth. A Personal Myth could be about gaining power over others or about learning from an encounter, participating in the space shared, playing, working, loving and protecting yourself on earth, with the music of emotion playing as your soundtrack to the adventure of performing your Myth.

Opening up the possibilities

Experiencing the flow, the charges, the bewilderment of emotion is a channel into the energetic wonder of reality, a connection to what's uncontrolled—the wild existence we appear in. It's a music that can play uncomfortably, even painfully, that can also play creatively.

Words assigned to emotions are not only limited, they can distance you from the experience by tagging it with a common word or with technical jargon. I'm supposed to consider the named emotion, like anxiety, as something familiar, enclosed within me. Once I believe it's the named emotion—sad, panicky, overwhelmed, ecstatic, happy—it can seem innately fixed. If I don't like it, I should think of a differently named emotion, one that feels more comfortable or happy. I can call up some person or image or mantra to bring on something more pleasant. But if I consider the experience as music, emotion isn't a thing to get out of or into. Choosing the music can be connected to the highest meaning to go for. It takes inspiration and skills. Can I find the notes, the harmony, the dissonance to create what's beautiful, to perform the most noble Myths? Can I understand what I'm feeling as an energy that dynamically connects me to my vulnerabilities and defenses, as well as to nature, to others, and to the cosmos?

Attuning to undercurrents of feeling or suddenly triggered reactions, I can sense tones, themes, energies playing in me, I can decide if this music is what I truly want to play in this moment. I can realize there are other ways to play my music of emotion, in other styles and genres I've made part of my repertoire. I can summon a different quality of feeling as shifts of playing and improvising to explore the possibilities of what notes and chords of emotion could create music of a Myth I deeply believe in. I could maybe even play two different melodies, two channels together for understanding myself and what's going on, for awareness and insights.

When I'm suddenly denied what I thought would be coming to me, when I feel a loved one turn away from me, the feeling could be identified as frustrated, angry, disappointed, betrayed. I could tell myself I'm feeling what those words are. But if I've known the infinite range of music that can arise from me, I can identify the limited music of self-protection going on—its primitive force, its ruminative lyrics. I can go to the source of the music, the boy who's been hurt or abandoned, who's scared. I can summon centering tones and rhythms, tapping into my body's sensing, vibrant, cool energies, maybe like a warm, slow movement of cellos, bass, violas and violins, or the reverberations from a guitar or harp. It's not those actual sounds that are necessary, but the feeling of their music that could help me. I can turn to the scared boy in me, allow him to feel what he's feeling and know I'm there for him. I can lead him to find a different song to play. If I've learned and felt how this world is held in its orbit with continual rhythms that hold me, how this planet is moving in a universe of 100 billion galaxies, I may summon that voice I've felt responding to this universe with a hymn of humility and awe. I may play a music of laughter at how misguided and limited my thinking was, ease the tensions felt, bring something different from the repertoire I've cultivated.

I propose the music of emotion as an aspect of what Hillman called the poetic basis of mind (which is also a conceptual blend). This poetic basis isn't superior to any other perspective. It includes an awareness and appreciation of the vast universe alive in me—my neural networks, neurochemistry, hormones, what I'll call the erotic concert of the nervous system, playing throughout my body and mind. I can tune into the amazing processes of the body, the networks of culture, present and past, the wonders of nature, and so much else that can be forgotten about this moment of living. Much of what I've been taught in current textbooks and trainings of psychology are based on their accepted cultural Mythology—the engineering of the human body and mind, the illusion of mastering reality.

Whether or not the reader finds truth in relating to emotion as music is an individual process and decision, which I respect. Each person would do so in her or his unique way, for each person feels and creates music differently. The process of understanding and living one's music of emotion can be through what I've acronymed AFAR: Awareness of the music of emotion (which I hope to facilitate by this book); Focusing on the new way of relating to experience (as music playing live in you); Acting on the new pattern (playing various forms of the music of your emotion in situations); and Repetition of this way of experiencing (regularly practicing your music). Learning to relate to your music of emotion is analogous to learning to play your instrument (of mind and body) well, to play compositions that are meaningful, to be creative and joyous in playing, to contribute to the beauty and good of the symphony of Being. May you find the practice to be a vibrant, meaningful adventure in the art of living.

CHAPTER 2: EMOTION AS MUSIC

Y OU are, right now and at every moment, receiving and playing the music of emotion. I don't mean a music listened to or the art performed on musical instruments or by the voice. It is how your body is relaxed or tightened or somewhere in between. It is how willing or timid you are when action is needed, how daring or doubting of yourself. It is how your gut, your breath, your flow of blood are part of a focus on or distraction from what you are doing and why. Emotion shows how your body and mind are not separate, but one instrument in your desiring and acting—whether for your control, protection, appetite, or for what's beyond all that, caring and standing for the good. It is the feeling of taking risks for something worthy or for a transient thrill. You are attuning to reality. You've done so since coming out of your mother's womb.

By emotion, I mean *the multi-toned sensations and rhythms flowing through the body, infusing the mind's interpretive responses to whatever situation a person is in*. If I'm lying on my couch, reading a book, the flow of emotion includes how safe I feel, how pleasing or not are the contents and temperature of the room, whether I see and hear what's going on outside, how the book is or isn't engaging me, how hungry or tired or comfortable I am, what I anticipate, what I remember, and countless other factors affecting what my body, imagination and intelligence are up to. The music may be pleasant or disturbing, but it's not good or bad. Feel what it plays.

There are many theories about whether emotion guides thoughts or it's the other way around. I think it's impossible and unnecessary to tell. When you're transfixed by a song that's playing, is it the lyrics, the accompanying instruments, or the voice that affects you? Sometimes, one or the other has more attraction, but all the elements together really are the effect.

From observing infant-mother interactions, Daniel Stern wrote about "affective attunement" as the sharing of felt experience between a mother and child.[1] When an infant is playing on the lap of a parent, staring eyes to eyes, each becomes attuned to the music played by their bodies and minds as well as the music of what's happening in the universe that holds them. The attunement doesn't stop when the infant is separated from the mother and it doesn't stop when the child grows beyond infancy and childhood. Affective attunement occurs along the human spectrum of experience every moment in our relation to others and to the environments and events we move through.

---

[1]   Daniel Stern, *The Interpersonal World of the Infant: A View from Psychoanalysis and Developmental Psychology* (New York: Basic Books, 1985)

Our culture, including its sciences, doesn't give good ways to be aware of our continual affective attunement to reality. Stern's groundbreaking study is more important for focusing upon and naming attunement than proving it, for the felt interrelation of mother to child has needed no proof. I will explore in this book how living involves continual attunement through the instrument of our mind and body, how emotion is experienced and played as music of the meanings we participate in creating every day. By realizing the range and quality of how that participation feels, we can ask ourselves: How do I want to attune to myself, others and the world every moment? What do I feel as meaningful, as beautiful? What quality of experience do I want to create with others, with the world? Many answers are given to these questions in religions, ideologies, psychotherapies and stories told about how to live. A good way to consider the meanings you live and feel is to know the Myth you live by.

Living Myths and Mythologies

We usually think of myths as beliefs from the past, told as stories to explain the creation of the world and other natural phenomena. The term has become innocuous, associated with old books or new superhero movies. But even myths of past societies weren't about entertainment, or explanations. Neither were they dogma to be believed. They were people's living relation to their reality in a horizon extending beyond the individual. Their gods, goddesses, devis and daimons were felt as highly charged presences—in reality, not in a fantasy. Myths were live metaphors of how and why people experienced reality.

The myths we live by today are mostly unrecognized, perhaps because they aren't felt and imagined with the grandeur of pre-modern myths. D. Stephenson Bond writes about how we can recognize the myths of our daily life:

> To me, the most vital form of mythology is not found in the stories of gods and goddesses long ago, nor in the psychological truths those stories reflect, but rather in the contemporary framework of images and meaning that are found in our own lifestyles. There is an intimate connection between our way of life—the rhythm and structure of our weekly, monthly and yearly cycles—and the myth that informs our life.[2]

The metaphors of Personal Myth and Mythology[3] I draw upon throughout this book are different from the conventional meaning of myth, which Wikipedia states as "a folklore genre consisting of narratives that play a fundamental role in a society, such as foundational tales or origin myths." Rather than folklore or narratives, I will refer to Myth as each person's enacted meanings, beliefs, purposes and inspirations. By Mythology, I mean social myths—the common beliefs, stories, symbols, norms and motives by which a society is organized for its members to enact. For example, to learn about the Mythology of Ancient Rome, I wouldn't focus just on the tales of gods, heroes, legends, etc., as told by Virgil, Ovid and others. I'd look at how Romans had faith in and enacted values of imperialism, patriarchy and social classes stratified by financial wealth.

---

[2] *Living Myth: Personal Meaning as a Way of Life* (Boston: Shambhala Publications, 1993), p. 1 (emphasis in original)

[3] Capitalizing the terms distinguishes how I use the terms from the conventional uses.

Because our modern worldview considers mythology to be irrational and irrelevant or entertaining stories for kids, it may be hard to recognize a Myth one lives by and its accompanying music. How one lives may summon the music of stress, worry and fear. Those notes may be played in the course of risks for a noble endeavor like sacrificing for love, or in habitual exaggerated fears over petty concerns, or trembling when overcome with awe. When exposed to the overwhelming forces of the universe, vastly beyond the human, wildly sublime, an experience of fear can come within a larger music, like the shocks of notes and rhythms in Stravinsky's Rites of Spring. In each case, the mind-body's fear systems are triggered, the quality of the different experiences reflect different meanings of the feelings. The style and quality of the music one feels depends on one's Personal Myth. The music of emotion always plays some aspect of one's Personal Myth.

A Personal Myth is how each individual creates and lives meaning. Your Myth is more about how you respond to what happens and what could happen than the stories you tell yourself and others. Your Myth consists of actions you choose, have chosen, and have forsaken for purposes embedded in your patterns of acting, thinking and feeling. Those purposes may be completely different from the reasons you tell yourself or others about what you do. The multitude of factors influencing you mostly aren't conscious. You're likely not aware of what's happening in your body, why certain sensations are happening, why you naturally respond to a situation. I may have many reasons for not going to a dinner party my partner wants to go to. I may say I have nothing in common with the people there, especially a certain someone I don't like. I won't say I won't go because I'm afraid of being considered inadequate or that there's a wholly unfounded feeling I'd be rejected. I may not even know about these fears because I haven't understood the music they play in me. I may not realize there's a soundtrack playing in me in that situation. If I do realize I'm protecting myself and don't reject those vulnerabilities, if instead I care for them, I may stand by my cover story as part of caring for myself, go to the party, be curious to see how my music will play.

Your Personal Myth isn't just a story. It includes a multiplicity of sometimes chaotic processes of energies, ideas, desires and potential, playing its music of emotion, often out of balance, not always pretty, many times awkward and embarrassing. You are happening as a living Myth, with boundless potential and imagination and wackiness, right now. Even if you don't know the roots of your perceptions, vulnerabilities and defenses, you can accept and care for them. Rather than a story told by you or others about you, your Myth is a living, biological, active presence participating in the mystery of the cosmos in your peculiar style. The Myth is continually created and lived in what you do and allow to be done every moment, how much you dare, within a continual flow of presences and events, under the spell of your music of emotion.

We usually want our Personal Myths to be understood by others, even to impress them. So we add or delete many details when telling about ourselves as a character. We want the story to be intelligible and maybe entertaining. For all those reasons, we'll probably tell it with a certain amount of dishonesty. It's hard to be honest in telling of one's Myth, not only because there's so much we can't observe about ourselves, but the urge to make it presentable and likeable distorts it. And that's usually okay. Revealing vulnerabilities could result in pathologizing them. A Personal Myth isn't fixed or contained by any narrative. It's not subject to judicial review or confession of your sins. What's more honest and interesting than the accuracy of your narrative is your Myth's music of emotion.

Preliterate myths were sung or recited as aesthetic expressions of emotion adequate to the myths' cosmic significance. The aesthetic dimension continues to be alive in us, continues to inspire songs and performed music that reflect how Myths are energized with emotion. I'll explore how the sacredness or divinity of a Myth has nothing to do with believing or following a religion or anything supernatural. Divinity is what would rip you into an opening of reality greater than needs, wants and fears of the self. Your culture may be of no help in the quest to live a divine Myth. When your culture's Mythology loses cosmic significance, you may be left with stories of living by and for money or popularity for the greedy, boring ego. Transcending the ego can come about through experiences of intense meaning, such as falling into an abyss of tragedy, the sacrifices and joys of love, experiences of genuine humility and reverence, or a self-subverting sense of humor. Rather than cowering before overwhelming forces or an omnipotent deity, humility and reverence for the sacred can provide thresholds into what Nietzsche calls "the eternal joy of existence":

> We are forced to gaze directly into the terror of individual existence but, in the process, must not become paralyzed. … For a short time we really are the primordial essence itself and feel its unbridled lust for and joy in existence. The struggle, torment, and destruction of appearances we now consider necessary, on account of the excess

of countless forms of existence forcefully thrusting themselves into life, and of the exuberant fecundity of the world's will. We are transfixed by the raging barbs of this torment in the very moment when we become, as it were, one with the immeasurable primordial delight in existence and when we sense the indestructible and eternal nature of this Dionysian joy. In spite of fear and compassion, we are fortunate vital beings, not as individuals, but as the one force of Life, with whose procreative joy we have been fused.[4]

Living your Myth may allow access to this "procreative joy." This doesn't mean simple pleasure or enjoyment. It means your Myth is about aspiring and daring to create and co-create with others living joy. Your Personal Myth could plunge you into and out of a music of emotion which can disrupt, inspire, transform and deepen your Myth.

Why music?

Emotion is present at every moment of life, even when we're vegging out, doing what seems to be nothing. That may be the feeling of being safe, mellow, care-free or just plain lazy.

What is there about music that makes it a great metaphor for relating to the continual flow of emotion? The philosopher Susanne Langer summarized her research to find that "there are aspects of the so-called 'inner life'—physical or mental—which have formal properties similar to those of music—patterns of motion and rest, of tension and release, of agreement and

---

[4]   Friedrich Nietzsche, *The Birth of Tragedy Out of the Spirit of Music*, sec. 17 (originally published in 1872, translation by Blackmask Online, 2003)

disagreement, preparation, fulfilment, excitation, sudden change, etc."[5] I fully agree with Langer's conclusion: "Because the forms of human feeling are much more congruent with musical forms than with the forms of language music can reveal the nature of feelings with a detail and truth that language cannot approach."[6] The emotion of your Personal Myth isn't felt abstractly, as words or text, but is directly experienced, as music is. Your Myth's continual struggle for and enjoyment of meaning depends on the music that moves you in your life.

How I affectively attune to daily life gives rise to the quality of meanings I live by. Developing meanings beyond survival, which I can imagine and test in action, is the continual process of forming the dynamic Myth. The quality of the music of emotion I play infuses the process. Mark Johnson notes the way "music is meaningful because it can present the flow of human experience, feeling and thinking in concrete, embodied forms— and this is meaning in its deepest sense."[7] Johnson quotes the music composer Roger Sessions, who described how music is affectively attuned through bodily processes and movement:

> … it is easy to trace our primary musical responses to the most primitive movement of our being—to those movements which are indeed at the very basis of animate existence. The feeling for tempo, so often derived from the dance, has, in reality, a much more primitive basis in the involuntary movements of the nervous system

---

[5]   Susanne K. Langer, *Philosophy in a New Key* (New York: A Mentor Book, New American Library, 1954) p. 185

[6]   Id. p. 191

[7]   Mark Johnson, *The Meaning of the Body: Aesthetics of Human Understanding* (Chicago: University of Chicago Press, 2007), p. 236

and the body in the beating of the heart and, more consciously in breathing, later in walking.[8]

The music of your Myth attunes to reality howsoever you've cultivated the instrument of the body and mind. Wherever you are, you can slow down the mind, open attention to your experience. What we consider objects and things can be sensed as playing their music. Trees, grasses, houses, the falling snow aren't pictures at an exhibition for you; they are playing tones you may not hear or understand, but nevertheless their silent music may join with your own. You may experience sadness or bitterness at the music of destruction and violence. You may feel rhythms of hope and optimism at fresh experiences of life. You may be knocked over by a devastating tragedy.

Meanings of the world and my life aren't abstractions but are felt and lived as Myth continually being created and performed. It's created from my body's complex living cells and systems, my history of relating to others and the world since infancy, the scope I allow my imagination and courage, my exposures to symphonic movements of air, wind, stones, trees, animals, loved ones, strangers, galaxies.

The music of my Myth can be limited by how muffled and distorted I attune to my potential and to what is happening within the range of my senses, perceptions and interpretations. The strength and flexibility of my mind-body affects how I respond to what's just triggered or awakened desires, fears and defenses. I must care for the potential quality of my Personal Myth, understand how it's affected by how I've loved and been loved, how I've lived in a technologically advanced society that's provided a high degree of comfort, protection and convenience.

---

[8]   Id., p. 237

While I take ample advantage of these amenities, I realize they can obscure much of the singing, pulsating, enlivening reality I can attune to.

We have been educated and conditioned to go for a state of more or less happiness and avoidance of pain. We are taught to play the music of emotion to function in an artificially constructed modern society. While technological progress has brought incredible progress in so many ways, it's disconnected us from the natural world that has enlivened the myths of humanity. The comforts and diversions given by industry and technology infuse our Myths. I'm offered ways to select what emotional states I want to get to, whether through ingesting chemicals, controlling the environment, or various practices to control what I think and feel. These offerings can promote arrogant illusions of mastery of the natural world, its rhythms and tones, its forces, tensions and challenges. We can become satisfied with words that tell us whether we're emotionally okay or not.

When we believe the world and its people are there to serve our needs and desires, when we try to pin down experiences in an immature Myth of Me, we're stepping back from the fluid, continually germinating movement of reality that extends beyond our own self-centered place. Using standardized words and concepts to capture our dynamic, sometimes disturbing, flow of experience, we try to interrupt the movement of experience to label it into intelligible units or symbols or dissected parts for Me, for my practical manipulations and control. Every moment, there are innumerable, interpenetrating phenomena, vibrations of reality happening. We usually don't realize we are creating certain rhythmic and tonal effects in the Myth by which to live. By mentally separating the emotional reality of experience into chunks like "depressed," "happy," etc., we are missing a deeper potential and magic for the ever-changing flow, the multiple tones of melodies for the greatest potential of a Myth to live by.

Emotional energy

I've thought of emotion as energy that reverberates, similar to how music's sound has a range of reverberations. However, we don't really know what "energy" is; thus, it also is a metaphor. I thought physicists knew exactly what energy is. But no less a luminary than Richard Feynman, known for the mathematical rigor of his explanations of physics, says:

> It is important to realize that in physics today, we have no knowledge of what energy is. We do not have a picture that energy comes in little blobs of a definite amount. It is not that way. However, we do have formulas for calculating some numerical quantity. ... It is an abstract thing in that it doesn't tell us the mechanism or the reasons for the various formulas.[9]

I wish many of the teachers, writers and practitioners of psychology would speak with such humility and clarity. Many would have you believe the energy of emotion is from the chemistry and hormones that shoot up and down in us. I'll discuss in a later chapter the magnificent concert of neurobiology in the brain, nervous system and body. But to describe emotional experience as the chemical, physiological or material actions and reactions within us is like describing a

---

[9]   *The Feynman Lectures on Physics* (Reading, MA: Addison-Wesley Publishing Co. 1963), p. 4-2

Beethoven symphony as soundwaves analyzed in detail. That isn't music. Energy is simply another metaphor to evoke an aspect of emotion.

Similar to Feynman's conclusion, I don't think we really know what the energy of emotion is. Rather than the mistaken notion that emotional energy is chemical or brainwaves or other pseudo-scientific guesses, I associate the felt energy with mythic concepts from ancient religious traditions, like ch'i (Daoist) or prana (Hindu). When I use the terms "emotional energy" or "Creative Energy," I mean a mysterious felt movement through the body and mind, streaming into the event that's happening. Words can evoke the experience but can't pin it down. The flow of the universe occurring to a person eludes the mind's attempt to capture it in a net. Like the effects of light waves recounted by physics, like the waves of sound from instruments or voices, we feel emotional energy as waves within, from and to us. Waves of the music of emotion from your past, your ancestors, your culture, your ecosystem, your possibilities are happening every moment. They're attuning you to reality. I'm not advocating a truth or belief. I'm inviting you to allow yourself to relate to each moment as experiential music, forming and blending complex, overlapping structures and qualities of thoughts, imagination and acts that form your Personal Myth, your performance of meanings, through a multitude of sources and capacities. You may allow a greater range, richness and vitality of composing or improvising your music for the highest potential of your dynamic Myth. You can learn what skill, experience and inspiration is needed to better play the music that's true to and transforming the Myth each moment.

Like performed or heard music, the music of emotion can't be translated exactly into words. It's felt and created in our lives by how we choose to live and take action, how attuned we are to so many sources and forces, how we respond to the music of others, the culture and ecosystem every moment. The music plays in a continuity of the past as part of what is happening and what comes next. By relating to emotion as non-verbal music flowing each moment through our instrument of body and mind, we can understand what concertos of joy, gluttony, greed, peace, etc. we play as the soundtrack of our dynamic Myths.

To reiterate, I don't mean that emotional experience is the same as whatever music we *listen to*. I don't mean to *directly map* experience with a musical score. Melodies, rhythms and harmonies of aural music are metaphors and analogies to flows of the body, mind and nervous system—what are typically called moods, sensations, feelings, states. On the other hand, I'd venture to say that most of us have listened to music of songs and passages of orchestral or instrumental music for therapeutic effects. Someone told me how she couldn't have gotten through the heartbreak from a relationship without certain Bill Withers songs. In counseling, I've used music's dynamic metaphors to allow people to relate to their experience as having various tones, rhythms, intensities and inspirations, with patterns as complex as harmony, polyphony and dissonance. I've also suggested considering interactions with others as ensembles of who and what is present.

The music of emotion is created and resonates through shifting ideas, thoughts, acts, images, urges, laughter, curses that enter the events of experience. While we can and inevitably do use words and concepts to describe our experiences and observations of reality, we commonly mistake the words and concepts for the complex processes happening within and around us. Feeling events and moments as music can allow greater attunement to reality and to ourselves.

We perform the music of emotion through the instrument of our particular processes of body and mind, which I'll call, to reduce the words, "mind-body." I don't mean mind-body as a thing, but as an intimate presence and process of a person in the world. Mind and body aren't two separate entities, as clarified by Mark Johnson: "What we call a 'person' is a certain kind of bodily organism that has a brain operating within its body, a body that is continually interacting with aspects of its environments (material and social) in an ever-changing process of experience."[10] We play our instrument almost always without even knowing that we're creating a music or being aware of its meanings, its infusion with what we encounter—rain falling, sun blazing, a child crying, interactions with loved ones and those who seem to have power over us. At times, all may seem still and silent, though the silence is a music. Words can come out of this music, analogous to lyrics or a libretto. Sometimes the words are stupid. Sometimes they help us perform our music. Words can be part of beautiful melodies or clumsy squawks.

Our music plays in our Personal Myths in genres that are as diverse as the climates, cultures and ecosystems of the world. The emotional styles of people can vary as much as Indian Ragas differ from country western, which differ from preludes of Chopin. Though the music of emotion doesn't play exactly

---

[10] Mark Johnson, *The Meaning of the Body: Aesthetics of Human Understanding* (Chicago: University of Chicago Press 2007), p. 11

like such musical genres, its styles may be considered as a varied repertoire for the mind-body, styles of enacting meanings in our Myths. I believe the metaphorical framework of music offers greater potential than current psycho-jargon to allow awareness of how and why one plays the instrument of mind-body. Whatever the style, we each can reflect on how well we play in the art of how we live, and for what qualities and meanings.

We usually don't realize how we're enacting our potential, with what effects in the world, every moment. The mind-body modulates and shifts to diverse levels of rhythms and tones, from different sources of thinking, feeling and acting. You can find yourself playing music you realize is not in accord with nature or with your potential, that isn't serving you or others, that may be keeping you stuck in the same deadening tune. You can discover new ways of playing, new lyrics to your composed meanings in the soundtrack of the adventure of living your dynamically creative Myth. The themes and styles likely change throughout your life, as you learn to face the challenges, discoveries and possibilities in the wonder of Being.

Before music became an industry, a commodity available at the touch of a screen or dial, music played a more meaningful role in culture. There are still times when music enacts important meanings, as when the playing of "Taps" deeply moves soldiers in honoring the death of a comrade. People can still sing, move to and play music that reflects feelings and expressions of reverence, seduction, joy, love, or tragedy. There are styles of emotion that at times may be analogous to ballet, ballroom dancing and mosh pit bruising. The styles are developed and refined in different timelines, from minutes up to a lifetime.

The quality of the emotion we compose and play comes from our life histories, our internal vulnerabilities and protective forces, and how we're aware of, caring and compassionate for those sources within us. We can create music of passionate maturity, even when surrounded by superficial or confused themes, through actions we take toward or away from integrity and fulfillment. The music of passionate maturity doesn't play by obeying commandments or rules, nor through non-stop pleasures or occasional ecstasies, but through cultivating virtues, especially humility, loving, allowing ourselves to be loved and taking a stand for the natural wholeness of the human and non-human symphony. Meanings of our Personal Mythology are not abstract, not just thoughts or words, but are uniquely experienced with tones, intensities and tempos, patterned and associated with how we strive and stand for ethical life purposes.

The metaphor of music is meant to give a sense of a person's potential to attune with the mystery of Being in the ordinary and extraordinary experiences of living a Personal Myth every day. We learn to play the music of emotion initially from the people and forces we experience in childhood. We can develop more repertoires and skills, leave behind the family's dead ends or negativity, by choosing traditions, teachers and practices in aspiring to grace, creativity and excellence. With help from others, we can learn how to come through the music of shame, confusion and trauma. We can realize structures to the music of emotion from the many themes and effects we've lived through, from sad, tragic, pleasurable and beautiful adventures in life.

Premodern myths weren't fixed into propaganda or belief systems. They were sung or recited by a music fitting their cosmic significance. They took unpredictable and non-linear turns. How else explain the myth of the divine Prometheus, who scorned the pantheon of gods, stole their liberating fire for humanity. What music plays to him as he lay exposed, cruelly chained on the rocks as the eternal price he pays?

Vibrant waves

Like atomic waves that light up what we see, that incite charges in and around everyone, we're unaware of the micro-waves of the music of emotion flowing around and through us. The quality of what we feel is created in processes we can't directly know, just as we can't perceive the flow of energies happening within each cell, each molecule of us. But we can know the effects of these processes as music that can be sluggish, disappointing, confusing, or joyous.

In our culture, we tend to think of reality as a set of standalone objects. These things, we learn, have hidden mechanisms and can work as parts of bigger things. We can try to predict and prescribe the behavior of a person as a stand-alone unit. But there are many excellent books on physics, biology and even psychology that show we aren't things or units, but processes that interrelate in networks of dynamically moving systems. While the science is beyond the scope of this book, I'll just mention that this perspective also can be found in ancient ways of thinking. For example, the dynamic flow of Being was understood as the Cosmic Dance of Shiva, the Hindu deity, as Fritjof Capra recounts: "Through his dance, Shiva sustains the manifold phenomena in the world, unifying all things by immersing in his rhythm and making them participate in the dance—a magnificent image of the dynamic unity of the universe."[11]

The Cosmic Dance is to a music that may be sensed, not as something heard, but as the mystery of the cosmos received with humility and reverence, as the potential and play given to us in the wonder. We may understand the Dance as the continual process of interrelating of all beings. From the sub-atomic level to the organic processes of a body and an ecosystem, we can learn how nothing is a stand-alone, self-sustaining unit or substance, how all of reality consists of continually creative processes of interrelation. This may seem to contradict our senses, especially vision, by which we see the world as separated, solid objects, moved around by the linear forces explained by Isaac Newton.

Modern physics has shown that visible things are not solid units and the atoms comprising "things" aren't solid particles. We see light as a linear ray of a beam. In 1801, an intensely curious physician and amateur physicist, Thomas Young, did an experiment to show that light is something different than how we see it. He turned light onto a screen that had two parallel slits. Instead of two rays of light, the light produced segmented bands, which, with many confirming experiments, would show that light consists of waves in motion, which we don't see. Eventually, experiments with electrons resulted in the development of quantum physics, which has shown that material objects are events, not things, of complicated processes that don't follow the model of how we perceive reality.

The progress of biology has shown how bodies consist of trillions of cells, each with amazing processes of taking in and

---

[11]   Fritjof Capra, *The Tao of Physics* (Boulder: Shambala, 1975), p. 191

transforming energies, coordinating intricate systems within us, so we can take in and respond to astounding forces and networks around us. All of nature is a continual resonance of (still mysterious) energies in processes of creation and transformation. However, emotion is usually described and understood by psychology and the public in ways that reduce feelings to separated internal states, moods, symptoms that not only fail to give a sense of the dynamic flow and possibilities of emotion, but mislead people to consider emotion as a self-enclosed, simplified state or syndrome, identified with brain chemistry, brain parts, tagged with single words, phrases and diagnoses. It amounts to a creed for people to believe themselves to be clusters of mechanical parts and operations.

Just as our description of light as we see it won't allow us to know light as it is, our descriptions of emotions don't really help us understand the experience and potentials of human emotion. I believe the metaphor of music is a more accurate and sensitive way to relate to the processes of emotion. Music is a way to relate to the polyphonic dynamism of experiencing the flow of reality. Science can be understood as revelations that can expand imagination. We can incorporate its discoveries into our Personal Myths as meaningful ways to feel and direct the energies flowing through us, the rippling, invisible waves of life forces that aren't always smooth and harmonious.

The tones, rhythms and notes of emotion flowing through your mind-body are how you attune to reality. How quick or slow the breath comes, how blood beats in the veins, how all physical elements interfuse with thoughts, images, memories and desires where you are, in a world that's always in fluctuations of change or resistance to change: this is how your music plays. It can

play, in clear or distorted pitches, your attempts to make sense
of what's happening, your desires and fears about the future,
words and images from a past. It moves your dance of time,
whether that is a dance of worry about money, relationships,
health, a dance of ordinary or forbidden desires, a dance of
despair or hope. The dance may be clumsy, beautiful or boring,
excellent or a waste of time. It's the dance of your Personal
Myth, moving toward its potential in the Cosmic Dance of
Shiva. Your steps, gestures and movement won't be those of
Shiva. They'll be uniquely your own.

We can think of the continually created and creating
notes of emotion playing together in patterns, perhaps in
movements of allegro, staccato, adagio, bop or thrash. Terms
used to describe performed music aren't exact definitions of
the musical experience; they're indicators of the patterns of
notes of the music. Musical terms aren't necessary to be moved
by and interpret the music one hears. However, I love using
musical terms for how life experience is felt. Susanne Langer
realized the connection: "Wolfgang Kohler, the great pioneer
of Gestalt psychology, remarks the usefulness of so-called
musical 'dynamics' to describe the forms of mental life. 'Quite
generally,' he says, 'the inner processes, whether emotional or
intellectual, show types of development which may be given
names, usually applied to musical events, such as: crescendo
and diminuendo, accelerando and ritardando'."[12] If I rely on
words like "depressed" or "anxiety," I don't focus on the fine-
grained shifts, rhythmic patterns and tones, the intensities or
speeds of my feelings, how the energy changes, is played with
others, and how I might alter what it plays. Instead, the emotion

[12]   *Philosophy in a New Key*, op. cit., pg. 184

words would cram me into a category as a static state, blocking various possibilities to play my instrument.

In his book on the philosophy of Henri Bergson, G. William Barnard notes how music is a particularly apt metaphor for reality:

> The similarities between music/melody and the nature of physical reality (at least as revealed by quantum physics) are striking. For instance, melody and physical reality (at least in its pulsational, vibratory, subatomic dimension) are both ever-changing, complexly organized, and inherently temporal. Both manifest themselves as an onrush of overlapping, interpenetrating, and resonant vibratory fields. ...
>
> "Hearing" the world through the metaphor of music and melody, it becomes easier to grasp how the world might well be such that individuality (whether in persons, things, or events) can and does coexist with some sort of underlying, even if hidden, connection and continuity. For instance, while it is tempting to think of a melody as an aggregate of separate, clearly delineated tones, if we look (or rather, listen) more carefully, what we discover is that each individual tone, while it maintains its uniqueness and distinctness, is not abruptly cut off from the other tones. Instead, each tone, during the time while it physically sounds, infuses and overlaps with the other tones that are concurrently sounding. What is more, even after each tone has physically faded, it continues to linger in memory, it continues to persist

in the mind—in fact, it is this very persistence in the memory that creates a melodic phrase.[13]

In each moment, reality is experienced in tones that engage human senses, interpretations, memories and desires. At times, the music is felt in multiple or conflictive melodies. Like an ensemble or symphony that has multiple instruments and instrument sections playing different notes and phrases, we can experience, interact with and create overlapping melodic phrases that criss-cross, harmonize, interrupt or clash with each other. Each individual follows meanings that may or may not be conscious, but are felt. The music of emotion played in her or his felt contexts can develop or get stuck, lead toward fulfillment or chaotic anguish, or it can demoralize one into quitting.

---

[13] G. William Barnard, *Living Consciousness* (Albany: State University of New York Press, 2011) pgs. 89 - 90

Chapter 3: Soundtracks

———◦⊶∿⊷◦———

T HE music of emotion is always playing in the background of the breathing, thinking, imagining and feeling mind-body. It is the soundtrack of your Personal Myth. While the music may play without your intention or awareness, it affects your vitality, sustains or strains your life purpose. You can take time to feel and interpret what your music is expressing. When you wake up in a daze, shuffle toward the coffee, it may be like playing a violin underwater. When you get to work, it may be a familiar, cheerful or annoying tune. You can choose what music you would rather play. While the music responds to each uncontrolled moment of reality from your memories, desires, meanings, and guts, you can interpret its meanings, assess its beauty, dullness, or self-absorption. You can determine what may be needed to inspire courage, joy and care in responding to reality with the dynamic creativity of your Personal Myth.

Understanding emotion as music of the mind-body, you can feel and perceive the rhythms, tonalities, notes, melodies and themes being played as the soundtrack of the Myth you are living. The soundtrack isn't fixed in your brain or genes, no matter what diagnosis or personality traits you've been tested for or assessed. You can learn to alter the soundtrack. The music can be played in different styles, awakening and energizing different meanings, reverberating in memory, imagination and the body. The emotional patterns of the soundtrack can be shaped and even severely limited by many factors, from the political and cultural to the genetic. However, by practicing honest self-reflection, curiosity and integrity, you can adapt to or overcome limitations, seek the soundtrack of adventurous living for Beauty and the Good. In body and mind, person and reality continually interpenetrate each other in ever-changing vibrant waves. The music is always being played in concert with the rhythms, tones, melodies and meanings of all others existing, each event influencing and being influenced by histories, possibilities and choices each moment.

Matthew Ratcliffe identifies the always present feelings of orienting to the world as "existential feelings," which are "ways of finding oneself in a world that act as a background to all experience."[1] I prefer to call this background the soundtrack of emotion. It may be of feeling loved, safe, humble, hopeful or, at the other extreme, feeling overwhelmed, unworthy, empty, hostile, so threatened or alienated as not to feel safe (as in a war zone). The music may be of a loss of contact with reality, as when the chaotic music of psychosis plays. And we can get stuck

---

[1]   Matthew Ratcliffe, *Feelings of Being: Phenomenology, Psychiatry and the Sense of Reality* (Oxford: Oxford University Press, 2008), p. 37

in the music of the Me Myth of a narcissistic style. I uniquely respond to, and somehow participate in, the music of reality around me. It takes imagination and integrity to get beyond the immature myth of Me, to participate in nobler music.

The soundtrack of existential feelings includes possibilities felt in each moment. We can be open and inspired or closed off and demoralized about our potential in each experience. Ratcliffe describes this as:

> styles of anticipation that permeate one's engagement with the world as a whole, which can open up or shut down types of possibility. A world where everything is anticipated in the guise of dread and where other people fail to offer the prospect of communion or support is a world in which goal-directed projects are unsustainable and where things are no longer experienced as practically significant in the ways they once were. Thus, a pervasive, dynamic, style of engagement with the social world can also be described in terms of a possibility space.[2]

These existential feelings continually affect and are affected by one's Personal Myth. They play their music in a "possibility space," while bearing the influences of childhood development. The soundtrack of one's Myth can dynamically change in different circumstances, such as felt threats. While the music plays meanings of the current situation, it reflects one's unique template of fears, defenses, values, and inspirations. These influences will be discussed in later chapters. The soundtrack can be reinvigorated throughout our lives to play beautifully,

---

[2] *The Routledge Handbook of Phenomenology of Emotion* (New York: Routledge, 2020), ed. Thomas Szanto and Hilge Landweer Kindle Edition. Chapter 22: "Existential Feelings" by Matthew Ratliffe

but this is never far from the replay of self-protective measures. How we learn to compose the music as beautiful, ugly, noble or dreary, will also be addressed in later chapters.

How the mental health industry doesn't help

To understand emotion, we usually look to experts from neurobiology, psychology and psychiatry. Rarely if ever do they, at least in their writings and teachings, discuss anything like emotional soundtracks of joy, love, or moral beauty.[3] The sciences have important parts to play in understanding the complexities of the music. Neuroscience researchers have helped me understand how emotion isn't separated from thinking, rationality and the body. However, most of clinical psychology's empirical research and popular writings present "emotion" in different categories, as if brain states happen to you through neurochemistry or cognitions so that you "have" emotions like depression, anxiety, stress and happiness. Psychiatric, therapeutic or self-helpful professionals or books offer you ways to get out of the less pleasant states and into pleasanter ones. They can't seem to do without the labels, categories or diagnoses. Labeling yourself as a state or condition not only is deceptive but can keep you stuck or dull by identifying with the label, playing music of emotion to fit its theme. The label can mislead you into considering yourself a victim of emotion, with the hope that the expert knows how to fix or change feelings to a label like "happy."

---

[3]   Notable exceptions include psychologists offering astounding work on love (Barbara Fredrickson), self-compassion (Kristin Neff) and joy (Laurel Mellin).

Understanding emotion as different qualities of experience that are part of encountering the world through my Personal Myth is very different from understanding emotion as mechanical operations of brain states that happen to me. When I get overly scared or stressed, it's tempting to try to apply diagnosable symptoms and labels. Instead, I could pay attention to what music my instrument of mind-body is playing. I could try to approach its source in me with caring, figure out what role I'm trying to play in the situation. This can lead to breaking out of what seems to be a self-enclosed solo. I may then begin to play a tender soundtrack of compassion toward myself and the world. That soundtrack can allow me to act in line with values of the Myth I'm living or trying to discover or refine. I can realize the importance of experiencing and practicing a soundtrack that's more playful, noble or loving.

Feeling inadequate is a soundtrack that comes to most of us at times. Knowing it's a soundtrack that's been triggered, rather than a state that I'm stuck in, can allow me to identify it as the "I'm not good enough" song and do what's needed to learn from it about my vulnerability and need for compassion. If I realize the song of inadequacy, playing and replaying, is based on vulnerabilities that arise and get stuck, I can realize I'm composing and sustaining the music, I can play notes of caring for those vulnerabilities and the protective forces arising from them, accepting myself completely, and look for what can inspire and support other authentic and interesting compositions in the key of loving.

Realizing my feelings as a non-aural music whose themes can be chaotic, inspiring, self-promoting or demoralizing gives me a better sense of how sensations, thoughts and reactions move dynamically, how the flow of notes and lyrics can be altered, rather than labeling myself in single words, implying a static state, like "depressed" or "happy." Realizing my music isn't static, that I can influence what is playing by how intelligently and creatively I want to live, I can experiment with different movements of emotion. The soundtrack can play in differently felt styles, themes and genres of meaningful living.

By forcing into labels an ever-shifting processing from my neural-cognitive-imaginative-bodily responses to reality, I can convince myself it's only a symptom that needs a mental health fix, for a price. The labels, categories and words for emotions and moods are given nowadays for the sake of a professional who defines emotion in order to try to get rid of (by techniques or medications) certain feelings. I'd submit to the diagnoses and treatments because I'd understand myself as a machine with the clinician as a mechanic whose operating manual I should trust.

The mental health professions—including psychiatry, clinical psychology, clinical social work and psychiatric nursing—have been greatly influenced by managed care institutions, especially insurance companies, which require mechanical fixes. This has given rise to a dominant professional model that reduces emotions to effects of brain chemistry and irrational thoughts and beliefs. Moods and emotions are categorized as symptoms in a DSM (Diagnostic and Statistical Manual). The model persuades "patients" to consider themselves in different categories called diagnoses, and to purchase remedies—pills or therapeutic "treatments"—to reduce felt intensities, to do away with unpleasant feelings or moods and to adjust people to function in our economic and social system. Professionals who follow this model wouldn't facilitate an exploration of the moral purposes and meanings of a person's life being expressed, the socioeconomic structures influencing an emotional soundtrack, the possibility spaces and natural goodness within each of us.

The soundtrack of fulfillment

Instead of looking to psychiatrists for diagnoses and symptoms, we can look to wise voices and guides, from ancient to modern times, who explore ways not only to survive, but to live for what goes beyond survival, in harmony with the rhythms and life forces of nature. Instead of taking pills to feel good, we can learn to cultivate personal skills and qualities to be responsible for ethical ways of life, responsive to what's given to us every moment—a beautiful, sacred music. Emotion is always playing in us and from us. It's playing our Personal Myth live every moment in thoughts, desires, memories and aspirations from so many sources of our mind-bodies and the surrounding cultures and ecosystems.

There are infinite possibilities of how to move our bodies, thoughts and expressions in rhythms and patterns of meaning, responding to the flow of rhythms and meanings around us. Our culture and dominant psychological models encourage us to go for no more than "feeling good." This doesn't come close to aspiring to fulfillment of one's human potential. Opening to the feeling of how the elements and inhabitants of the universe sustain and energize us in each moment allows a realization of how the soundtrack to our lives is interactive, not fully within our control. In the frantic pace of making a living and caring for loved ones, we can ignore or become oblivious to how interactive and complex life is, how emotion can be influenced and triggered. We may not realize how we create qualities of experience, how this is forming our Personal Myth, how we can envision and enact a Myth of fulfillment of ourselves by transcending our selves.

We are taught to think and act for linear outcomes (e.g., salaries, investment size, performance metrics), that time is to be used, not meaningfully experienced. Meanings can become shallowed into individual marks of success. When individuals feel they're not progressing by linear measures, they can feel demoralized, hopeless or desperate. Accomplishing outcomes can foster delusions of false grandeur. Transcendent rhythms of love aren't measured in quantities and aren't given for rewards. When we relate to the body as a wondrous instrument of love, we'll want to treat our own and others' with reverent care, rather than as an object to be used, counted as data, exploited for profits.

Taking the plunge into the music of loving is for a power that isn't power over anyone or anything. In the most moving and tender moments you may reach, this power allows you to go beyond assumed limits to recognize and revere the reality beyond yourself. Love is no squirt of oxytocin or serotonin. Nor is it a goal for rewards. It isn't necessarily an advantage. It is an opening of your heart, head and body to the other, tenderly touching and giving, caring deeply so that courage, wisdom and generosity arise before even thinking about it. Opening yourself to give and receive love goes against the natural instinct to protect yourself from vulnerability, from the unknown, from what's out of your control. You may consider this just an ideal. You may find it especially hard to turn unconditional acceptance and compassion toward yourself.

The Myth we live forms on the foundation of how we relate to and treat ourselves as part of the world we live in. Self-compassion can open our mind-body instrument to better play the feeling of open hearts. It isn't about esteeming or pumping ourselves up. It is moving toward transcendent excellence from a position of accepting, rather than rejecting, any part of ourselves. Self-acceptance can reveal patterns of Personal Myths that hold us back. It can also show how courage, kindness, support and creativity can correct and transform the pattern.

To play the most meaningful music, I'd best care for and keep tuned the bodily aspect of my instrument in health, fitness and strength, while accepting help for whatever may be my limitations, pains and illnesses. With warmth and humor, I hope to discover new music of mind-body and Soul (which I discuss later) and develop the genres most suitable to my Myth. Each day can be a continual process of learning through experiences, study, conversation, experimentation, devotion and creativity. It can involve mistakes, pain and suffering. A Personal Myth expands and transforms through experiences. Different levels of mind-body can be phased in and out, while acknowledging whatever painful and dark music may play, whatever clarity and passion of life purpose I can summon in living my Myth.

Of course, there are lots of obstacles to living for fulfillment of one's potential. They are mostly within us. We might think emotion can be an obstacle that overtakes us, erupts against our will, and can lead into temptation, a downward spiral or a startling into fears. The feelings can seem to come from somewhere else. Someone, especially someone close to me, or some unfair setback or roadblock can sure make me frustrated, angry or demoralized, can keep me stuck, right? Maybe not. I can feel haunted by themes that scare me, narrow my focus to self-doubt or gloom. I can feel I'm the victim of emotion or mood. I am then playing the songs of victimhood in thoughts and stories from my mind. I can assess whether these notes and melodies are helpful or hindering. I can realize the music is being played by me. I can use the obstacles to learn about myself and the world, to build confidence in my ability to take on adversity. I can create a different score from learning and practicing different compositions and methods of playing my instrument. I can allow a more noble and joyous music to play through me.

As explored in the next chapter, we all have sources of fears and the effects of suffering past harm and continuing vulnerabilities. When these sources are activated, various emotional forces can be set off to try to evade feared threats, pain or helplessness. The triggered protective and primitive forces can create various forms of music like aggression, escapism, grandiosity, or ways to dominate others or ourselves. We can realize a more mature and playful way of understanding and responding from a different level. We can learn to compose a soundtrack that leads us beyond self-protection, to allow the passion of Soul to play.

Music of meaning in The Wild

A Personal Myth of creative living involves experimenting, taking risks, making mistakes, suffering harm and setbacks. Its soundtrack plays with a sense of adventure in the flow of what I call "the Wild." *"The Wild" refers to the experience of the moment in which you'll take action in a world you don't control, a moment full of possibility from your vast potential. You can summon your highest purposes and gifts for what's called upon from you in the uncontrolled Wild.* Rather than follow others or sit on the side, rather than stick with the music of victimhood or mere survival, you can meet the moment, *open to the mystery with Creative Energy*, to play music of the Good and the Beautiful in the soundtrack of your Myth.

Calling upon your highest Mythic purposes—such as love, integrity, nobility—you can prepare to respond to challenging situations by centering body and mind in self-compassion and creativity. The Wild doesn't call for chaos, anarchy or domination. Order and structure may be the most natural, creative response. By cultivating prudence, courage and integrity in the soundtrack of your life, you can act with self-confidence, equipoise and vitality in the moment of whoever and whatever may be happening in the Wild. *From there, you can sense freedom and possibilities emerging. You can choose to creatively play for noble stakes through the passion and creativity of your Myth.* Creative Energy can flow toward connection, solutions and joy. You can feel yourself opening to and enacting your highest potential in beautifully played music. The music calls for focus, self-discipline and good decision-making, like a great conductor of a symphony, then perhaps relaxation and enjoyment of your response in the Wild.

To play at your best, you must care for the instrument of your body and mind. To produce interesting and moving music, not only must the instrument be kept healthy, vigorous and well-tuned, as well as you can, you'll need to learn from others—people around you and from the past whose lives resonate with your loving heart and curious mind—and from experiences, including failings, mistakes, tragedies and triumphs in the Wild.

In our times of offices, factories, wages, entertainments, wealthy celebrities, it's easy to think of how much money it takes to encounter the Wild. I need adequate safety and comfort and will pay for it. I try to be responsible for resources I use, messes I make. But comfort and convenience can become an unnecessary burden on others and the environment. I can desensitize my response to the natural world by dependence on artificial safeguards and comforts. Yet, like all animals, I need a home, community and environment that's trustworthy and nurturing. Knowing that reality is actually Wild, I realize life isn't what's created artificially, that I'm connected every moment to the vast universe, the minute elements that sustain life every moment. To open to and enter into the Wild with Creative Energy, I have to distinguish from reality the continual chatter, noise and distracting notes played from the culture and the mind.

Routine interactions with others can be so habitual as to obscure awareness of how we're creating a soundtrack with them. We choose how much of ourselves to disclose, how much to inquire into, how strong, subtle, warm or cool to play the notes of emotion. We can be aware of different levels of comfort, confidence and adventure in interactions. We can be aware of the emotional styles of interactions enacted in our Myths— friendly, distant, suspicious, hostile, helpful, seductive, supportive, calculating, vivacious, engaging, curious, defensive, caring, controlling, polite, submissive, assertive, accommodating. We can alter the style through self-aware practice and feedback from others, to go for greater qualities and fulfillment in our Personal Myths.

Industrialized perspectives measure time by a clock and schedule, people as data and statistics. In living a creative Myth, time is experienced in the now, which isn't digitized; before it can be counted, it's gone. The moment is in the Wild. The Wild isn't a measurable object. It's a dimension of possibilities of the moment.

The soundtrack of your adventure of living isn't self-contained or self-composed. Even if you live a very isolated life, your soundtrack is continually receiving from and emanating toward other human and non-human beings, with different qualities of harmony, tonality, rhythm, subtlety and intensity. Your choices of purpose, focus and practice may allow it to be a soundtrack of fulfilling your highest potential in the Wild, gracefully playing for love, sacrificing for the good, creating beauty, even in money economies. You may have to reject and go beyond many aspects of your culture in ways that make sense to you, then follow the rhythms and meanings of the music you cultivate. The music flows within and from the mind-body as a means of connecting with and feeling nature's reality even in an urbanized society that's permeated by alienated, regulated ways of living. Your Myth can continually transform in change and growth, allowing you to produce unique compositions and experience new music from others in your life in the Wild.

Chapter 4: Composing the Music and Myth

Awoman—let's call her Angie—is astonished at how life is turning out. She's broken up with a lover she lived with for several years. She quit her job as a clinical psychologist in a clinic because she couldn't work any longer with the contradictions of her profession. She's found less security but more integrity after deciding she had to live differently. She's opened herself to the calling of her Personal Myth. It plays in her a music she can't give up and wants to share.

In the mental health clinics Angie's worked in, professionals tried to impress each other with how they weren't just "treating" diagnoses (rather than people) but, regulating or refueling dopamine surges, serotonin drains, dazzling their patients with talk of brain neurochemistry. The pitch seemed to work for most patients and for each other. Angie stopped buying it long ago.

As a counselor, Angie attended many trainings and conducted thousands of sessions with individuals, groups and couples. The trainings mostly treated emotion as a set of problems to fix with efficient therapies. She noticed right away they never actually spoke or wrote about the experience of emotion as it happens. They abstracted emotion into symptoms of diagnoses—fixing anxiety by mindfulness and CBT, absolving anyone of responsibility or freedom because of the dogma of "chemical imbalance" in the brain.[1] She made the mistake only once of raising her hand in a large room to ask a trainer if he ever thought of emotion as playing the music of meaning. He asked her if there was any research about this. She said she hadn't seen any. He said, "There's a reason for that. Therapy is too serious to allow you to follow just anything you dream up." The hundred or so people in the room stared at her as if she were a strange beast that had wandered in and should be ushered out.

Angie tried to follow the manuals and trainings her first few years in practice. It got pretty boring. She began asking a selected handful of her clients to tune into what might be playing in them as if it were music. Usually, they smiled and named songs or types of music they liked. An old man surprised her by saying he feels like he's a conductor of an orchestra. She

---

[1] The dogma has recently been officially dispelled: "The major new umbrella review – an overview of existing meta-analyses and systematic reviews – was published on July 20, 2022 in the journal *Molecular Psychiatry*. It suggests that depression is not likely caused by a chemical imbalance, and calls into question what antidepressant medications do." https://scitechdaily.com/scientists-find-no-evidence-that-depression-is-caused-by-chemical-imbalance-or-low-serotonin-levels/?utm_source=substack&utm_medium=email

would guess what music she was playing for him. She got better at tuning into what tones and melodies flowed from people and from herself. She tried to inspire herself by opening to the ethereal choirs of loving she'd summon for herself, then weave the notes into whatever events people related to her. She asked a man who'd been utterly demoralized to imagine what his heart was trying to sing to him. When he said he couldn't, she quietly hummed what she imagined it was singing. He smiled and said "Not bad." "What," she replied, "my voice or your heart?" He dropped his head down and when it rose, he just smiled.

In sessions, she got away from applying techniques or interpretations to the person, even away from any goal. She tried to pick up the person's tune, then feel it go wayward, sometimes becoming harmonious, sometimes not. The main thing, she thought, was the process of the notes bringing something into being from somewhere outside of each of them, riffing away from whatever too familiar song the person was stuck in. Sometimes she recognized the music needed her to just shut up. As she got better and better at this, her own music affected her in ways that deepened her Personal Myth.

She's discovered how the music of emotion is composed from many sources. Since college, she's been fascinated by just what emotion may be. Her master's thesis traced the metaphors of emotion, from ancient times to now, from philosophers like Plato through psychology's big breakthrough with Freud, on down to neuroscientists who mapped out the brain. In her thesis, she wrote of how most of the theories separated feelings from thinking and reason, how emotion was portrayed as dangerous, uncivilized. Plato used the image of a chariot to contrast the primal emotional energy of the horses (fierce passions and appetites) with the charioteer who skillfully trains and directs them to his purposes. Modern theorists speak in images that aren't as vivid, but they carry forward much the same beliefs, with the charioteer called something like "rational mind" or "executive function." Angie has let the horses loose. She wrote of how, in the 17th century, René Descartes firmly separated the body from the mind, leading centuries of theorists to advocate control of emotion by thinking rationally. Angie's mind and body flow into each other. And of course, Sigmund Freud famously invented a model of three kinds of mind: at the higher level is the "I" or ego (logical, in control); at the lowest level, the Id, or "it" (instinctive, pleasure driven, chaotic, amoral, irrational), with the superego, or "over-I," (guilt, pride, conscience) somewhere in between. Angie has allowed all three to perform on stage, while dancing in the wings.

She really got into neuroscience. At first, she was amazed at its version of separating emotion from thinking, placing a higher level of thinking literally at the height of the brain— the cerebral cortex. Emotions were set lower, in the limbic region. Most unruly of all was the "reptilian brain" way down at the brain stem. What's made more sense to her is what the neuropsychologist Lisa Feldman Barrett said about how the brain isn't so compartmentalized, how feeling and thinking, interrelated with the body, are indivisibly creating a dynamic process of emotion: "Modern neuroscience ... has shown that the so-called limbic system is a fiction, which is not surprising because no single brain area is dedicated to emotion."[2]

---

[2]   *How Emotions Are Made* (New York: Houghton Mifflin Harcourt 2017), p. 168

While everywhere, scientific and popular articles on emotion focus mostly on the brain, Angie thinks the brain is just one part (an amazing one) of the instrument that allows improvising and composing in ways that are still mysterious. She invited her clients to let imagination roam into whatever style of playing could best showcase their talents. She knew she had to treat those moments like her deeper experiences of reality—with humility and reverence, realizing the explosive potential of very tiny moments of human life in the universe.

She got the message that the brain is the guide to living a good life, like an operator of a machine or the software of a computer. But she never really bought that idea. Since grad school, she's been frustrated by how psychology, as a profession and as a theory, treats people as standalone units, separately functioning. She refused to implement therapies that were based on measuring feelings and regulating behavior with rewards or punishments. She's seen how that model, originated by B. F. Skinner's behaviorism, still pervades the mental health industry, even though it's been debunked by science. The most promoted therapy, cognitive behavioral therapy (CBT) continues to treat people as machines. The clinics gave her operating manuals to train people's thoughts and behaviors. She asked the last expert at a workshop, "What's the purpose of these techniques? Who or what am I serving?" He said, "It serves your life." She answered, "I don't want that kind of life."

Discovering her living Myth

What's missing in the psychology she studied and practiced, Angie realized, has been a lack of imagination and guts.

A friend of hers who's a Jungian therapist gave her the book, *Living Myth*. Though written by a Jungian, it spoke to her more than Carl Jung ever did. She went into therapy with a Jungian analyst, but couldn't remember her dreams. The analyst told her to have a notebook by her bed to write them down. The dreams she reported were interpreted in ways that got predictable. The notebook was creating bad insomnia. So she quit the therapy, which was her last.

What was important to Angie from Jung and certain writers in that tradition was not so much the concepts of "psyche" and "collective unconscious" as the validation of her imagination. From Jung's own autobiographical writings, she found that he also went through a crisis about the psychology he had studied and practiced. He said the most important teacher he had was a guy named Théodore Flournoy, who stressed the importance of *"imagination créatrice"*—creative imagination. Angie crossed a line then. She allowed herself to fully trust the imagination that had been so important to her throughout her life. She wondered why American psychology had never recognized the creative imagination.

Her imagination opened Angie's mind not only to images and dreams, which Jungians focused on, but to what she felt in her body while experiencing the sunlight and darkness, the trees and the buildings she walked among. Her imagination led Angie to allow wonder to connect her to everything she sensed and remembered and desired. She opened her body and mind to feelings that could affect her as music. She saw and felt everything and everyone as creating, every moment, a work of art. She realized how the artists, writers and composers she loved had given openings to the imagination. For her, imagination isn't just for private fantasies. It's shown her the Mythology she was participating in, how so much of it isn't right for who she is, the Myth she wants to live. She's found music to inspirit every moment of her Myth, to live in the mystery of Being.

Paying attention to her music of emotion, Angie's realized melodies that can be noble, banal, intelligent or stupid, with the potential to enact beauty, love and irony in her unique way. Trusting the art, philosophies and science that clarify her Myth, she's responded to what her imagination and gut were calling for—striving for qualities of herself that could enact beautiful, noble, courageous and excellent responses to life. She's determined to develop the instrument of her mind-body to live those qualities, not as the operator of a machine, but as a creative artist. Knowing her life as a Myth and the challenges it presents, she can be more clear about what norms and purposes she wants to follow. She assesses actions, words and thoughts aesthetically. As the artist of her Myth, she composes tones, intensities and other qualities of the music of her emotion that attune with an encompassing Mythology of Being, revealed by the natural world and certain artists, scientists and philosophers. It became clear to her how that Mythology differs from the Mythology of her culture, which keeps people chasing different ways to substitute drama, within themselves and their daily theaters, for truly meaningful action in the world. She gave up the dramas of avant-garde art and punk clubs, wanted to feel fierce winds on hikes, watch thunderstorms, spellbound. The Mythology of Being demanded that she recognize the reality outside herself, realize it doesn't center on her, but invites her to participate in its vast self-creation, to enact the dignity and beauty of herself, others, the earth and universe. Each day, she goes for this participation in Being, watching so many other possible choices for comfortable, conforming survival.

But she also produces songs and compositions that are mediocre, often inspired by fear and self-protection. She's been compelled to explore and understand the sources of the rhythms, tones and themes of all the music of emotion—from the ennobling and transcendent to the petty and limiting. In counseling, she's tried to evoke the most inspiring soundtracks of meaning, daring clients to live their unique role in the symphony of Being. She's had to study and experiment with a range of ideas her colleagues and employers would find scandalous. She got in trouble for not forcing people into what they called "evidence-based therapies." She took her stand and got knocked out of a really secure job. In what follows, she shares notes of her experiences and studies, her mistakes and experiments.

Unchosen music

It's not like a songwriter or composer. I don't write a script or a score to bring about any emotion. Emotion's music can arise without warning. I don't always want it. It can be confusing. It's led me into mistakes. I'm glad I made them, though. At any moment, I can feel so many different tones and forces that aren't consciously composed, some of which can spiral into rhythms of panic, boredom, overwhelm, despair, and, yes, also courage, also joy.

The music can inspire me to create or destroy. I have to be careful. I've seen how it can lead people to dominate or to love. I've had to get a good understanding of where this comes from. I've been able to help people see how the sources of the music of emotion can lead to decisions that are careful and caring or stupid and self-defeating.

Let me tell you about some of what I've learned, first for my own life. The sources of the music are embedded in mind and body. They could be movements for the creative art of living. When I realize those sources and my potential to create from them, I can form structures and styles to play the original music of my living Myth in relationships, work, responsibilities and chance. It's not always easy. I have to deal with my two minds.

I've had to unlearn so much of what I was taught in psychology. The key that unlocked so much for me was learning how metaphors structure how we think, imagine and live. The metaphors illuminate the Myth I live by. I was inspired by some wise people in psychology that were never mentioned in any of my trainings. One of the most important is Steven Stosny, a clinical psychologist who's written books about some of the most difficult issues in counseling. He wrote about cases that were a lot like my own.

I started out in a clinic that got referrals from courts ordering guys into counseling who were sentenced to probation for domestic violence. I thought it would be a way to intervene in some of the most important battles going on out there— violence against women. I soon had that ideal crushed. The women counselors would shame the men, force them to confess their sins, to admit they were guilty not just of what they were accused of, but also of thoughts about women they shouldn't have. If they didn't give the right answers, they wouldn't pass probation. I talked with some of those guys. They said they knew what they had to say in the groups, they just wanted it to be over. When I raised this with the women, they turned as cold as they were in the groups. They told me I can't enable them. I didn't dare say I just wanted them to be able to speak honestly. I saw how those groups weren't doing any of those men any good, so I got out of there.

Stosny worked with court ordered cases like those. But he helped the men understand the sources of their behaviors and alternatives. And he helped me understand the two minds. He uses the metaphors "Adult Brain" and "Toddler Brain."[3] Those terms emphasize a certain distinction, but I prefer the more general term, "Primitive," over "Toddler" for qualities of thinking and behavior formed even beyond the Toddler years. And I mean "Mind" as wholly in connection with the body, not confined to the skull. The model echoes the age-old distinction between higher and lower levels of the mind. He means by Adult Mind the capacities of the mind that fully develop sometime after the age of twenty, maybe mid-twenties. I use the term "Primitive Mind" to cover those sources of emotion that are about survival—the well-known 4 F's, feeding, fighting, fleeing and fucking—which are always there within us throughout life. I call "Pre-Adult" those patterns of thinking, acting and emotional energy formed in our first couple of decades of life. They also stay with us throughout life.

Stosny describes how the Adult Mind "provides a level of self-awareness and awareness of others ... the ability to ascribe mental states, such as beliefs, feelings, motives, and desires, to self and others. ... [and] enhances our most humane qualities, such as appreciation and higher order compassion—

---

[3]   Stosny's excellent book exploring this way of thinking is *Soar Above* (Deerfield Beach, FL: Health Communications, Inc., 2016)

sympathies for vulnerabilities that we do not share."[4] Although my discoveries of more current neuroscience would lead to some quarrels with Stosny's narrowing the Adult Mind to certain areas of the brain, his terms have been very useful as metaphors to help people understand the basis for certain feelings and behaviors they didn't understand or want. The Adult Mind allows full exercise of our more complex cognitive functions, like predicting consequences, analyzing, planning and strategizing for goals and values. If I've developed skills and awareness in the more complex thinking and strategizing from the Adult Mind, I can intercept Primitive impulses, shift to a perspective that cares about the future and other people or a cause greater than me, then choose to act with more flexibility and effectiveness.

Distinguishing and intimately knowing my own Adult and Primitive Minds can be quite helpful. If I'm aware of how sensations can arise from my body and mind for the sake of Primitive highs or Pre-Adult comforts and satisfactions, I can assess it as part of decision making. If I'm tempted to go for some junk food or some body, I can pause, bring my Adult Mind online, consider the consequences before making that decision. I know these distinctions can oversimplify the complexities of the mind's flow, but the terms are practical as metaphors. I've really come to know my Primitive Mind in relationships: acting like a big baby when my partner would come home late or not give me the attention I think I need; listening from my perspective, not my lover's; what, do I have to compromise again? With awareness of the two levels, I can engage in more Adult perceptions, interpretations and choices, like imagining

4   *Soar Above*, p. 3

what it's like to have my partner's point-of-view, listening and communicating in ways that overcome the biases and impulses of my inner Toddler.

The Adult Mind helps me realize meanings after illusions are shattered or terrible things have happened. I can be with myself warmly and intimately, no matter what I've done or what's been done to me. If I imagine and realize how my emotional energy could be engaged physically and creatively for something good in the world, I can focus for something greater than satisfying wants and needs or manipulating others and the earth to maximize pleasure, comfort or profits.

Despite the instinctive wish to be in control of my life, the Myth I live continually roils me in forces and tensions I feel but don't control. By learning about the sources of that unchosen music, I can relate to them, care for them, help them transform. I can choose notes and rhythms to infuse the sources with broader ranges of meaning. The music of caring and reverence is amazing. I can wisely choose pleasures. I can envision the freedom and responsibility needed to enact the Myth.

Stosny's work shows how we all have the potential every moment to erupt or escape into Pre-Adult and Primitive behaviors because these have been our natural repertoire for at least the first couple of decades of life. To play at a more meaningful and complex level, we have to focus on learning, imagining, practicing, rehearsing and performing from the Adult level. This isn't to exclude or disfavor the Primitive in us, but to integrate it for greater potential and choices. We get there by cultivating and enacting Adult meanings and values as part of a full repertoire of experience and action.

The Primitive, Pre-Adult Mind mostly serves our self-centered, immature, self-gratifying or survival purposes. Aggression, temper tantrums, insisting on being right, efforts to control or dominate, acting on all kinds of urges and addictions, are reactive behaviors and energies from the Primitive level. The reactions may be attempts to protect myself or someone else out of instinct or attempts to impress, or they can serve my natural greed to possess, dominate, consume or stockpile. Usually, I'm not aware I'm serving these Primitive purposes. Whether I like it or not, the Primitive is alive and well in the Personal Myth I live.

Primitive music can arise from early years as needy children, from painful or traumatic experiences, from learning according to Primitive models (in the family and culture) or out of the need to survive. Pre-Adult experiences become habits of thinking and behaving that remain, to various degrees, even when we cultivate more complex, mature and humane practices from the Adult Mind. I can play styles of more sophisticated Adult music for meanings that include Primitive riffs and rhythms. I can acknowledge a lot of patterns and habits of thinking and behaving I should outgrow, reduce or eliminate for more meaningful habits and styles of playing. Every day, I can choose actions guided by the Adult Mind, based on values and purposes from my Myth, even while riding the uncontrolled waves of Primitive forces. By pausing, focusing and cultivating skills, I can alter the music's quality, its organization and performance or its entire genre. A lot of Pre-Adult patterns can be transformed to become more interesting and fulfilling as I aspire to care for and contribute to people and the world outside me, while appreciating Primitive forces for the right situations and pleasures.

No one is guided by the Adult level of thinking, feeling and acting all the time. All of us will make mistakes, sometimes grave ones. The mistakes can be met with forgiveness, learning and humility about ourselves and others. We should help each other with avoiding serious mistakes that can be harmful and to recover and learn from bad choices and misfortunes. We can also learn how to care for and allow Primitive surges to enrich and intensify experiences as part of forming and playing music of Myths we want to live by.

The music of vulnerabilities, protection and the Soul

When I discovered the amazing usefulness of metaphors and metaphorical concepts, my understanding of people opened much wider. I felt that all I'd been learning was dry and about control. Those metaphors weren't mine. I didn't care that I was counseling people who were really tough, many without much motivation. My metaphors led me to share my curiosity, my jokes, my frustrations and people sitting with me began to share theirs. I was attentive, even reverent in my irreverent style, toward the vulnerabilities in their Myths. When anger or fear or dejection would play its music, I knew the vulnerability was important.

I talked to people about their vulnerabilities, even if they denied they had any. I never asked anyone to believe what I said. I never pretended to know exactly where the vulnerabilities came from. I knew it was a mix of genetics and dramas we grow up with and then later create on our own. My new understanding made so much sense, I had to offer it to people who'd come to my office. And so I offer it to you. You can decide if it's helpful or not.

We usually aren't aware of how or when our vulnerabilities are activated. Experiences of being hurt, lost, abused, abandoned, frightened, threatened and demoralized are wounds that re-open in certain situations. We can get good at insecurity. We've acquired a range of protective forces in an attempt to defend ourselves from or avoid the vulnerabilities. We're not heroes in ideal myths, not so cool or strong. We all can be idiots at times, bringing out aspects of our Myths that aren't too flattering. The protective forces triggered by vulnerabilities can play tunes of fight or flight, panicky sensations, shame, silly vanity, and other reactions that can lead us into consequences that aren't so good. They're just as much a part of our Personal Myths as the ideal stuff we'd rather publicize Here's the list of what I think are the sources of the music of emotion.

HIDDEN VULNERABILITIES:

- Fears – fortissimo shocks and strains of reacting to or anticipating threats
- Outcries of inner wounds from past trauma, abuse and hurt
- Undercurrents from abandonment, rejection and early denial of love
- The blues of loneliness
- Tones of powerlessness or helplessness fueled by beliefs and memories
- Recurrent themes of guilt and shame
- Dirges of grief and loss
- Self-defeating songs of self-denigration or regrets

- Recurrent themes of inadequacy, inferiority
- Disorganized, out of control noise

And here are some of the Primitive forces that can be automatically triggered, usually without intention, often without awareness, to protect me from experiencing those vulnerabilities:

ESCAPISM: Siren songs drawing me away or into a fake reality:

- Avoiding experiences, people, responsibilities, risks, opportunities
- Addictions (substances, gaming, shopping, sex, gambling, eating, etc.)
- Obsessions and compulsions
- Suicide and self-injury
- Withdrawal (from others, the world)
- Pessimism
- Numbing or shutting down
- Paranoia
- Fantasy in place of reality

I MUST CONTROL: Tonalities of control, domination, criticism:

- Overly Controlling/Calculating/Managing
- Harsh mental pushing, criticizing, judging of myself or others

FIGHTING SONGS: played forcefully or intensely:

- Fierce blares of aggression, intimidation
- Angry, even abusive, acting out (verbal, physical, relational)
- Violence
- Hypervigilant, Survivalist reactions

EGO TUNES: attempts to compensate for, rise above or protect from vulnerability:
- Performing to be admired, #1, the hero, the smart one
- Perfectionism
- High-charged performance/Ruthless competition
- Overselling or proving how great I am/Undervaluing or finding fault with others
- Comic operas of blinding self-regard

But we all have the potential to care for our vulnerabilities, to accept and transform our protective energies with:

CENTERED IMPROVISATIONS: I open to, recognize, accept and care for my vulnerabilities and protective forces. I can transform their energies by focused playing of:
- Curious, exploratory openings and overtures to what's within me
- Compassionate forgiveness of others and myself
- Creative, imaginative solos or polyphonies and jam sessions with others
- Embodied hymns of courage for the good
- Deep harmonies of love and connection (to myself & others)
- Rondos of enacting virtues, purposes, leadership
- Free, passionate playing of radical responsibility

And there can be music that arises from the boundless potential of my living Myth, which allows the living, embodied dimension of Soul to flow through and from me.

SOUL'S TRANSCENDING FLOWS:
- Luminous, felt presence and energy of love
- Soulful spirituals lifting me beyond self-interest

- Transcendent hymns of beauty and goodness in the world
- Devotional works of reverence, sacrifice and play beyond myself
- Rhythms of enacting my open potential in the now

As an example of how these sources of emotion may play, I've let songs of self-doubt and escape hold me back from asserting myself in meetings or social gatherings because of how I've been rejected or felt inferior in groups when I was young, as well as some shame I felt about aspects of my family. Therefore, I didn't know how to be confident and lead myself in the world, take risks or even show up in situations and opportunities. I withdrew into myself. Too much time was wasted binging on video games and movies. I tried to learn how to impress others into admiring me by winning competitive events and sounding like I knew more than others. I tried to be sexy or impressive to people who'd go for that sort of thing. With wise guides and caring others, I became more aware of the scared kid in me. Finally, I felt the choice of accepting myself unconditionally about all of it. I began to care for the fears and self-protection that would play in me. I practiced ways to center myself, allowing my music to play authentically regardless of who may dislike or reject it. I tried to choose caring people to be with. I would speak up at most meetings and dare myself to voice my values and resist guarding them. I've learned to compose music of love, beauty and humor from the Adult and Primitive Minds playing together.

Living the potential of my Myth comes by how I attune to the world and to my vulnerabilities and protective forces, how I allow creativity, love and humor in the art of living my

Personal Myth. Art which is just about the artist is narcissistic. Art that's created to be sold to others is a commodity. Art that goes beyond self-satisfaction and sentimentality, that moves with inspiring emotion, that attunes to subtle and vibrant experiences of reality, is art that transcends my self through my imperfect self. Being honest to myself about my sources of emotion is part of allowing my Myth its freedom, even if it may embarrass me, even if no one else likes the notes and chords that play from me.

The Personal Myth I embody is continually transforming. It isn't limited by "I" or fixed categories. The Myth of who I am interrelates with others' Personal Myths and the Mythology of Being through attunement, learning from science, history, works of art, experiences. As I act upon my Mythic values, I learn and test them. I spend time recomposing whatever music plays badly in my actions. I learn how the soundtrack of emotion arises from memories and traditions, how patterns of feeling, thinking and acting grew out of an earlier history of interactions with my family, and how current cultural norms and actions of others can affect the music every day. It's important to tune in to the cultural forces I move in, but I don't have to conform to them. I reject the nonsense and distractions of a lot of popular culture. I try to do so respectfully. I know how my ego can play know-it-all tunes. I've composed new music of emotion through taking risks for noble stakes. I can create and co-create something beautiful.

Though the effects of vulnerabilities and protective forces may not be deliberate or even conscious, I don't need complete understanding of them or their sources. I only need to be honest and aware of when I'm triggered by those forces and do my best to call up Centered Improvising and the Soul's Transcending Flows. It takes practice and learning from mistakes to be aware of what music I'm creating with others. From experiencing the flaws and mistakes of my Myth, I can get to better understand and deal with sources of violence, grandiosity, manipulation and escape in myself and others. I can learn ways to compose and improvise music of emotion that inspires and fortifies me to let go of and try to prevent disconnection, misery, greed and evil, to struggle for the good and endure the boring and the painful.

Reconciling the mature and primitive levels

We respond to every moment from possibilities of our Adult, Primitive and Pre-Adult levels, usually in some combination of the modes. All of us will have times of being hurt, afraid, confused, frustrated, full of doubt. My setbacks, obstacles and failures might move me further into my Primitive, Pre-Adult Mind and styles of behaving. Without Adult guidance, this can go to ridiculous lengths, such as forms of addiction, withdrawal, even destructive or self-destructive tendencies. But the Primitive level also allows passion in daring for noble objectives and ways of living. I believe we each can develop a unique, flexible and optimal balance of the Adult and Primitive modes to act responsibly and playfully, accenting one or the other, mixing and changing the modes in responding to situations. Allowing a balance that's true to my temperament and history, together with aspiring to excellence, generates my living Myth.

There's a strange cultural denial of the distinction and possible integration of the Adult and Primitive/Pre-Adult Minds. We tend to either deny or celebrate the Primitive.

Imagine telling your child you can act and think like a child or adolescent yourself—afraid, trying to escape hard stuff, egotistic, less than mature. Such a conversation could be a liberating and learning moment for both. It would've been so good if my father could've told me of his fears and mistakes rather than try to hide them with booze. Whether parents acknowledge it or not, they'll show their kids their Primitive and Pre-Adult levels. At times, it won't look pretty. A parent can show how her or his selfish or excessive behaviors come from a Primitive/Pre-Adult level and can be remedied or atoned. The child can learn from a parent being honest about acting from Primitive and Pre-Adult Minds, with the Adult available to apologize and correct as needed. A child can learn how we're all works in progress.

With the precision and creative qualities of my Adult Mind, I can bring complexity and subtlety to Primitive thinking, feeling and acting. Henry David Thoreau said he found in himself a "higher, or, as it is named, spiritual life, as do most men, and another toward a primitive rank and savage one, and I reverence them both. I love the wild not less than the good."[5] I don't want to get rid of my Primitive and Pre-Adult Minds. They're essential to any interesting development of my Myth, which really is a life-long work or, better yet, play, in progress. Primitive rhythms and passions are necessary to play the instrument of mind-body at its full potential. I want to keep very much alive the imagination and curiosity of a child, a readiness to loosen the Adult Mind to play, to open me to Primitive passion and spontaneity for riffs that can be vibrant,

---

[5]   Henry David Thoreau, *Walden, Civil Disobedience and Other Writings*, 3 edn. ed. William Rossi (New York: W. W. Norton & Co., 2008), pp. 143 (Kindle Locations 2572-2573)

thrilling and fun, and to Soulfully play the blues and spirituals. The Adult in me can come and help out when I get scared or really angry or lost. Together, they can give meaning and creative energy for the motifs, variations and improvisations of my Personal Myth. Psychology has no description of "well-being" or "mental health" comparable to Whitney Balliet's description of the New Orleans jazz music of Red Allen:

> His full, often declamatory tone was suitably crimped by growls or piercing high notes; his basically legato approach was enlivened by rushes of on-the-beat notes; his seemingly straightforward melodic content was enriched by long, sagacious phrases and by a daring choice of notes. Allen was particularly striking at slow tempos. He would linger over his notes, holding them far longer than any trumpeter, and would bend them and press them, coloring them with a distinct and disturbing melancholy. His slow solos were often requiems.[6]

To play my music of emotion well, I have to learn and practice skills of communication and try to be aware of the vulnerabilities and potential of myself and others. I know that strict linear progress and disciplined rationality can create robotic or bureaucratic notes and styles; it may be more efficient, but less human. I need Primitive impetus at times to cut loose from too much calculation or worry. My Childish side must be allowed to get around the Adult Mind to take myself and the world less seriously, to allow me to play more imaginative, funny and meaningful music.

---

[6]   Whitney Balliet, *Improvising* (New York: Oxford University Press, 1977), p. 3

From my Pre-adult Mind, I let out the little kid to freshly step up into the snowy foothills, unconcerned with earlier or later in the day or with what she's supposed to do. She's freed of notions from her Adult Mind. She'll let almost anything happen. I need to let her out as often as I can. She isn't so innocent. She can do the wrong thing many times. She thinks without a lot of my Adult skills, but she can free me of stifling reasons to hold back. She can allow me to try what the Adult Mind thinks I wouldn't be good at, help me get past its worries and calculations. I need her to let down my guards, explore without agendas, let go of expectations. The kid doesn't worry about looking awkward or unattractive at doing something, even if doing it badly. I want her openness and carefree instincts to work and play well with others, with my Adult Mind still there to manage her urges.

Keying into the life purposes of my Myth can inspire my music of emotion. My Centered Improvisations can allow me to respond flexibly in scary situations and play with a greater range of ideas and melodies. By experimenting with, rather than mastering, reality, I can expand the capacity of my Personal Myth. I can enjoy the process. I can play in the mystery of Being, not to beat others or just survive, but to appreciate the Myths of others—Myths of love, death, beauty. A playful Myth allows me to do what I choose to do with ease and trust, for the good.

The Adult, Primitive and Pre-Adult Minds can play their roles together to help me consciously realize I have nothing I need to defend about myself, no need for anyone else's approval. They can bring to my heart an assurance that I am enough. I can then better focus on what I can do to help with problems out in the world or in some project at which I may be pursuing some hazardous or losing strategy. I can feel how usually there's less to fear.

No perfect balance

When is it best to go Primitive? When is it worse? How do I know the Adult isn't just scared or indecisive? Do I decide these things?

At any moment, deciding what quality and intensity of emotion should come out isn't like selecting a song or album to play. At least, not usually. It's important to have become familiar with the many different styles, genres and possible virtuosities of my music of emotion to know what can play. Right now, I'm in a busy airport, having left a fiasco and waiting to see if my flight will be cancelled as warned. I call up the long, tragic notes of a Japanese flute of my mind and nerve endings. The music sets it all in better perspective, tells me there are far worse times, far more beautiful notes, ahead in life. The music invites me to contemplate how much worse so many are having it in the world right now. It settles me.

I can tell by the emotional music playing in me when protective forces are triggered in my Primitive Mind. Because I know it's mostly my Primitive Mind and not the world that's pushing me, I can determine whether it's helping me with its niggling static or its flood of righteous fanfare or its blaring emergency and escape sirens. I can try to cut into its music with a soundtrack that would bring calmness, focus, analytic clarity or metaphysical truth.

Identifying the music playing, its usefulness or unnecessary noise is itself a skill that takes practice. Opening a different, more meaningful channel of the music of emotion is an art. It's rarely performed perfectly. If I worry about doing it right, much less perfectly, I'll have a harder time playing the music I may need.

Credible studies have shown the self-protective energies—from sources such as fear, abandonment, betrayal, anger, loneliness—are far stronger and more quickly triggered than positive energies such as compassion or joy.[7] This helps me realize that disturbing music is playing from myself, not from others, and how hard it can be to alter the force of those energies. To cultivate the skills of self-monitoring and assessing the music that can play requires a commitment to being reflective and honest with myself. I also have to seek and be willing to hear feedback from trusted others. I have to devote time and attention to exemplars and texts that demonstrate the transcendent way to love in difficult situations. Even while striving to do my best, it helps to be humble, to seek the support and guidance of caring and loving people.

There are ways I can learn and practice to play rhythms and tones from the Primitive, Pre-Adult Mind for the Myth of love, so the immature wants and demands can be calmed, directed or modified. Methods of playing can be learned from counselors, teachers, good books, as well as from those caring and loving people around us living the best imperfect lives they can. Learning good coping methods and strategies are for the care, fine-tuning and skillful playing of the instrument of body and mind in a world that actually doesn't center on me.

---

[7] Roy F. Baumeister, Ellen Bratslavsky, Catrin Finkenauer, Kathleen D. Vohs (2001) "Bad is Stronger than Good," *Review of General Psychology*, Vol. 5, No. 4, 323-370

In my important relationships, the Adult and Primitive/Pre-Adult levels get continually out of balance and need correction, communication and contrition. The difference between Adult and Primitive abilities to communicate is the difference between what Steven Stosny calls monocular v. binocular vision. Monocular vision is how I see, sense, feel and interpret everything and everyone naturally—from the perspective of Me at the center of the universe. Binocular vision is holding, next to my own lens on everything, a realization of and care for the perspectives and Myths of others. Trying to listen, perceive and understand with binocular vision is hard. It'll involve checking with the other person(s) to see if I got it right, if I need to know more to understand, to make sense of how others interpret me and our context. In intimate relationships, I've learned the hard way how my partner's vision is often very different from my own. Rather than worry about whose stories about the world and ourselves is more true, I try to call up curiosity about each of our minds and listen to the music my partner plays without countering it. It's rare for anyone to do binocular perspective taking really well. We can only continually practice and get better. From my Adult Mind, I try to get better at seeing how others interpret shared situations, then try to play my music in accompaniment, not just solo, in explaining myself. I need to be aware that what I observe and interpret and want is likely from the orientation of the limited, egocentric Me. There's much more difficulty and depth in playing music that takes account of others' different perspectives, vulnerabilities and desires. The challenge invites a caring dialogue and dance.

A tricky and essential aspect of emotional maturing is trusting myself and others. I've been able to trust those with whom there's assurance of safety, while allowing for our mutual flaws and mistakes. There's always risk in trusting. The risk need not be foolish or reckless. I always have my coping and capacities to fall back on when someone fails me or hurts me, which usually isn't intentional on their part. But there's no way to play the music of my most noble values and purposes without daring to take risks in relationships and, at times, getting at least bruised. I welcome the tough times, even when I lose, otherwise I can't get better. Finely attuning to others can start with being honest and open with myself about my own vulnerabilities, wounds and fears, and the innumerable ways I've tried to protect myself. This can allow flexibility, prudence and forgiveness in dealing with others, as well as a sense of humor, irony and optimism as styles of my Myth. I can cultivate confidence and resilience in order to trust, and to recover from betrayals or hurt or failures. I do none of this perfectly.

The calling

My Personal Myth, let's see ... It isn't a story about me or my past. It's what I'm doing in my life. It could easily become only a tale I tell myself. It could conform to the Mythology of my culture—financial success, commercial entertainment, status, the esteem of others and myself. It could even be a delusion. So, it's important that I carefully tune it in to what life's calling for from me, which isn't about conforming. It requires help from wise guides and inspirations, experimenting, practicing Centered Improvisations, until my emotion music plays tones of mystery and beauty in the Wild. When it plays for something greater than me, it can take a while to understand its reverberations, what it calls for from me. I'm called to play this music of love with exacting, exciting, and forgiving, standards. The music is essential to my Personal Myth.

How I treat the people I'm close to, how I treat the earth and its creatures, how I sacrifice and take risks for the sake of love, for Beauty and the Good (as imagined by Plato and blessed by the incredible Iris Murdoch) and for my own learning and development, how I do all that will let me know how I'm responding to the calling. There's no voice or text that tells me what to do. There is no belief system that'll guarantee I'm doing it right, tapping into my greatest potential. I can't always get it right, but I can be responsible for effects of my actions, I can be curious about what I can learn even from misfortunes, which can come out in primal chords. Sometimes I just have to holler.

What I do and how I do it constitutes my Personal Myth. How beautiful or ugly or dull its music of emotion feels will tell me, and certain other people too, if the Myth is calling me out, if it smacks me for how lousy or stupid or uptight the music plays. My Personal Myth wants music from the world's Mythology of greatness. Example: how Ezra Pound defined a "classic": "It is classic because of a certain eternal and irrepressible freshness." [8]

How do I play that music of emotion? When I act with courage without even thinking of the word. When I make the right sacrifices, create the right order needed for a loving relationship with someone. When I, in some way, usually minuscule, uphold the flourishing of others, human and non-

---

[8]   *The ABC of Reading* (New York: New Directions Books, 1934/1960), p. 14

human, and live in natural accord with the earth and universe every day.

Sometimes, I'm called to express my Myth, as I'm doing here. I could try to put up a story to be proud of myself, to justify my life or way of life. That would be a Myth of self-satisfaction. People can get a lot of mileage out of that. Or, what a lot of dreams are made of: I could write something, maybe a memoir, try to sell it to a lot of people, make a tidy sum of money, get recognition and respect from my peers or the larger society. That would be a Myth of scoring a commodity for prestige, fame or financial success. My Myth won't let me get away with those. My Myth calls for expressing only to create a passage into a realm of Beauty and the Good. When I give myself to this calling, I'm never sure if expressing is self-indulgent, but I aspire to the standards of a classic: "a certain eternal and irrepressible freshness."

Even though I can feel the calling of my Myth, I can be deceived by my needy, greedy ego, effects from a less than rosy childhood, the stupidities I've been taught and made up on my own. And the calling changes at different times of life. What's needed to keep it fresh is to expose myself to many kinds of challenges. I have a lot to learn about relationships, ethical economic and political orders, and the natural world. I have to maintain a strong, responsible Adult Mind without pathologizing the Primitive and Child in me. I can feel how creative, adventurous and Soulful I am in improvising my daily life, how my protective forces and self-satisfaction can make the music stale and mediocre.

Just as music I listen to can be amazing and inspiring, I want the music of my emotion to take me well beyond the easy average, beyond junk from the past and the American Mythology of materialism. I'll keep learning styles of Centered Improvising and I'll create new music when needed. My Myth keeps calling, inviting me to play from the dimension of Soul.

Epilogue

Angie's paying her bills by free-lance substitute teaching at some grade schools. She doesn't know if she'll go back to her role as counselor. After giving up on trying to date, she approached a pianist who played brilliantly, who in turn finds Angie's music to be extraordinary. They're in love. She hopes it'll be more than that, for each of them, whatever happens. She's careful about it and everything else. But she knows she'll have to take risks for the noble stakes of her Myth.

CHAPTER 5: THE EROTIC CONCERT OF THE NERVOUS SYSTEM

━◦◦◦◦◦◦◦━

I F YOU are chaste, puritanical, ascetic, you may be shocked that there's an erotic game of stimulating, exciting and connecting going on in you. Scintillating charges shoot through your brain, blood, nerves, gut and muscles, calling and responding to your senses, your imagination and the world. Intricately aroused libertines and nymphs, called neurons, flirt with, seduce, ravish and relish each other. They set off a fireworks of ignited orgasms to arouse and inspire your body and your consciousness. Rather than quick thrills of adolescent lust, they may procreate ideas and passion for a life in harmony with the cosmos.

If you've read thus far, you'll know that "erotic" here is metaphorical, not literal. Need I clarify that I don't impute sexuality to neurons? I do impute the magic and energy of the erotic to the nervous system. I employ the term "erotic" knowing full well it's mostly used these days for something close to the pornographic, which focuses on male fantasies of women as body parts. The nervous system is often analyzed and written about in a pornographic way—as parts to be used. Rather than pornographic focus on components under the skull, I propose that our amazing neural firings and chemistry may be rendered metaphorically as energies symbolized by the Greek god Eros, biologically essential to human life, connecting us to the cosmos. Carl Jung introduced Eros into psychology as "psychic energy," as explained by Tjeu van den Berk:

> Psychic energy is a concentrated amount of cosmic energy. ... In mythology, we constantly perceive a transformation, a metamorphosis of this libidinal force, this lust. ... However, the sexual drive is only one aspect of the universal Eros, which permeates the entirety of reality like a dark irrational power, from the sub-atomic world to the cosmic realms. ... Jung repeatedly quoted from myths which portray the diversity of this force.[1]

Allowing poetic metaphor to animate our relationship to the nervous system does not substitute for the science. Rather, it substitutes for language and narratives that interpret the science in dry, mechanistic, porny terms that interpret our alive, organic forces as operations of parts within us. The neuro-pornographers' brain equipment needs no connection to nature, only mechanisms to keep the parts working. Buying into this popular rendition, the mechanical nervous system is disconnected from erotically charged contexts of living on earth.

---

[1]   Tjeu van den Berk, *Jung on Art: The Autonomy of the Creative Drive* (New York: Routledge, 2012), p. 25

The usual mechanistic perspective never gets to the significance of the nervous system as continually creating lived music of emotion. The melodies and improvisations are of one's Personal Myth, which may or may not be attuned to the harmonic systems of the natural universe. We don't need to believe in anything super- or non-natural to understand that music, which can't be limited to a mechanical model serving egocentric appetites. The metaphorical concepts in this chapter are meant to express the significance of what science reveals—a nervous system allowing humans to connect to and participate in the erotic energy of the natural world.

The nervous system creates forces within us, wakening and calling to us as the god Eros incited amorous energies into humans, inspiring them to risk all for love. Our instruments of mind-body are chemically and electrically charged by incessant orgies of neurons to create the music of emotion. Again, this is not a sexual fantasy about the nervous system. It is a rejection of the popular pornographic explanations of the brain as parts of a machine juiced by neurochemistry. The rigorous curiosity of science can reveal new metaphors.

Neural notes of the concert

Progress in neuroscience has begun to allow us to discover and understand the intricate, delicate neural networks throughout the mind-body, which act as erotic stimuli for moving, thinking, sensing and feeling. These networks have been explained according to the mechanical model put forth by writers and Youtubers—some of them neuroscientists, some popularizers of the science—who describe the brain and nervous system as if consisting of dissected parts injected with different chemical or hormonal fuels. Media outlets spread news to the public that their minds and bodies are operated by abstractly named parts (shown in colored diagrams of the brain) for specialized functions—something like porn's reductionistic portrayal of body parts.

As will be discussed in chapter 7, categorizing is an automatic process of the mind. It's become a means of perceiving reality as objects named with words, especially nouns. Objectifying the brain as the operation of parts objectifies processes of the mind such as emotion. Words used for brain parts are Latin relics that give a medicalized aura and are, at least for my taste, ugly. But they persist as part of the metaphor of humans as machines—a crude, easily understandable metaphor. Fortunately, some researchers see through objectifying tendencies:

> ... both the lay public and scientists exhibit strong predispositions to view the world through the lens of simple, objectified noun concepts. Contrary to this view, extensive evidence exists that the world does not work this way. Instead, the fundamental building blocks of everything, from genetics to culture, appear to be dynamic, context sensitive processes.[2]

Understanding ourselves as processes, including the process of reverberating, interactive waves of emotion, begins to clarify the invalidity of the metaphor of people as machines operated for mastery over nature and other people, wielding power over whoever and whatever one may want. That metaphor fits with

---

[2]   Lawrence W. Barsalou, Christine D. Wilson & Wendy Hasenkamp, "On the Vices of Nominalization and the Virtues of Contextualization," in *Mind In Context*, edited by Batja Mesquita, Lisa Feldman Barret, Eliot R. Smith (New York: Guilford Publications, 2010) pgs. 337, 339

a theological tradition of privileging man as dominator and manipulator of matter and nature, entitled to own women, slaves and patches of the earth. The narrative of man as master continues in an industrialized economy, with faith in very high tech, including technologies of pharmaceutical and behaviorist control of emotion. The mechanistic Mythology prevents a perspective that would value the energies of bodies and minds as sacred connections with the earth and the web of life, enabling participation in a cosmic dance. The Mythology of mainstream psychiatry[3] presents us as brain parts and chemicals, to be fixed according to diagnostic manuals to improve the functioning of the parts, especially to function in the economic machine.

I understand the nervous system through an alternative Mythology that features neurons interacting with each other and the world, not as separated objects, but as dynamic processes in the Wild. The processes in which neurons excitedly seek each other out in highly coordinated patterns are like an orchestra playing a complex biological concert in the concert hall of nature's interacting energies. By neurons' pulsating synapses, trillions of neural connections, forming complex networks, are going on each moment to allow you to see, hear, feel, think, digest and otherwise be alive to the world. The network is charged from 120 billion neurons[4] connecting and stimulating each other through various neurochemicals, carrying forces

[3] By *mainstream* I mean practitioners who dole out pills (esp. anti-depressants and tranquilizers) to practically anyone who pays to see them. I exclude those who serve people with damage or disease to the brain and the many psychiatrists who don't restrict themselves to the model of people as primarily diagnoses to be medicated.

[4] This scientific estimate is found in many reliable sources, though I'd like to see them counted.

that can create love, and not just the lusty or ethereal versions, as Anna Nalick sings in "Catalyst":

> When you say love, hmm
> Is a simple chemical reaction
> Can't say I agree
> 'Cause my chemical, yeah, yeah
> Left me a beautiful disaster

What happens in the brain and body is always connected to one's environment—the world in all its natural dimensions. In the Mythology of industrialized psychology, humans are portrayed as mere stimulus-response machines. We have lost the sense of creatively participating in a dynamic, alive artwork of Being, energized and inspired by a complex, passionate music. The world isn't here to passively listen to and applaud or boo your music. The world is indivisible from the creation of your music in the artwork of the senses, molecules of air, flows of expressions and productions, all interpreted and energized through your nervous system interacting with the music playing around and through you in the Wild.

Erasing the boundaries between emotion and reasoning

The mind-body's erotic firings and connections have been analyzed according to a neuroscience model that placed emotion and reason in different regions of the brain. The logic of that theory explained the human brain as divided into three areas: (1) at the lowest level, the brainstem area, often called the Reptilian Brain, neurons produce instinctive reactions, causing one to react before thinking, as in a quick pull away from a snake; (2) in the next area up from the brainstem, the limbic system, neurons radiate emotions; and (3) at the top of the brain, the neocortex, neurons form thinking capabilities of abstraction, analysis, planning, etc., sometimes called the Rational Mind. This theory was modeled in scientific terms as the "triune brain," by which the brain was established in three layers, graphically shown in Wikipedia[5] as:

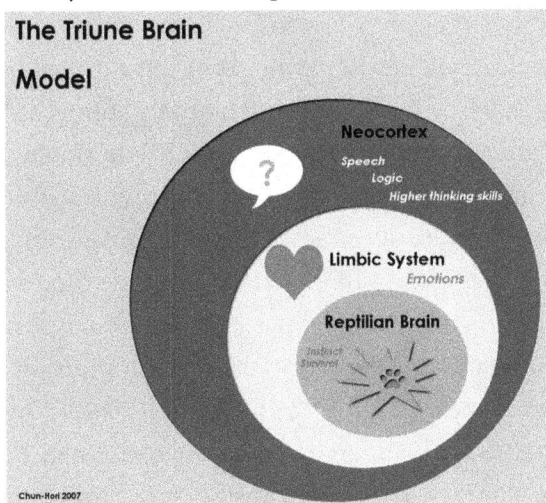

The model has been highly influential on the practice of psychotherapy or counseling. It made things simple: you could blame the Reptile Brain or limbic system for your bad choices or behavior. Early in my career as a therapist, I taught this model of the brain to people I counseled as a basis for individuals to distinguish and develop the Rational Mind to regulate disruptive forces from the Emotional and Reptile Minds. The metaphors of the Adult and Primitive Minds, discussed in

---

[5] Graphic by Lchunhori at English Wikipedia - Own work by the original uploader, CC BY-SA 2.5, https://commons.wikimedia.org/w/index.php?curid=42657486

the last chapter, are not strictly characterized as Rational v. Emotional or cordoned off in separate regions of the brain.

My understanding and my practice of counseling was dramatically corrected by work of neuroscience researchers such as Lisa Barrett Feldman, who made available to us knowledge of the far more complex systems of the brain, nervous system, and bodily processes. The science conclusively demonstrates that emotions are not separate from the rational operations of thinking but are interrelated and neurally connected. Responses, actions and meanings arise with both emotional and rational aspects infused in lightning fast coordinations of the neural network. The erotic concert plays from a neural orchestra of many sections: "The basic idea is that the observables of psychology—thoughts, feelings, actions are not driven by single causes but are the emergent results of multiple transactive processes."[6]

What a sophisticated, sometimes chaotic, concert plays from constantly firing synapses, flows of hormones and neurochemistry, intelligently following intricate systems of the genes we're born with and the world we're born into. The systems incite lusty neurons to have intercourse, form complex pathways in the brain for every feeling, movement, dream and thought we have. Much of the neural activity is devoted to the body's complex processes, which we don't consciously direct or even perceive. Neural networks are crackling right now, responding to whatever's happening outside and inside of your body's skin, driven by memories, fears, genes and needs, responding to the world, blooming curiosity, wonder, creativity

---

[6]   *The Mind in Context*, edited by Batja Mesquita, Lisa Feldman Barret, Eliot R. Smith (New York: Guilford Publications, 2010) p. 5

and cruelty, figuring out and sometimes solving the problems we fall into.

The sciences that have discovered the complexities of the nervous system are some of the highest achievements of human learning. Even if we could, we don't have to understand all the science. But we can appreciate the amazing biological miracles that, every moment, produce our ideas, fantasies, noble and ignoble fights for life and liberation, spiraling out songs of love and hate and indifference on a fast-moving earth. Though neural networks play the music, we each are responsible for whether the erotic concert is of beauty or brutality, love or evil.

How the concert plays

Lisa Feldman Barrett provides as concise an explanation as possible: "An emotion is your brain's creation of what your bodily sensations mean, in relation to what is going on around you in the world. … Emotions are not reactions to the world. You are not a passive receiver of sensory input but an active constructor of your emotions. From sensory input and past experience, your brain constructs meaning and prescribes action."[7]

Neural networks play like an orchestra shifting constantly in its hugely diverse sections to respond to experiences and predict what will happen. For example, we feel various intensities and tonal qualities of fear from various kinds of threat—from the violent to the banal. The threats are received as signals that trigger processes of prediction that are interpreting what's happening and preparing to respond with lightning speed of

---

[7] *How Emotions Are Made* (New York: Houghton Mifflin Harcourt 2017), pp. 30, 31

neural connections. Those responses depend on the patterns of music we've repeated, chosen and cultivated. So, if my partner threatens to leave me, the concerto can play as freak-out screeches, aggressive doom metal, drones of despair or, hopefully, warm movements of acceptance and caring to center me from the choruses of catastrophe. The erotic concert of the nervous system can begin with chaotic escapism, blaring cries of terror or aggression, then shift to more sober or soothing tempos to allow an Adult level of resetting, followed by orchestrated integrity.

It's not all in your head

The meanings and strategies I compose to respond to sensory signals are affected not just from patterns I've practiced or habitually repeated, but also by the music of others I interact with and the culture in which I move, maneuver, intuit, remember and interpret. The concert plays to and from the environment and action in which I'm engaged. And it plays through the body, not just the brain. To help me avoid self-defeating thoughts and actions, such as intense blaming of myself or others, I can focus on relocating the music from inside my skull, as just my state of mind, to awareness of my body's experience (e.g., the beating of my heart), the action happening between me and what's encountered in the world, and the sources of the music playing in me (the triggered vulnerabilities and protective forces). The emotional energies going on every moment in me are part of what I'm doing in an interaction with who or what I'm relating to—someone else, a work of art, some mind-numbing work, some ecstatic or fearful activity, etc. The erotic concert is never a self-enclosed masturbation of neurons.

I'll give an example from a session in which I was counseling a couple (with details changed to protect their identities). I'll call them Jill and Alex. Jill was contemplating a major change in her life, which would involve some financial risk, but would move her closer to fulfilling a potential of hers. The change could also benefit both of them as a couple concerning issues they'd been citing as problems. She spoke about the possibility of enacting this change with obvious excitement that had been missing in prior sessions. Alex was a bit shaken up by the risk which could affect their material standard of living. He brought up a lot of insightful factors to consider about the opportunity. Jill was silent, her smiles faded. She finally shouted out "Okay! You win! It's always been this way! I won't do it!" She abruptly left the room.

A standard way of describing what I witnessed would identify Jill as feeling enthusiasm, then gradually less so, then agitated, then angry, if not furious. I know therapists who'd see Jill not just in terms of those emotion words, but even try to label her with a diagnosis or as failing to "regulate affect." I know other therapists who'd interpret Alex as inconsiderate, perhaps deploying patriarchal power. Those approaches assume the problem was what was happening in their respective emotional states, generated in their brains. I saw them as playing music together without realizing how the notes they were playing were out of attunement and conflicting. Jill's abrupt exit from the room was a good move. I firmly believe in the benefit of calling time-outs to abruptly stop communication when the participants can't be sure of stopping an escalation of hostile music. Moving the body can help to recenter. Taking a walk alchemically changed Jill's music. When she returned, I gave cues to guide them to recenter themselves from the forceful music that arose: first, allowing awareness of their physical rhythms; then, realizing the vulnerabilities being triggered along with the protective forces, and how to accept and care for them; then, listening to each other, opening to the music of emotion from each other with curiosity, respect and appreciation, so that the music could be of connection and mutual understanding, not who was right or wrong. Ultimately, they were able to alter the music of that interchange and look at how to experiment with different styles that would allow more loving ways to listen to and learn from each other. Slowing down to a focused process, they felt how they could play a musical duet, not a determination of who wins or loses. It wasn't easy, but great music never is.

The ideas I write about in this book arose mostly from the limitations I found in how psychology explains people and how mental health professionals limit their formulations and prescriptions for the human problems presented to them. There are scholars and practitioners who don't treat the problems simply as encapsulated mental disorders or a "chemical imbalance." For example, Batja Mesquita doesn't confine emotions to the individual's brain or state: "... emotions are directed engagements with the [person's] social environments, relationship alignments, or strategic bids."[8] In other words, emotion isn't just within the mind, but also within a person's flow of action. The notes of my emotion are aesthetic enactments of my responses to notes played to me from Myths of others and the Mythology of the culture. Jill and Alex shifted from

---

[8] *The Mind in Context,* edited by Batja Mesquita, et al., Guilford Publications, 2010 p 95

seeing each other as problems to finding a wider range of music to play together, allowing for harmony and dissonance. By continual practice and opening to each other's music, they'll create compositions for loving Myths of each other and their cute family.

A concert of polarities and combinations

Reaching into and beyond neuroscience and dynamic systems theory, Evan Thompson began, in *Mind in Life*[9], "to sketch in a preliminary way what a neurophenomenology of emotion might look like." (p. 381) (I won't begin to try to describe "neurophenomenology" though it really is much more commonsensical than it sounds.) Thompson's account is valuable as pointing out the variety and dynamism of elements going on in the erotic concert of emotion. I've summarized and supplemented his analyses to describe how the individual's instrument of mind-body attunes to the world. While the description uses a lot of abstract terms, they're meant to indicate details of our attunements, flows of thinking and sensing, how we continually meet the world, feeling and playing a range of responses with others, playing our music in an interactional orchestra.

1. I'm always experiencing from current sensorimotor fluctuations, and the "'primordial dynamism' of the lived body" (p. 378), a live generator of Personal Myth, including "lasting interpretive-emotional habits specific to classes of situations" (p. 380).

---

9   *Mind in Life: Biology, Phenomenology and the Sciences of Mind* (Cambridge, MA: Belknap Press of Harvard University Press, 2007)

2. The "body's feeling and movement tendencies"
fluctuate in continual combinations of notes in the
soundtrack of emotion. The notes "exhibit movement
and posture valences—toward/away, approach/
withdrawal, engage/avoid, receptive/defensive. As
feeling tendencies, they exhibit affective and hedonic
valences—attraction/repulsion, like/dislike, pleasant/
unpleasant, and positive/negative. As socially situated,
they exhibit social valences—dominance/submission,
nurturance/rejection. And, as culturally situated, they
exhibit normative and cultural valences, that is to say,
values—good/bad, virtuous/unvirtuous, praiseworthy/
blameworthy. Valence, as manifested in these many
ways, needs to be understood not as a simple behavioral
or affective plus/minus sign, but rather as a complex
space of polarities and possible combinations..."
(p. 378) "[M]ood is always present as a background
setting or situation within which transient emotional
interpretations occur." (p. 379)

3. I am allured, in various ways, by what I encounter.
"Attention at any level is motivated by virtue of
something's affective allure. Depending on the nature
and force of the allure, as well as one's motivations,
one may yield to the allure passively or involuntarily,
voluntarily turn one's attention toward it, or have
one's attention captured or repulsed by it. ... [I]t
emerges into affective prominence, salience, or relief,
while something else becomes unnoticeable owing to
the weakness of its allure. This dynamic interplay ...

does not have an articulated subject-object structure." (p. 374)

4. The event has meaning for me, "reflecting an appraisal, which can take form before the experience of affect … just after (as a post-hoc appraisal), and can interact continually and reciprocally with affect, through processes of self-amplification and self-stabilization … The appraisal can be fleeting or detailed, realistic or distorted, empathetic or insensitive (and typically reflects some combination of these features). Much of the appraisal will be prereflective and/or unconscious." (p. 376)

5. My experience has a "feeling tone … along a pleasant/unpleasant polarity." (p. 376)

6. There are reactions in my body, externally (e.g., face, posture) and internally (e.g., pulse, skin heat, muscular tensions or relief, endocrine activity) as part of my "differential action tendencies or global intentions for acting on the world." (p. 376)

7. My thoughts and concepts move along various associations and interpretations, building on each other, shifting or thrown out, as part of experiencing.

8. In dynamic systems terms, the "affective allure amounts to a parameter that at a certain critical threshold induces a bifurcation from passive affection ('passivity') to an active and motivated orienting ('receptivity') toward something emerging as affectively salient or prominent." (pp. 377-378)

9. I take some kind of action (observable or not) that has effects on me, through the strata described above. The

action will likely result in a change, to some extent, in my Myth's long-term patterns of predicting, appraising and responding to situations. I may learn new ways to be receptive to and feel phenomena of different experiences, discriminate different factors, recognize obstacles and potentials, effects on others and on myself. This is how my Personal Myth continually expands or contracts.

Thompson's account of emotional experiencing includes the almost infinitely complex interplay of variables among neural, bodily, relational, cultural and ecological systems within which a person moves. Rather than explaining definite causes of feelings and actions, he points to "a complex space of polarities and possible combinations..." The music of emotion plays from an original score of social norms of good/bad learned and practiced in my family and culture, then my Myth and its music change as I interact with wider expanses of the world, as I critique Myths from my past and from my culture. From adventures in the Wild, I can go for those experiences that allow a richness and vitality of perception, feeling and ideas, with appraisals of what effects I want to create in myself and the world. I should take responsibility for how my Personal Myth forms, changes and affects me and the world.

Norms and values aren't simple rules programmed into the mind, but are played by our instruments in many ways, from passively submitting to them, to testing, experimenting with, or flouting the norms. One can be satisfied by the security of a well-paying job, social status, even a family trajectory that conforms to all the markers of success. Then, one day, or maybe over a number of days, something allures this conventional hero to risk it all—perhaps an insight that leads to a mystic withdrawal from society or, at the other end, a sexual seduction that leads to the cutting of secure anchors, then perhaps realizations that her or his sexual Myth is missing or limiting the full potential of love. Disrupting one's Personal Myth disrupts the erotic concert, creating chaos in the composition, perhaps a music of anguish or despair. For a life of continual challenge in the Wild, adapting to changes in one's various environments and situations will likely interrupt what may have been expected to be linear progress. This may be a necessary step to living for greater meanings or it may lead into a detour or worse. Just like music that becomes too standard and familiar, he or she may have to experiment with very different styles of living, figure out what soundtrack is right for the style. The right way to behave can be set out by religious or psychological or peer group Myths, but one can choose to question the norms and break the rules for what may be needed to find more creative ways of living. The wisdom of the ancients and the moderns (including neurophenomenologists) can prevent disastrous accidents and detours and guide us in understanding and adapting, as well as avoiding quacks.

Neural notes of concepts

The erotic process of charging neurons and exciting their connections unfolds in living one's Myth in the world. Neuronal networks are continually stimulated when responding to what's perceived and encountered, as "sketched" above. The erotic concert isn't just chaotically spewing out notes (except when disrupted by ingested chemicals or neural damage). The concert plays from information that's been processed into what we call concepts. Again, Lisa Feldman Barrett[10] concisely describes an enormous amount of complex neuroscience findings:

> … concepts are predictions. Early in life, you build up concepts from detailed sensory input (as prediction error) from your body and the world. Your brain efficiently compresses the sensory input it receives … extracting similarities out of differences, eventually creating an efficient, multisensory summary. Once your brain has learned a concept in this manner, it can run this process in reverse, expanding the similarities into differences to construct an instance of the concept … This is a prediction. Think of prediction as "applying" a concept, modifying the activity in your primary sensory and motor regions, and correcting or refining as needed. (p. 118)
>
> In real life, your brain never categorizes 100 percent with one concept and 0 percent with others. Predictions are more probabilistic than that. Your brain launches thousands of predictions simultaneously in every moment, in a storm of probabilities, and never lingers on a single winning instance. Each time you categorize with concepts, your brain creates many competing predictions while being bombarded by sensory input. Which predictions should be the winners? Which sensory input is important, and which is just noise? Your brain has a network to help resolve these uncertainties, known as your control network. (p. 122) Your control network … helps neurons to participate in certain constructions rather than others, and keeps some

---

[10]   In *How Emotions are Made*, op. cit.

concept instances alive while suppressing others. The result is akin to natural selection, in which the instances most suitable to the current environment survive to shape your perception and action. ... Your control network is more of an optimizer. It constantly tinkers with the information flow among neurons, ramping up the firing rate of some neurons and slowing down others, which moves sensory input in and out of your attentional spotlight, making some predictions fit while others become irrelevant. ... (p. 123)
Your brain has a mental model of the world as it will be in the next moment, developed from past experience. This is the phenomenon of making meaning from the world and the body using concepts. In every waking moment, your brain uses past experience, organized as concepts, to guide your actions and give your sensations meaning. (p. 125) Emotions are meaning. They explain your interoceptive changes and corresponding affective feelings, in relation to the situation. They are a prescription for action. (p. 126)

Meanings can come in the form of words or of non-verbally experienced themes and intuitions. The processes of the mind-body have a natural drive toward discovering answers to what we don't know. Questions can come from a complex spectrum of sources, from the very abstract (such as solving mathematical problems) to the very moral (how my conscience can bother me about my choices). Our drive to inquire, discover and solve is toward horizons of what we don't know or don't know how to solve, all happening with a soundtrack of emotion. Emotion's music, infused with the conceptual process, including words, continually moves us, calling us to aspire to our highest potential with a flow of Creative Energy.

As music, the erotic concert of the nervous system is playing many different notes and chords continually, attracted or repelled by what's encountered. The neural control networks of concepts, infused with energies of neurochemistry and hormones, calling up and recalibrating concepts, makes predictions and sense of what's encountered, which may be quite mistaken. It can be important to be aware of the Adult or Primitive qualities of the music's energy and themes. One's Personal Myth involves a mental model of oneself and the world, its soundtracks, its inspired predictions and directions, which are continually, imperceptibly changing from the polarities and combinations of notes playing in experience. When the predictions and meanings turn out to clash with reality, the Personal Myth and its music can adjust, correct, maladapt or stay stuck. The changes can be very subtle or dramatic.

Meanings are motifs of the music of emotion. They range in quality, complexity and integrity—from shallow and self-serving to profoundly inspired. The motifs, themes and finales of your life are part of the concerto of your Myth. It may be played with excellence, mediocrity or misery, based on what meanings are interpreted, created and enacted in your life.

Naturally negative notes

If you've watched daily lives of animals in their natural, wild habitat—for most of us, this is in "nature" documentaries— you'll know that much of their lives are Survivalist. They are hunting or foraging for food, being alert to and evasive of becoming food for predators. For many thousands of years, humans lived Survivalist lifestyles, developing skills and instincts to hunt, forage and escape predators. The human nervous system retains the capacity for those Survivalist instincts and skills in what I've called the Primitive Mind. The nervous system's amazing fine-tuning for terror, aggression, suspicion, defense and worry continues to play a nervy soundtrack in the background of awareness. In a post-industrial world that's unlike the natural environments and ways of life of our ancestors, we can see Survivalist instincts and skills activated and cultivated by financial or political predators and by cultic bands and conspiracy theorists conceiving themselves as entrenched against others, threatened by their own wacky concepts.

Conditions of most of the modern world are less physically dangerous than in Survivalist times, but situations become more complex and just as intense in the dramatic movements of finding relationships (from coworkers to lovers), being rejected or disillusioned, conforming to or being alienated from social norms, developing ambitions, forming endlessly varied appetites and fantasies for sexual excitement. Because we naturally need to cooperate and connect with people for survival, pleasure and joy, we will get hurt. The people with whom we want to share our music and myth can be unavailable, have different agendas, play a different genre of music. They can reject, frustrate or confuse us. We can react to these misconnections with hurt, bitterness and deepened vulnerabilities that endure. As Angie showed in chapter 4, we all have hidden vulnerabilities that are triggered to greater or lesser degrees throughout life. When vulnerabilities are triggered, motifs of threat and insecurity can play in the body and nervous system from memories and concepts to inspire us to choose to attack or escape or narcissitate. The motifs I go for determine how much of my emotional soundtrack is dominated by protective music. The more I develop those defensive patterns of music, the less free I'll feel to be myself and go for a greatness beyond myself.

In their paper, "Bad is Stronger than Good,"[11] Roy Baumeister, et al. document the multitude of interpretations, moods, beliefs and feelings that show the much greater strength of negative (mostly based on fear and its resonance) over positive (enjoyable, invigorating, etc.) music from our neural and behavioral system. So, what do I do with this negative music when it arises, pretty much every day? If I'm able to shift into Centering modes (described in Chapter 4), I can learn from what those negative tones, thoughts, moods and rhythms may reveal about the limits of myself and the prevailing norms of my society. I may learn how and why fearful or traumatic compositions played in the music of my family of origin, my ancestors, the environment I grew up in, how I adapted to this, how I can sympathize with and critique these influences as a comic music with dark overtones or a dark music with incidents of slapstick.

We're responsible for the compositions we create and play. If we only go for positive feelings in life, we could add to the culture's Disneyfied concerto. If we play superficial music to be happy, we should own up to the shallowness of the life. If we drone on in stuck tunes or noise of a neurotic or narcissist, we should honestly admit the limitation rather than blame others or the past or whatever. We can accept stupid or shameful

[11] Roy F. Baumeister, Ellen Bratslavsky, Catrin Finkenauer, Kathleen D. Vohs, "Bad is Stronger than Good," *Review of General Psychology* 5, no. 4 (2001): 323-370

things we've done, then perhaps caricature them, know them as imperfect, anarchic aspects of our concerto. But we should also look at the social and cultural norms that may have influenced our concepts and neural control network into compliance with social roles that limit, degrade or distort our potential.

Sensations and distortions of reality that flare from notes and rhythms of the concertos of fear, appetite and ego call for the prudent, caring, centered interventions of the Adult Mind. Especially if I've given importance to practice the skills and perspectives of the Adult sense of responsibility, poise and confidence, I can have a better chance of making realistic assessments and choosing effective actions to apply to the situation that may scare or seduce me.

Concertos of fear and courage

Like many of our words for emotion, "fear" is imprecise and can be misleading. It's applied to such divergent experiences as terror at gunpoint, a roller coaster ride, and fear of failure. Naturally, you might say, there's something common to all those experiences—the crazy sensations, racing thoughts, lowering of IQ. That commonality is believed to come from the amygdala region of the brain. Until I learned better neuroscience, I used to buy that conventional wisdom, telling the amazing story of how this small region of the brain (amygdala translates to almond) can radiate the most powerful emotional energy. The neuroscience story goes something like this: signals of danger from the world around us are received at the amygdala, which then shoots out synaptic signals to release hormones, especially adrenaline, through the body; the signals also create behavioral responses of fighting, fleeing or freezing; the system is from thousands of years of evolution as the essential human survival program. Brain scans have shown this brain region light up when people or rodents were frightened.

In 2018, a researcher from Stanford University, stimulated the public with finding a "courage switch" in a brain region. The research group of Andrew Huberman, Ph.D. subjected mice to a menacing overhead video simulation of a predatory raptor, like a hawk. They compared natural responses of mice. Their natural reaction was to scurry for escape. After manipulating the rodent's particular cluster of neurons targeted by the research, the treated mouse didn't run like hell but stood its ground with "courage." As Huberman put it, "You could hear their tails thumping against the side of the chamber. It's the mouse equivalent of slapping and beating your chest and saying, 'OK, let's fight!'"[12] He was pretty sure this finding could be applied to humans.

One of the problems with such neuro-reductionism is that fear doesn't exist without a context, which has an infinite range of variables. The situation of a sudden life threat is so obviously different from that of fear of losing money or a lover. The situation is affected by the person's history of being subjected to and dealing with threats and harm. The situation is affected by the cultural values of the person. An example is the culture of a combat soldier. In his book, The Mystery of Courage, William Ian Miller, gives an example of a soldier being cured of fear. It's a scene from Philip Caputo's book, A Rumor of War, in which a sergeant confronts a marine who had "collapsed in tears sobbing that he couldn't take any more combat":

[12]   https://neurosciencenews.com/fear-courage-8942/

Sergeant Horne bulled up to the marine, kicked him in the ribs, and pulled him to his feet … Horne's face was scarlet and fierce beneath his flaring mustache. He shook the marine violently. "You're a fucking coward, but you're going and you'll take it. You'll take it as long as I do." Holding the man by the front of the shirt, he shook him like a rag doll. "YOU HEAR THAT, YOU FUCKING COWARD? YOU'LL TAKE IT AS LONG AS I DO." And none of us did a thing to stop Horne because we felt the same terror. And we knew that that kind of fear was a contagion and the marine a carrier. So, shake the hell out of him, Sergeant Horne. Beat him, kick him, beat that virus out of him before it spreads.

The medicine worked. The marine recovered, his fear of battle overcome by a greater fear of the big, bull-chested Horne.

Miller comments, "Fear can prove to be its own sovereign remedy …"[13] I'm not sure that was a remedy or if what resulted was courage. It seems more like aggression inspiring aggression.

Contrast Miller's passage with the findings of Kelly McGonigal, Ph.D., another Stanford researcher. In her book, *The Upside of Stress*[14], she advocates meeting fears with responses that include "tend and befriend," using the energy from oxytocin (the so-called love hormone) to protect yourself or others, seek connection and support. The music of "tend and befriend" can motivate you to care for others while literally strengthening

---

[13]   *The Mystery of Courage* (Cambridge, MA: Harvard University Press, 2000), pp. 207-208

[14]   *The Upside of Stress* (New York: Avery/Penguin Random House, 2016)

your heart. For example, she tells how calling up memories of someone you love and trust, or just calling them, opens up neural networks and concepts that can reduce fear. Quite a different Mythology than Miller narrates in his book. Her research also shows the efficacy of playing the music of "The Challenge Response"—using the energy and biochemistry in your body's systems to perform under pressure as a challenge you willingly, purposefully take on.

The point of these examples is to show how "fear," "courage" and "coward" are terms that can have very different meanings from the perspectives of whoever's talking about it. Throughout my life, the perspective I've heard has mostly followed macho motifs. It's funny how Huberman defined fear and courage according to how rodents were threatened by raptors. Maybe he'd been watching too many violent movies or video games. Funny how it wasn't obvious to him or the reviewers of his paper that rodent contexts of fear are very different from what most humans face. As Lisa Feldman Barrett notes about much of the research on fear learning, "I've never been sure why they decided it's fear. Couldn't the rat be learning by surprise, or vigilance, or maybe just pain? If I were the rat, I'd be pretty pissed off about the shocks, so why isn't it 'anger learning'?"[15] So, projecting "fear" or "courage" of behaviors of lab rats onto human nervous systems isn't just inadequate and misleading, it's unfair to the rodents.

What's left out about the amygdala story of fear are so many other interactions of neural systems, such as the complicated story of how one interprets the situation and how different bodily states (like those of "tend and befriend")

---

[15] *How Emotions are Made*, p. 271

affect a response to threats. Remember, what's going on in the erotic neural concert is an intense process of predictions about what you're facing in the situation based on memories of past experiences that are similar, making the best guess about what might happen in the next moment, adding in coping songs, preparing you for your next action, all of which are affected by the music playing in the body. In this rapid process, the neural networks are coming up with concepts to apply to the situation to interpret what's happening and make the predictions. The concept is constructed from different memories and ideas in a process Barrett calls "conceptual combination."

Concertos in the key of fear are played from the Primitive Mind. Certain hormones, such as adrenaline, send sensations through the body, which can be conceived as neural notes and chords of the concerto. The Primitive Mind is continually scanning each moment for threats, playing like the rhythm section of an ensemble. This skill of the nervous system is inherited from the many thousands of years of human evolution that involved Survivalist lifestyles requiring skills and emotional soundtracks to hunt, forage and escape predators.

Real and perceived dangers can switch on the music of warnings and protective forces. It may play in full out overwhelm or in less intense rhythms of anxiety, worry and stress. Sensations are accompanied by the conceptual combinations that tend to give negative interpretations of who and what's around us in attempting to keep us safe. Safe from what? The Primitive Mind was developed over the vast majority of our history to keep a person safe from life threatening predators and hazards. Included in the dangers are other people who may be violent or actively exerting power over the individual. The Primitive Mind fashions meanings of one's history and living situations that can create tendencies to withdraw, become passive, even inert or, at the other polarity, aggressive and manipulative. While individuals and a society can cultivate passivity, aggression and greed, one can shift the concerto with motifs from the Adult Mind, which can interrupt the Primitive music, eventually shift to movements of responsible thinking, moving and creating, while the Primitive music can be blended or integrated into a concerto of fulfilling one's potential for the good.

How afraid I'll be and how I'll then respond depends on the conceptual combinations applied to the situation. If I've rehearsed and prepared for public speaking, especially if I've learned from past performances, I can have a concept maybe like, "I don't care if I look and sound like an idiot, I'm going to be that idiot having some fun." Going through uncomfortable or scary experiences, applying guidelines like "tend and befriend," filtering the situation according to values and virtues I want to stand for are major factors in responding optimally to scary and threatening situations. Of course, each situation is different from prior ones and I likely won't have the exactly fitting concepts available for it. The music of courage isn't to dominate one's own fear (like the marine sergeant was meant to show), but to improvise intelligent responses. An overall perspective such as unconditional self-acceptance can facilitate confidence and, if you prefer the term, courage.

The neural orchestra

The Mythology of neuroscience has been transforming. What was once set in its dominant model was a brain carved up into different parts, regions and hemispheres, with its discrete places for emotion, cognition, language, etc. The model is becoming more complex and wholistic. Especially important is how emotion forms, not just from the amygdala or limbic system, but with conceptual combinations adapting to a person's experiences of the world. The nervous system draws from many different sources in us, especially tunings of the body. The different sources are like different sections of an orchestra, though they can be playing in ways that can clash. With practice, they can create brilliant music.

The erotic concertos of the nervous system are not random. They're formed from movements of the different creative adaptations, vulnerabilities, protective forces, creative improvisations and soulful flows, described in chapter 4. Emanations of the Adult, Primitive and Pre-Adult Minds play together in pretty much every experience. As shown by the contrasting approaches of Miller and McGonigal to fear and courage, one can choose to play more in Primitive or Adult styles, with their corresponding narratives, tones and potentials.

There is something like a conductor of the neural orchestra, though it's not a self or inner entity; it's the "control network" which Barrett notes, "constantly tinkers with the information flow among neurons, ramping up the firing rate of some neurons and slowing down others, which moves sensory input in and out of your attentional spotlight, making some predictions fit while others become irrelevant."[16] The concertos played are meanings made through emotion to form a model of reality to guide a person's choices of what to focus and act upon and why.

If meanings are made and concertos are played through the complex networks of cells and chemistry of the body and

---

[16] *How Emotions are Made*, p. 123

nervous system, isn't the concept of "person" obsolete? Aren't I just a biological machine driven by rewards and punishments? This was the model B. F. Skinner urged in *Beyond Freedom and Dignity*, which continues to influence psychology. I believe that "person," "freedom," and "dignity," are metaphors and fictions useful to conceptualize complex human phenomena, to live toward our human potential. Everyone has the freedom and dignity to be responsible for the concertos they play, as brilliantly analyzed by Barrett:

> This [neural] network can only work with the concepts that you've got. So, the question of responsibility becomes, Are you responsible for your concepts? Not all of them, certainly. … as an adult, you do have choices about what you expose yourself to and therefore what you learn, which creates the concepts that ultimately drive your actions, whether they feel willful or not. So "responsibility" means making deliberate choices to change your concepts. …
>
> You are indeed partly responsible for your actions, even so-called emotional reactions that you experience as out of your control.
>
> It is your responsibility to learn concepts that, through prediction, steer you away from harmful actions. You also bear some responsibility for others, because your actions shape other people's concepts and behaviors, creating the environment that turns genes on and off to wire their brains, including the brains of the next generation. Social reality implies that we are all partly responsible for one another's behavior …[17]

---

[17]   *How Emotions are Made*, pp. 154, 155

In the Wild, you, as a person, can be reactive against what you encounter or you may conform to what others or the culture expect of you. You can also be responsibly creative in making your moves as part of the artwork of what happens in reality. I'll be exploring ways we can exercise responsible creativity as cultivating qualities of character in the art of living.

A different Mythology

Electrified cells seek each other out to procreate into networks resulting in the concert we know as visions and ideas, felt in tones and rhythms, noiselessly flaring out of human animals. What if we were to choose a Mythic model that interprets neural charges as a surging of waves of the oceanic music of love, which can become distorted, consummated, disappointed or corrupted? This music of love may create ultimate meaning, in each person's Myth, within nature, as Irving Singer described:

> We live in a world that in its totality seems to have no meaning to it, a world that exists in accordance with natural laws that are not themselves capable of expressing love or meaning or anything like them. Yet life itself, even among human beings who have become demoralized or have little or no sense of purpose, is always creating value and new forms of meaningfulness. These arise from within, as part of what it is to be alive, and in organisms such as ours they tend to issue into a need for love of one sort or another. These facts of nature are most evident in creatures endowed with imagination that enables them to entertain varied possibilities beyond their actual existence from moment to moment. Our species has this capacity to an extraordinary degree, and

that is why love and the quest for value-laden meaning matter so much to us.[18]

The flow of the music of love takes nonlinear turns in human dramas. It inspires songs of vulnerability that don't rely on the protections of idealized spirituality or commercialized fantasy, as well as the many songs of escape, aggression or addiction. The genuine music of love includes darkness and light, as in Orzabal Roland's song "Mad World":

And I find it kind of funny

I find it kind of sad

The dreams in which I'm dying

Are the best I've ever had

Neural firings allow the instrument of the body and mind to play each person's part in the cosmic dance and music of love. The nervous system provides our ability to experience and create meaning, to play it into the world, not like machines or robots, but like messy, excited, inspired or despondent human embodiments of the cosmic energy of eros.

---

[18] Singer, Irving, *Meaning in Life, Vol. 3: The Harmony of Nature and Spirit*, (Cambridge, MA: MIT Press, 2010), pp. 8 - 9

Chapter 6: Culture's Concert

C ULTURE is how we learn to live. It is also the effect of the way we live. Societies are held together by family, religious and economic practices, language, recognized borders and culture. People learn patterns of practices, beliefs, and feelings by Mythologies of their culture. In the beginning, we have no choice about adopting the culture's Mythology. It happens through the child's attunement with caregivers, relations with family and friends, schools, and, of course, TV, the internet, and high-tech mass media. To become aware of how and why your music of emotion plays and how to discover music that's more meaningful and inspiring, it's important to know how your music has been composed according to the the norms and styles of your culture, how much you want to continue to follow them, how to compose something different.

Culture is often identified as certain types of artistic productions, such as "high," "low," "pop," or "mass" cultures.

Culture is broader than artistic productions. Some mean by culture a refined style of living, from table manners to opera season tickets. That sense of culture is mostly made fun of anymore. The word's often associated with one's particular national or racial or ethnic group. What I mean by culture is crisply defined by Jesse Prinz:

> Cultures consist in those things that are socially learned. Social learning is learning through the help of other individuals or through things that have been created by other individuals. More specifically cultures consist in things that are learned by a process that one might call conforming; members of a culture do things in virtue of the fact that other individuals do those things. Conformity may be conscious or unconscious. Cultures can consist of many different psychological and behavioral traits (habits, skills, ideas, values, etc.) because these things can all be transmitted socially. ... Culture can include things that have both a human and a biological origin. Language skills may be an example. ... [T]hings that are acquired through genuine social learning ... cannot be entirely driven by biology.[1]

If I identify myself as a part of French or American or African-American or masculine culture, I have in mind a living portrait with features of certain foods I eat, music I listen to, ways of speaking, relating to family, mourning, believing, etc. There can be pride in one's identified culture, a sense of solidarity with other members of the group. But the portrait doesn't do justice to the complex history of how one's body, imagination

---

[1]   Jesse J. Prinz, *The Emotional Construction of Morals* (Oxford, UK: Oxford Univ. Press, 2007), p. 184

and feelings interact with the culture, its members and its Mythology. While distinctions of individual identities can be exaggerated—e.g., grouping people into a few simple colors—people within differently named social groups can be quite diverse. Hardly anyone speaks for those who aren't certain of or agreeable with their grouped identity, who don't feel right in any of the offered brands of groups.

A Personal Myth is always related to the Mythology of a culture within which one is born and raised. A Mythology consists of shared practices, beliefs, values, and ideals that compel or inspire individuals to follow norms of thinking and acting. The culture is driven and conveyed by the living, interactive stories and norms of behavior comprising its Mythology, which may be relatively static or, at times, transforming. American Mythology features capitalist practices of amassing wealth, faith in practices of investment and business, structuring and compensating work, etc. The Mythology calls for a shared faith (even if not conscious) that current capitalist practices are necessary for high material standards of living and the security of individuals and families. The economic and political rationales are sold as necessary to avoid misery or lack of freedom like that in North Korea. Faith in the Mythology is assumed to be a matter of life and death, or at least the loss of freedom to watch whatever you want on TV or the internet.

Everyone plays their music of emotion, enacts their Personal Myths in particular styles, which may stay pretty much the same or continually develop and change throughout life. American culture has inculcated in me countless ways of acting, imagining and believing. From historians, critics and exiles of the culture I've learned to critique and overcome many of those influences. The ways I individually embody and act upon beliefs, values and ideals is through my Personal Myth, which diverges from the culture's Mythology.

An example of a cultural Myth is the meaning of "nature." Mostly, it's what we call that which isn't manufactured by humans, that's separate from human culture, such as the lives of non-human animals in their natural habitat. Different cultural voices interpret nature differently. In the values of business, nature is a given supply of "resources" to be exploited for human uses, as in mining, real estate development, economic growth. From an interpretation based upon scientific research and analysis, James Lovelock introduced the meaning of the earth as a living environment of dynamic phenomena he called Gaia. Gaia symbolizes living systems not created or governed by humans yet granting life to humans. It doesn't mean that nature is friendly, nice, pretty or even safe, for humans. It means nature is in living relationship with us every moment. Its reality isn't compatible with business culture's Myth of nature. We can learn the Myth of Gaia through science and by opening to Gaia's majestic, potentially terrifying, emotional music.

I'm always in some kind of relation to the culture I live within. It's like the sea in which marine creatures swim. For humans, the sea isn't aquatic but does consist of waves of energies, especially the cultural undertow to conform, waves of cultural information flowing in sensations, symbols, meanings felt around and in us. The sea is interpreted and expressed by us in our Myths. We have no say about the kinds of currents we're born and raised in. We don't realize how much we're affected by and dependent upon culture because we're immersed in it. When playing our music of emotion, we do so within an affective music of the culture—an engagement with the social environment of shared values, motivations and interrelationships. It gets interesting when the music of emotion playing from my Personal Myth isn't harmonious with the surrounding cultural waves in which I swim, which may not be reverberating in the same genre.

How culture enters and influences us

While each of us is unique, meanings aren't made in an isolated mind. There is no person without a culture. There's no such thing as a brain without a daily environment of social interactions and relationships (current and remembered), an ecosystem, personal practices of daily life, all experienced through culture. We live our particular Myths within a surrounding Mythology of cultural stories, symbols, beliefs and behavioral norms. For a music of emotion that feels much more meaningful than what plays from my culture's norms, I've had to experiment, play badly at first, learn from others, to find intelligible and inspiring compositions.

As discussed in the last chapter, the erotic concert of the nervous system involves the mind's continual calling up of concepts to make sense of the world and what to do next in it. Concepts form from categorizing and explaining to ourselves what we encounter (always with feeling), calling up information from the past, relating, comparing and distinguishing differently perceived phenomena, and the need to act upon what we experience. Though we're sure this is what really happened and how the world really is, what we know is only our mind's model of the world and its inhabitants. This model and the concepts it's made of will be called up in memory to interpret myself and the world, predict what may happen, and decide what action to take. Nothing has meaning without mental concepts. Cultural concepts are learned by adapting to the Mythology(ies) in which we're socialized, then distinguishing qualities and values of what's there. Caregivers who raise us, networks of friends and family we belong to, and the formal and idiosyncratic teachings we're exposed to have various degrees of influence on concepts we form and choose to live by. But we each are responsible for the quality of our concepts.

Concepts are used for a person's conscious and unconscious goals. We try out concepts, throw many of them out, commit to some, all in a process so lightning fast we can't be aware of it. Through the neural network's current complex of concepts, we make meanings of the flow of sensory inputs, bodily sensations, words, ideas, overlain with memories and goals. The meanings can be guided by desires and vulnerabilities, played perhaps in protective and threatening refrains or reverberant waves of pleasure. Defensive lyrics can be in conflict with questing songs of caring and loving, resulting in anguish that may resolved by tones of withdrawal or domination, or in heartbreak or rapture. Meanings are chosen, may be risked.

A baby begins to make sense of what is being sensed with the help of caregivers and how safe and nurturing the social and physical environments are. Conceptual structures are shaped by whatever cultural values guide the caregivers and social environments. The mighty baby brain makes predictions from patterns experienced, initially about physical edges, shapes and movements, but also about humans from the attunement of caregivers. Learning progresses when the amazing miracle of language develops, always affected by how caregivers attune to and treat the child. The child's goals develop from moving about to getting what feels good, avoiding what feels bad. The child's mental model of the world expands, not just with thoughts, but through tonal qualities of how music of emotion plays to and from the people and environments in which he or she breathes, feels and moves, within enveloping, multilayered, forms of culture.

Throughout development, a child's concepts are continually being forged through interactions with family, friends, teachers, the internet and, hopefully, books. The society in which these interactions occur has its own goals, involving rules, norms and meanings usually not explicitly stated. These are supported by cultural concepts, transmitted by stories that are either told, read or watched, and from the lived practices and structures of one's family, religious and social groups, education, work and leisure activities, including pop culture playing in technologized media, which gives little importance to the long traditions of prior societies.

We don't usually notice the Mythology being incorporated into the erotic concert of our nervous system, how it's part of the soundtrack of emotion always playing in us, how much it can lure, elevate or conform our music. We choose among various concepts presented in particular contexts of playing, working, conversing, and in short- and long-term relationships with others, informed by motifs from the past and calculations of the future. What a person chooses to do and interpret each day contributes to the quality of her or his mental model of reality, excluding or altering some concepts, channeling goals into paths that may bring one closer to or veer away from the greatest music. We seek and commit to living for certain purposes and goals, whether aware of it or not. This is how our Personal Myths are formed and continually transform. In his landmark work, *Acts of Meaning*, Jerome Bruner describes the enactment of one's Personal Myth:

> When we enter human life, it is as if we walk on stage into a play whose enactment is already in progress—a play whose somewhat open plot determines what parts we may play and toward what denouements we may be heading. ... [I]t is culture, not biology, that shapes human life and the human mind, that gives meaning to action by situating its underlying intentional states in an interpretive system. It does this by imposing the patterns inherent in the culture's symbolic system—its language and discourse modes, the forms of logical and narrative explication, and the patterns of mutually dependent communal life.[2]

Cultural patterns are learned uniquely within family, educational, economic and romantic ensembles, in performances of work, family and leisure activities, in groups or in solitude.

Imagination

Cultural patterns are taken up or rejected through the mind's process of conceptualization. Concepts are continually formed in our neural networks without our awareness of how or even when they form at lightning speed. Most of psychology has ignored or oversimplified the importance of imagination in forming and transforming an individual's concepts. Imagination

---

[2] Jerome Bruner, *Acts of Meaning* (Cambridge MA: Harvard University Press, 1990), p. 34

is an essential and creative aspect of the instrument of mind-body.

Behaviorism was based on a person's learning by being "reinforced": you follow the dictates of stimuli, which rewards or punishes you for your responses, forming habitual actions. Behaviorists initially didn't care about mental concepts. The mind's processing was called a "black box," and deemed unnecessary to controlling behaviors of yourself or others. That mechanistic orientation is still present in psychology, such as CBT, that includes cognitions—thoughts, beliefs, interpretations—but assumes the cognitions act like stimuli to determine behavior. Stimuli are classified by this theory as appetitive v. aversive—what I naturally like, what's pleasurable v. what I don't like and want to get away from. Under the behaviorist operant conditioning, my behavior can be "shaped" by the dictates of rewarding or punishing consequences. B. F. Skinner wrote a lot about how designers of a culture should follow his behaviorist operation manual, forsaking such outdated ideas as freedom and dignity, to eliminate problematic behaviors and even create a utopian society, as set out in his book *Walden Two*.

However, the mind isn't so simple. While conditioning works for a lot of behavior, it isn't the only way we work. Rewards and punishments work primarily with our Primitive Minds, especially its Survivalist forces. While I often form habits of behavior on the basis of conditioning, I also can think from the Adult Mind, from which I can be discerning and aspiring about my motivations, choosing on the basis of whether they serve the kind of values and style I want in my Personal Myth. I can interpret what happens beyond immediate stimuli, beyond even the pleasurable, beyond the meanings of the dominant Mythology of the culture which loves to condition its citizens by offering all sorts of rewards. Aware that what I perceive and evaluate in situations may be alluring or unpalatable, how cues promise pleasure or threaten pain, I need not be limited to satisfying immediate appetites or aversions. I can imaginatively consider multiple meanings and comparisons of what is happening. At the same time, I can be honest about how I'm feeling about what's happening and the quality of character I want to enact in my behavior. I can do all that through imagination.

Fauconnier and Turner compare the mind's conceptualizing process to the forming of molecules: through "integration networks," concepts that are related or alternative to input stimuli combine, or blend, with the stimuli perceptions in ways that experiment with how they work in interpreting what's happening and predicting what may happen. The combinations of concepts can result in a new concept "with emergent structure that is not in the inputs."[3] I can evaluate the offered input of a rewarding concept by imagining and combining it with other concepts, like whether that reward (what feels nice and advantageous) upholds values important to me. I can choose what alternate outcome seems true to values I want to stand for.

Thus, we aren't doomed to obey and conform to cultural beliefs and Myths. We can better evaluate all beliefs and Myths by applying an active, creative imagination for the most meaningful responses to situations. The more concepts we've learned and cultivated, the more combinations, alternatives

---

[3]   *The Way We Think*, op. cit., p. 42

and innovations we can choose to implement. Like a virtuoso musician who's learned to play many compositions, who can create rich, inspiring improvisations, each individual can cultivate abilities to play the complex instrument of mind-body for the music of noble, playful, loving emotion in acting in the Wild.

Situations, social and economic structures

Oh, if only you could always play the music you want to play, when and where you want. If only you didn't have to conform to requirements of an economic market and an employer, to common, boring conventions of behavior, so you'd be free to play in your authentic style always. How great that could feel. Instead, your style often isn't appreciated. You may be given so little chance. You may have to play with people unlike you. But maybe the challenges can push you to play for the right reasons, regardless of dominant cultural meanings and structures, to become a virtuoso of the best music of emotion you can play. And maybe, just maybe, you find people who want to play in an ensemble with you and, with dedication, compromise, conflicts and effort, you wind up playing beautiful music together.

No matter how reclusive you may be, you still must interact with others. If you happen to find a cave with vacancies, others will invade it from your mind. The conversations and interactions you have involve some degree of shared contexts, common ground or background. The activities, groups, communities, traditions and interests you're drawn to affect who you select for different kinds of relationships and dedicated activities. How much you conform, conflict or synchronize to each other's values will greatly influence the depth and activities of the relationship. All these activities, evaluations, choices and commitments influence your Personal Myth and the forms, intensities and possibilities for the music of emotion you can play.

In situations you're involved in, you can understand and direct your choices of action based on your mental model and conceptualizations of the purpose of the situation and the roles you play in it. The character formations of your Personal Myth lead to various responses to what's happening: passive or active, inhibited or influential, intelligently chosen or impulsive. The music of emotion played in the situation may be familiar and predictable or bold, perhaps innovative. Choosing the predictable may be appropriate or may be a retreat from opening to possibilities in the Wild with curiosity, bravery and creativity. You may find it hard to express yourself, to be recognized, to be wise in harmonizing with others' played parts. When you're unaware of the music playing within you or how you may choose other notes and melodies, when you inhibit yourself out of fear or shyness, you may miss out on a potential quality of experience and action that would be deeply meaningful.

Styles and contents of conversation, codes of conduct, motivations, ways of taking on risks and coping with stresses, all play out in workplaces, the home, relationships and artistic activities. Motifs of the music of individual lives arise in ambitions, disciplines, beliefs and commitments that seem necessary to maintain emotional and economic stability, like caring for a home and a family, keeping a job, paying bills, budgeting, selling street drugs or committing crimes for a living. Fortunate, suppressed, and traumatic experiences go into individuals' styles of ambition, productivity, socializing, parenting, sexuality, artistic tastes, and creativity.

A child is completely dependent on the music of emotion provided by caretakers and the immediate environment in which he or she grows up. The child can experience the music of caring and love or that of deprivation and violence. The child learns a Mythic style that's trusting and expressive or submissive, frightened, defensive. The style carries forward as the child grows older. One chooses concepts and models to rely upon, at times without realizing the choice. At some point of passage into adulthood, he or she will be making decisions critical to forming her or his Personal Myth. A culture can help or hinder the development of qualities of character that structure a Personal Myth. We can judge people as bad or evil because of their harmful behavior without understanding the Mythology he or she learned from and followed.

Where a person's culture does not show caring and love as a dominant style of relations, where instead, the society enacts and facilitates exploitation, cut-throat competition, neglect of disadvantaged members, those styles will affect the development of individuals' concepts, emotional capacities, strengths and potential. Elijah Anderson wrote of how the environment of people in inner-city ghettos produces a "despair [that] is pervasive enough to spawn an oppositional culture, that of the 'streets' … [T]he street culture has evolved what may be called a code of the streets, which amounts to a set of informal rules governing interpersonal public behavior, including violence."[4] He goes into detail about how children are forced to fight from

---

[4]   Elijah Anderson, "The code of the streets", *Atlantic Monthly*, May 1994, p. 82

an early age, often without caregivers who can provide the care they need, and naturally grow in social groupings that rely on violence for self-worth, survival and opportunity.

Visions, models and opportunities for the potential of a Personal Myth can be limited by one's culture. Though we all are subject to influences and opportunities, with just enough Adult maturity and guidance we can question and critique the cultural norms and concepts we've incorporated and seek alternatives through imagination and investigations of other Mythologies. The imagination needs mental concepts to reach alternatives to a Mythology that leads to destructive or despairing or superficial paths. To enrich one's range of concepts, the individual must have access to cultural sources of the highest human life purposes. The sources may be found through teachers, books, counselors, or other guides.

The styles by which each of us feels, thinks and acts are energized by a corresponding music of emotion, which affects how one's Myth is formed. If I get good at taking advantage of others or violence, my music will play in those styles. I may find that I follow styles, lyrics, melodies and movements that conform to the economic roles I play—e.g., working routine jobs for the paycheck, managing or marketing to increase sales, the bottom line, etc.—that affect the motivations, limits and structures of my feelings, thoughts and actions. I may be creating or joining in a music that's narrow in range, thrilling, dulling or deadening or reduced to trivial surfaces of experience. I may unknowingly constrain my thinking and energy to take on the role of a cog in an organization and carry the constraints with me after work.

Was it different in times before the industrial age of capitalism? I once thought people in certain pre-industrial societies worked, played and lived in rhythms that are closer to nature, involving the cycles of seasons and fertility, myths and practices that united people and produced natural aesthetic experiences and artefacts. My parents and relatives grew up on farms that would be considered fairly primitive now. While visits to those rural environments are still meaningful and exotic in my memory, I saw how it didn't overcome many petty and ugly patterns people's lives could fall into. I look with a realistic eye on pre-capitalist economic systems and see: harsh violence and social conditions; the poverty of ancient and medieval economic systems regulated by religious and traditional beliefs and practices; submission to royalty and upper-classes; centuries of economies that relied on raids, war, slavery and beliefs that validated violence.

The music of money

There's a popular sense that America is multi-cultural, meaning there are many different cultures rather than one, and everyone is free to follow, or even found, their preferred cultures. Certainly, there are diverse cultural styles in language, cooking, the arts, fashion in clothing, hairstyles, etc. Examples of American multiculturalism can resemble a diversity of brands of products or TV channels. Despite the many varieties of ethnic offerings, there are common values by which people in this society live their lives, whether consciously or not. I offer the following elements as a profile of what I'll be referring to as the dominant Mythology:

- Money pervades values of daily living, including work, education, leisure, sense of security and worth, measures of success in performance and artistic efforts.

- The world is perceived as resources for human appetites rather than respecting our place in the natural cosmos, the interrelation of systems of beings and bio-chemical processes.
- The predominant goal of life is power for the individual, family, social and political groups, rather than living harmoniously with human and non-human beings, caring for the natural world, addressing and resolving conflicts by respectful consensus.
- Violence and its overtones arise as manifestations of power in a range of activities, from entertainment to war.

These anchors of the dominant Mythology produce values that guide human activities of living.

My profile of our dominant Mythology isn't intended to be complete nor completely rejecting of a market economy. It is the Mythology rather than the economics or political structure I address. I don't believe in the kind of revolution that got short-lived traction among the young (like me) in the 1960's to '70's. I believe that the economic system and culture should be responsibly critiqued, by methods of science, history, moral philosophy and aesthetics, and allowed to evolve without violent means.

Does modern capitalism facilitate freedom and creativity? Industrial capitalism created a system dependent upon money. Money became more than a medium of exchange; it became a medium for valuing and reducing people and the earth to dollars. The capitalist Myth is that individuals are allowed to free themselves from servitude through negotiating for wages, starting one's own business, wisely investing one's own savings, owning one's own property. One would do so through ambitious making, using, saving and investing money. Arguably, capitalism provided openings for more individuals to choose their life purposes, how and what to play on the instruments of body and mind. However, the individual's choices are highly influenced and limited, in current culture, by the dominant meanings and motivations of consumerism, the world as marketplace, as investment opportunity and "resources" to be used for individual power and security, and the comforts and conveniences of individual self-satisfaction and wealth. The political system is dominated by money from oligarchs and their networks.

Critics, defenders and ordinary people should continue to examine, debate and think about whether and how market economies are the most progressive structures to allow individual and collective freedom and progress. Capitalism shouldn't just be examined as theory, but in the practice of it—namely, the reduction of value (of people, nature, art, etc.) to dollars, a business's methods of increasing sales and profits. We should continually examine how this economic system can create a culture to serve the market's main force—money—the increase of which dictates values like beating the competition and maximizing profits, even if this means manipulating and dominating people with far less money, disregarding values not measured by money, destroying natural habitat, getting away with unfair advantages. Meanings of work and entertainment in our society are measured in money. Justice usually takes the form of financial compensation in the form of jury verdicts of big bucks, payoffs, disability checks, etc. Music and other arts take the form of commodities packaged, mass marketed and sold, favoring artists or entertainers who generate the highest revenues regardless of aesthetic depth and creativity.

Our socioeconomic system has fostered norms of ego and monetary rewards to winners, no matter how they win or what they're winning. The market gives monetary rewards to the most marketably innovative—those who capture the most customers who pay or generate ad revenue. Artistic pursuits are judged in box-office or other sales metrics. The market mentality promotes motivations to use others and nature as means to profits, accumulation, and getting ahead for one's own ends, for the advancement of oneself and one's family or group. Faith in the quasi-divine force of Technology, especially High Technology, for the sake of material comforts and conveniences helps erase any sense of a sacred connection to the earth and universe. It's hard for the individual to be aware of, much less overcome such norms, to be genuinely and spontaneously reverent toward others and the earth when one has to depend on exploitive activity to make a living. Mainstream methods of psychiatry and psychology are based on the individual's self-centered interest in feeling good without regard to the whole.

The algorithms of monetizing people as consumers, workers and owners—tracked in sales, profits, expenses, stock exchanges, etc.—calculate values of people and "resources" in sales and costs. The system's justified by rising material standards of living and the wealth of esteemed individuals and corporations. The motivating music of money has been accepted as a part of American life, a life that promises comfort, convenience, entertainment and security. Much scholarly work shows how those in economic power throughout history (including tribal chiefs, kings, royal families, dictators, monopolies) have the dominant influence over the culture of their subject population. The influence can be understood as a system of concepts believed in—i.e., ideology—serving those in power. The ideology can be explicit or hidden and succeeds by people accepting and enacting its concepts, knowingly or not. Standup comics, late night shows and entertainers make jokes about the rich and the stupidities in our culture, but the critique seldom goes beyond the laughs. There's little interest in developing models that would provide a modern Mythology of norms to counter those of monetizing people and the non-human world. Alternative models are usually confined to academia or marginalized mavericks.

Does anyone doubt that American politics and government is run by cash? For US federal elections in 2020, $14 billion was spent by the candidates. Most of this, of course, is spent on hyperstimulating ads on TV, social media, other media, which is how most Americans must inform themselves to vote. When candidates have to qualify by raising enormous amounts of money, can this legitimately be called a democracy? There doesn't seem to be serious concern, much less shame, about it among the majority of citizens.

The culture of rewarding or punishing with money has prevailed with its norms of material self-interest and self-satisfaction. It plays a music that's usually superficial, that doesn't question or imagine alternatives to the status quo, much less play from an integrity of values that recognizes destructive and deceitful practices of the culture. The music of money has little interest in tradition unless it can be packaged to sell. It has the vibe of advertising—upbeat, driven by hype to stimulate, entitle and satisfy our wants. Money gives motivation to the ambitious, hope to the downhearted, happiness to consumers. Life purpose is centered upon material comforts, pleasures, satisfactions, though the messaging doesn't overtly identify these values. Artistic productions are measured by mass consumption. Rather than a means to produce art, money becomes the end. Popular entertainment has been the solution, though outbreaks of pop culture have demonstrated values of justice, integrity and love.

The music of money can't be composed for what's unpriceable, like taking risks and sacrificing for love, justice and beauty, even if its lyrics and themes use those terms for sentimentalized versions that scale to a mass market for the right price. However, imagination and Creative Energy do arise among many artists, even in pop culture, who can vitalize consumers like me, if not the culture. Like all of us, they have to get paid. But if their inspiration is the pay, their influence is corrupt.

Kitschy emotion

It can be helpful to understand our culture's effects upon one's Personal Myth from the literature on kitsch. The term was originally used in the 19th century for cheap mass-produced art that was meant to elicit pleasant, superficial emotional responses. Kitsch relies upon immediate effects and gratification, much like addiction, for mass appeal. Popular movies and video gaming rely on hyperstimulating effects such as special effects and violence, common ingredients of our culture's kitsch. Tomas Kulka wrote a seminal work on the subject, *Kitsch and Art*, in which he noted, "If works of art were judged democratically—that is, according to how many people like them—kitsch would easily defeat all its competitors."[5] In the novel, *The Unbearable Lightness of Being*, Milan Kundera's narrator says kitsch is "the aesthetic ideal of all politicians and all political parties and movements." Kundera's novel focused on kitsch in communist Czech life, showing how capitalism has no exclusive rights to the style.

More than just in artistic productions, kitsch can characterize individual personal styles and entire ways of life, what Roger Scruton called "the Disneyfication of everyday life," involving sentimentality and narcissism, cheap stimulation for cheap thrills, "permitting us to pay passing tribute to love and sorrow without the trouble of feeling them."[6] "Love you" becomes a phrase of sentimental endearment. Special effects are more important than Soul in cultural productions. People bond together over kitschy movies and TV series.

Scruton contrasts the kitschy style of art and daily living with a level of values from "another realm, in which human life is endowed with an emotional logic that makes suffering noble and love worthwhile."[7] To go for this logic is a choice of how much of yourself you're willing to give—in creating and appreciating vital, noble art, in sacrificing for someone or some cause you love. Striving to live from the level of Soul has a certain emotional soundtrack that moves you for what is greater than a comfortable life of self-satisfaction.

---

[5]   Thomas Kulka, *Kitsch and Art* (University Park, PA: Pennsylvania University Press, 1996), p. 17

[6]   Roger Scruton, *Beauty A Very Short Introduction* (Oxford: Oxford University Press, 2009) p. 191

[7]   Id. p. 188

This may seem too highbrow, grandiloquent or high-falutin. Doesn't sharing kitsch culture allow social cohesion? And if a capitalist economy relies on a consumer culture that produces kitsch, that keeps people satisfied with kitschy values and entertaining conversations, that may be accepted as the cultural price to pay for living in a capitalist society. There's no denying what progress has occurred in capitalist societies. People's lifespans have increased impressively. Access to consumer goods, including one's own home, has freed up people's time and choices. People seem to be free to think and express themselves to a degree unparalleled in history. Why would anyone not conform to such an economic and social system that offers and delivers material abundance, high-tech innovations, personal security and fun? Our consumer culture allows for, even commercializes, non-conformists, such as the hippies and underground movements of the 60's and the swash-buckling adventurers of Silicon Valley. If people want kitsch in their goals and styles of living, shouldn't the market satisfy their demand?

The culture affects everyone. You may adopt the mainstream ideology and style of living without even knowing it. You may very consciously affirm and advocate for the modern capitalist society, now promising a tech utopia, without caring about its superficial aesthetic values. People always seem to value entertainment and sports more than the arts. The dominant Mythology plays its music of meaning through you or may be countered by the music played from your dimension of Soul. How will you know the quality of your style of living? From the qualities of your emotion. We all can revert to kitsch when we don't go for more beauty, depth and breadth of meaning to enact care and reverence for others and the earth. We all need help in learning to critique our own music of emotion and the culture's Mythology. Learning from schools and colleges is often hit or miss. You may have to look hard for individuals who live and die for excellence, integrity, beauty and love. There are artistic, philosophic and religious works that responsibly move people to transcend the needy, greedy, self-satisfying ego, that inspire imagining and experimenting with alternative Myths of living. We can be like composers who choose what style of music to create, what traditions are important, what innovations are needed.

Shall your music conform to styles of the dominant Mythology to share in popularity and, possibly, profits? If so, you'll learn to play the role and shape your style to succeed in making money, to be featured and even admired in mass media. You can consciously decide which cultural norms can be followed. You can challenge the dynamic Mythology with alternative ideas and experiments for dynamic combinations of concepts to be offered for others' imagination. Your decision to live by a style is carried into the habits, roles, vocations and Creative Energy of your Personal Myth, inspired by and inspiring your music of emotion.

Your Personal Myth includes dealing with economic demands. Choosing your economic role isn't always clear cut or free. We're all influenced by the culture and how our social networks follow norms. The most meaningful, original and creative ways to live usually aren't supported by the profit-making necessities of our economic system. Business leaders and entrepreneurs are emulated, if not worshipped, in our culture. Their success is measured, of course, in making money.

A market economy may offer many opportunities to make a living, but they're constrained by demand for the product or service. The demand has been shaped by the power of corporations to squeeze out independent or subversive norms and styles that don't maximize immediate monetary returns. Success in the economic system is through a mass market. The mass market is based on appealing to consumers' quick and easy responsiveness to products—i.e., kitsch. Submitting to the norms of a mass market inevitably is to submit to the superficial or deadening effects of money on your originality, creativity and integrity, directly affecting your music of emotion.

Beyond the currents of capitalist culture

There's nothing intrinsically wrong with money, technology or, for that matter, comfort and convenience. I partake of them all, as does pretty much everyone. I don't think I'm entitled to them and I try not to take them for granted. I'm amazed at the economic organizing and innovating that brings them. I want to honestly use money without being used by it. I want to be aware of how my culture and its economy can influence how I perceive and act in my working and leisure spaces, my roles, relationships and goals. I want to know how habitually measuring my time and myself may limit the music of my experience, the creativity and vibrancy with which I can live. I want to be as courageous and honest as Thoreau was in honestly calling out the culture for desecrating nature and exploiting bodies and minds to serve a consumer market.

What can I do about the influence of the social and cultural orders? Not much. How do I call myself out on submitting to the commercial norms of this culture? How do I try to find alternatives under its influence? Through awareness of my perspectives and the potential of imagination, I can understand and relate to the influences. I can also be confused and overreactive. All of that's necessary, as is going out to another source of the music playing without need of me—outside of meanings that serve myself, environments fashioned for humans—where massive waves of earth's music resounds beyond human needs. In one of his few public addresses, Robinson Jeffers told of this music playing not for us:

> The whole human race spends too much attention on itself. The happiest and freest man is the scientist investigating nature, or the artist admiring it, the person who is interested in things that are not human. Or if he is interested in human things, let him regard them objectively, as a small part of great music.[8]

By taking a stand for the "great music," I have less need to protect my little self from others' opinions, rejections or infidelities. With personally realized humility, I can turn away from a Mythology of strength through exploitation, the innate craving for power of selves like mine. Attaining humility that allows access to the "great music" is a personal journey for each individual. Choosing against the dominant Mythology means taking on challenges and risks that are peculiar to each person. There will be more mistakes and failures than heroic feats. My own quest has involved realizing I was serving the dominant Mythology while conflicted about what I was doing in the business world, hearing men speak crudely of women, playing a part in a system of survival of the greediest. I finally

---

[8]   Quoted in Robert Hass, *What Light Can Do* (New York: Harper Collins, 2012) p.143

broke with it to find work that wasn't run by sovereign rules of profit. Through my daily choices and discoveries, I continue to learn how to open to that "great music" of the earth and allow it to lead to a Personal Myth that may transcend my egocentric tendencies without denying my individual desires, vulnerabilities and defenses.

I've witnessed in myself and my history how hard it is to acknowledge how deeply one can be motivated by and devoted to the music of money and the cultural influence it creates. The influence is transmitted, in various ways, through family, schools, mass media, making a living, owning, investing. Good economic, legal and educational systems require good institutions that protect and encourage creativity, order and freedom. The systems and institutions should be continually evaluated by experts who communicate with common people. I can't just blame the powers of the culture, systems and institutions. I have to honestly acknowledge that life everyday happens by and through me. It's my responsibility to cultivate my music of emotion to give effective, responsible meaning to my daily choices that continually form my Personal Myth.

My choices can't be blamed on how the culture doesn't make it easy. I can't complain too much about people not having the patience or priority to care much about our culture. Those who create music outside commercial norms struggle to be heard. Yet there are and always have been people who don't conform to kitsch and the religion of the gods, Comfort and Convenience. It might be as hard as it was for that crazy fish who, millions of years ago, jumped out of the water and crawled onto land to create a whole different way of living.

Crawling out of a dominant cultural ocean and living by norms of excellence in this consumer society requires humility, imagination and courage, but it certainly can be done. Artists now recognized as great created in conditions of poverty. Mozart died buried in debts. Van Gogh painted in conditions we'd consider wretched, never imagining his painting would be sold at New York auction houses for millions of dollars each. Creative Energy is available despite a lack of funding. Opening to our highest potential for creativity, meaning and beauty is possible without a lot of money. It requires a music of emotion that's composed by rules of living for beauty and the good rather than money. It requires me to evaluate how I'm playing the instrument of my mind-body, and what I need to learn. There are plenty of libraries and teachers that can offer me ways to cultivate my mind and Soul. There are plenty of ways for me to choose to act with courage, to create beautiful experiences every day.

With awareness of what aspects of the dominant Mythology I don't want to live by, I can choose what values to live for. I can make difficult decisions about the kind of work, friends and activities in which and for whom I choose to participate, what music of emotion I can go for. I can muffle or forego my Creative Energy, compromise my higher life purposes, conform to the values of profiteering. Or I can dare to go into the Wild with my heart, my head and my original style, finding traditions of integrity and beauty, countering any forces of domination that would co-opt my music. Some say that strategic resistance may allow one to play a part in subverting a dominant cultural order. I don't know about that. At times, the best I can do is duck out of the way of traps and disasters.

What can be helpful is to realize living is an art and we each live it with a style. Each moment, each day, I choose the quality of meaning I enact, the risks I take or avoid, the style by which I feel, think and move. The style forms by what I manage to discover, learn and practice. At each moment, I can dare to play the music of emotion that's at my highest level, no matter what music is playing from the culture.

Progress

Though I find little of interest in the dominant Mythology of America, I'm not advocating battles for one economic system against the other, nor am I morally judging anyone caught up in the Mythology. There seems to me to be no possible quick fix. Great efforts for a more rational, just and civilized society have been made, both in theory and in activism, but progress has been quite limited. Progress is primarily needed on a cultural level. Generally, this would parallel personal development: cultivating and practicing mature Adult capacities and values in political, economic and artistic practices, which would at least entail far less appeal to the Primitive and Pre-Adult level of public values in business, politics and the arts.

The cultural shift in Europe known as the Enlightenment was a revolution that affected the whole world. It was based on intelligence and passion, not violence. Revolutions like that in France in 1792 and Russia in 1917 involved unjustifiable bloodshed. While the perspectives and values from the Enlightenment freely developed, progress hasn't been linear or flawless. Cultural and political actors now can't claim ignorance of how to seek truth, moral goodness and beauty. But the forces of the Primitive levels of human social, political and cultural actions have and will continue to be potential destroyers and distorters of progress. There is so much vulnerability and responsibility for humans as the most intelligent beings on earth. Yet, Primitive power still holds sway in politics and business. It's amazing how wars, greed, irreverence, the befoulment of earth and its atmosphere, seem to be unstoppable. Adolescent, egocentric tendencies seem to spread more rapidly in modern cultures than mature ways of thinking and acting.

Breaking free of the dominant Mythology

The culture of capitalism is based upon a Mythology of profit-making—making a profit from people's appetites and fears, from buying anything (from land to credit default swaps) to sell it at a profit, from the labor of people priced as cheaply as possible, etc. Its Myths play out as rational, ruthless, foolish, triumphant, pretentious. The economic logic turns land and people into things—real estate, consumers, employees—priced in numeric values, related to markets rather than to an ecosystem or tradition. There's not much serious challenging of the supremacy of the Mythology because it seems to make everyone more well off than ever. Being well off is, of course, measured by money. The Mythology empowers and is empowered by social hierarchies. One of its greatest myths has tales of people rising from lower social ranks to reach hierarchies and attain great wealth if they get good at the game of profit-making.

In a *Wall Street Journal* article dated March 3, 2022, titled "These Americans Own European-Style Castles in Their Own Backyards," there are photos and descriptions of single family homes, sold and bought in the real estate market in different parts of the US, described as: a "$60 million listing for a fairy-tale castle in Woodstock, Conn., with a moat and a dungeon"; "a replica of a 15th-century castle in County Cork, Ireland, resemble[ing] a fort or some kind of citadel with two imposing crenelated towers on either side"; a Colorado chateau with "a lighted colonnade, a turret and 12 dormer windows flanked by statues modeled after ones the sellers had seen in Monaco. Inside, there were 126 custom-made chandeliers." There's nothing noble about the architecture or the acquisitions of these imitations. The suburban edifices are trying to impress, to be dominantly decorative. The main narrative is of prices for which they're bought and listed. They are rewards that seem to prove the Mythology of America as the land of opportunity. While the super-rich aren't always so conspicuous about their wealth and comics could make jokes about the castles and mansions, there's no question that such wasteful, vain expenditures are accepted in the Mythology. I've been a part of serving the dominant Mythology that sustains such wealth. I finally broke free of it.

My history shows how a Personal Myth can form despite a lack of early knowledge or guidance and can transform through my aesthetic dimension, which I'll more fully discuss in a later chapter. I discovered the magic of aesthetics as a young kid, haphazardly. Like everyone else in my working-class family and neighborhood, my mind-body absorbed the dominant Mythology from family, TV, movies, games and sports I played and followed. I was about six when a couple of jazz records came free with our new stereo. I played them incessantly. I devoured books of Greek myths that were part of the encyclopedia set my parents bought. The radio brought the early music of Bob Dylan. From some anthologies we were given in high school and my searches of the local library, I discovered avant-garde literature and art. No one else in my family, neighborhood or school had heard of it. I didn't know what the aesthetic dimension was, but so much of my life would change because of it.

After high school, I worked in a factory, in a couple of years became a forklift driver extraordinaire. My music of emotion called me away. I entered college to study literature. After graduation and just before a marriage, I felt compelled to choose a path that would provide financial stability and growth, wound up as a business lawyer. As a young adult in the 1970's, I didn't know much about the Mythology of capitalism. Still, I trusted it and my Personal Myth formed within it. In the 13 years I was a lawyer, the music playing in my Personal Myth was often morally discordant. I saw how greed corrupted the choices made by individuals and my society, how the dignity of people, non-humans and the earth was not part of the profit-making logic of the Mythology I was supporting. Though the music of my emotion was calling me away, it was hard to see an alternative way of living that would work. I studied critiques of capitalism. I was drawn more and more to philosophical and artistic traditions, from ancient to avant-garde, that were alien to the dominant Mythology. In the last few years of practicing law, I got involved in pro bono work on behalf of refugees and women who'd been subjected to sexual harassment. I finally left to become a clinical social worker. I was guided to a different Personal Myth by imagination and passion in the aesthetic dimension that had never died in me.

I have to continue to cultivate skills to activate and expand this dimension of my Personal Myth. Being true to my aesthetic potential motivates me to be reverent, creative and exhilarated by what I experience and do in the Wild. I'm called and challenged to go for what is beautiful and good, for values that transcend the self, and to join a deeper dimension of the Wild.

I suspect it's become much harder for young people these days to find alternatives to the dominant Mythology. Research by Patricia Greenfield, UCLA professor of psychology and director of the Children's Digital Media Center, Los Angeles, found that skills in critical thinking and analysis have declined with the pervasive use of computer or television based visual media and a corresponding decrease in reading.[9] Socrates roamed the public spaces of Athens, focusing on people's language and ideas, challenging citizens to think critically, verbally cracking assumptions open in an attempt to help them better think. Of course, he did so without benefit of low or high tech.

Toward an aesthetic scientific Mythology

Is a Mythology that counters that of capitalism desirable and possible? Not only because of the clear signs of waste and destruction, but with the potential of human imagination and intelligence, the answer is yes. For quite some time now, scientists, philosophers and creative artists have begun to imagine and enact meanings of living in ways that would sustain, enhance and celebrate the eco-symphony of human and non-human

---

[9]   University of California - Los Angeles. "Is Technology Producing A Decline In Critical Thinking And Analysis?." ScienceDaily. ScienceDaily, 29 January 2009. www.sciencedaily.com/ releases/2009/01/090128092341.htm

inhabitants of earth through a reverent yet realistic relationship with the actual, wondrous, mysterious universe.

One of the symbols of the new Mythology was from a scientist, James Lovelock, who identified the intricately interrelated systems of the earth as a living planet, affecting and affected by its inhabitants. He named the theory Gaia, the earth mother goddess of ancient Greek religion. Rather than reverence for Gaia, profit-making has led us into trying to choke her to death. Humans can be recognized as participants in the harmonics of the living earth. How we affect its biological systems is revealed by the sciences. How we're responsible for harm to its natural systems is shown by ethics and common sense. Lovelock describes it well:

> We have made this appalling mess of the planet and mostly with rampant liberal good intentions. Even now, when the bell has started tolling to mark our ending, we still talk of sustainable development and renewable energy as if these feeble offerings would be accepted by Gaia as an appropriate and affordable sacrifice. We are like a careless and thoughtless family member whose presence is destructive and who seems to think that an apology is enough. We are part of the Gaian family, and valued as such, but until we stop acting as if human welfare was all that mattered, and was the excuse for our bad behaviour, all talk of further development of any kind is unacceptable.[10]

I don't think science alone could create a Mythology that would move most people because its education and literature

---

[10] James Lovelock, *The Revenge of Gaia: Why the Earth is Fighting Back – and How We Can Still Save Humanity*, (London: Penguin, 2007), p. 189

are anchored in so much abstraction, featuring collections of data and complex mathematized theories. The music of such expressions is, for most of us at least, pretty uninspiring. The reality of ecosystems, of the physics of the universe can't be captured and confined in abstract, ossified language, for the complexities, dynamic flows, transformations, and recombinations of what we call matter and energies inherently exceed abstractions and defy exact definitions in technical language. Is it a dodge of coherent, rigorous thinking to suggest that technical and descriptive words aren't sufficient? Long ago, Daoists accepted the inadequacy of words alone, as expressed in the first chapter of the *Daodejing*:

> Way-making (dao) that can be put into words is not really way-making.
> And naming that can assign fixed reference to things is not really naming.
> The nameless is the fetal beginnings of everything that is happening,
> While that which is named is their mother.[11]

And the mother has been named Gaia.

So, am I suggesting we do without words? Of course not. What about objectivity, which science relies upon to prevent political, economic or personal bias and manipulation of observed evidence? Does the Mythology change with each subjectivity? Every "objective" observation is infused with a perspective and with the music of emotion (yes, there's feeling to differential equations). If you've ever been questioned and

---

[11] Roger T. Ames and David L. Hall, *Daodejing "Making This Life Significant": a Philosophical Translation* (New York: Ballantine Books, 2003), p. 77

observed by some "objective" assessor, such as a psychiatric assessment, you could probably feel how cold and controlling the observation was. The proper role of objectivity is in discerning the validity and feasibility of concepts according to unbiased criteria. But science need not be coldly insensitive. We have to be aware of the perspectives and morality within which we try to objectively observe and assess. A surgeon has to treat a body on the operating table as objectively as possible but can do so from a perspective of reverence for life. Though science itself can be plagued by biases, its basic process invites critique of its claims. Its methods and continually refined or transformed concepts are a model for a new Mythology that would be self-critiquing and corrective, especially about those seeking to use science for self-aggrandizing power.

The aesthetic dimension of the Mythology wouldn't simply translate the concepts of science into easier words or ideas, but would express its findings and values artistically, poetically. The late pioneering biologist, Edward O. Wilson called for a consilience, or conceptual blending, between scientific and aesthetic ways of knowing and expressing—an "Ionian Enchantment." He said the consilience wouldn't be "hybridization, not some unpleasantly self-conscious form of scientific art or artistic science, but reinvigoration of interpretation with the knowledge of science..."[12]

The call for consilience has been answered by Donald A. Crosby, a professor of theology, who's synthesized many concepts into what he's called religious naturalism, which

---

[12] Edward O. Wilson, *Consilience: The Unity of Knowledge* (New York: Alfred A. Knopf, 1998) p. 211

has no belief in or devotion to God, Goddess, gods, or goddesses. For it, nature in some shape or form is all there is, ever has been, or ever will be. ... In the perspective of religious naturalism, human beings are integral parts of nature, one particular species of life amid the vast numbers of such species and their members that presently dwell or have previously dwelt on this planet. Humans are linked with all other creatures in a common evolutionary history based on a common DNA template, and they are bound together with them in intimate, crucial relations of ecological dependency.[13]

Crosby has committed to the responsibility to give adequate concepts and "non-discursive symbolic modes of expression" to allow each individual a unique, intimate relation to the natural world through "symbolic forms of intuition and expression in our everyday lives."

The dominant Mythology of capitalist culture has its roots in Judeo-Christian religion. The creation myth of this religion was summarized by the late philosopher David Hall:

... in the context of Genesis myths ... God is primarily construed in terms of Power... 'Nature' is the object of God's creation. ... the world remains under his complete control. But this control is qualified by the fact that man

---

[13] Donald A. Crosby, *The Thou of Nature : Religious Naturalism and Reverence for Sentient Life,* (Albany: State University of New York Press, 2013) p. 2

was made God's 'deputy.' As such, nature is an *object* of *man's* control. He must establish power over it.[14]
This Mythology's commandment of power and control over nature has taken the form of power and control over beliefs for a mass consumer market and labor force. It's culturally transmitted mostly as kitsch in the mass media. Nature is sentimentalized as nice landscapes, entertaining videos of animals and tableaus playing on screens. Gaia is irrelevant in movie extravaganzas and video games.

Developing a Mythology that would be true to the sciences (not including the social sciences, which only mimic real science) and expressed aesthetically could allow a natural sense of connection and interrelatedness with the continual self-creativity of nature. It would be a big shift from the dominant Mythology of our consumer culture. A listing of a property for sale would include descriptions of its ecosystem, the amount of polluting energy needed to build and maintain it, the history of the people who've dwelled before upon the land. I hope for a Mythology like that which must have inspired Robinson Jeffers in his poem upon building his stone dwelling on the Pacific coast, "To the Rock That Will Be a Cornerstone of the House":

> Old garden of grayish and ochre lichen,
> How long a time since the brown people who have vanished from here
> Built fires beside you and nestled by you
> Out of the ranging sea-wind?
> ...

---

14 David L. Hall, *The Uncertain Phoenix: Adventures Toward a Post-Cultural Sensibility* (New York: Fordham University Press, 1982), pp. 85, 86

Lend me the stone strength of the past and I will lend you
The wings of the future, for I have them.
How dear you will be to me when I too grow old, old comrade.

Chapter 7: Words and Styles

———————

Words may be taken, not literally, but as signs of something out of nowhere, out of a song, this life or death promise or fantasy. Measures are taken for honesty or control, for technical precision or laughed at, kept in files and records of the mind. Styles of emotion can be graceful and distasteful, bringing you and others to an earthly realm of heaven or hell or satires of either.

Words can automatically come out of us, at times unfortunately. They range from the banal to the sacred. They may burst, leak or articulate from collections in your Personal Myth. They can try to limit, denigrate or inspire yourself and others. They can take you into or beyond a Primitive level, toward brutality or beauty.

The culture's Mythology gives styles of living from movie stars, sports and other celebrities showing how to feel attractive, popular, powerful. Media stars can dissolve any importance of past artistic or philosophic traditions. Yet, on the edge of the stage are styles of grace, beauty, infinity.

Words for emotion

We like to be sure of what happens, so we pin names, words, and categories onto experience. Naming emotions with the certainty of a defining word or phrase, especially a medical term, can give a sense of certainty for myself and others. I can simplify myself by words like "happy," "sad," "nervous," "angry," "depressed." I may try on labels for categories acceptable to myself and others. The label may allow mental healthians to prescribe ways to move into a differently named emotion like "contentment," "mental health," or "in a good mood." They can offer the pride, deception and limitation of an identity.

We usually don't question the usual use of words to designate emotion or mood. Why do we so easily think reality can be captured by a single word or phrase or label? An astute researcher confirms what centuries of critical thinkers have been saying: "A word can function like an 'essence placeholder,' encouraging psychological essentialism: A word can convince the perceiver that there is some deep reality to the category in the material world."[1] From infancy, human perceptions become biased to see the world as separated, manipulable objects, made easier to identify by discrete words rather than as processes and interrelationships:

> Not only do manipulable object categories have physical properties that make them easy to individuate, but they

---

[1]   *The Mind in Context,* edited by Batja Mesquita, Lisa Feldman Barret, Eliot R. Smith (New York: Guilford Publications, 2010) p. 1

also benefit from biological predispositions that anticipate these properties. At an early age, infants expect objects to have clear boundaries, to remain relatively constant across time and context, to be easily manipulable, and to exhibit contact causality. ... Prototypically, a noun comes to mean categories whose members have clear boundaries, remain relatively constant across time and contexts, are manipulable, and exhibit simple contact causality.[2]

Thus, words, especially nouns, as "manipulable object categories," can naturally and convincingly become truths about the world. Human experience is categorized and understood in units of words, which string together into abstract concepts. Understanding and moving about in the world seems easier when we believe physical phenomena are objects or things to take account of and manipulate. The same perceptual process automatically designates non-physical phenomena, such as emotion, into "manipulable object categories." Words also make it easier for poisonous beliefs to become convincing, such as racism, sexism, nationalism, anti-semitism, etc.

We rarely think about how words can simplify reality in everyday life. Perceptions and sensations that don't have clear, distinct labels can get ignored in describing experience. We can understand ourselves within a grid of practical and entertaining words and dialogues for productive, functional lives in work, family and social life. Not so practical dimensions of human experience, such as the transcendent and the aesthetic, don't

---

[2]   Lawrence W. Barsalou, Christine D. Wilson & Wendy Hasenkamp, "On the Vices of Nominalization and the Virtues of Contextualization," in *Mind In Context*, p. 337, 339

find a place in that grid. Feelings and thoughts of the music of emotion which don't smoothly lead to "feeling good" can be categorized as problems that may confuse or disrupt a person's carrying out culturally assigned roles. Feelings are usually dealt with by simplifying them so that influences of the past and future, culture and conflict can be resolved into words like "happy," "healthy," "sad," "sick" or psychiatric terms that assign experience to categories of functioning or malfunctioning.

An alternative to the model of the world as objects, units mechanically operating, came from process philosophy. The process view is of everything continually, imperceptibly becoming, developing, changing. Reality as process isn't a new perspective. We have only surviving fragments of his philosophy, but the Greek pre-Socratic sage Heraclitus (born ca. 560 B.C.E.) understood reality as continually in flux. Plotinus (204 – 270 C.E.) considered the dynamic process of existence to be "emanations of the divine."

Words and divinity

In our culture, the name "God" implies a being separate not only from humans, but from everything—all of His creation. Millennia of beliefs and practices of monotheistic religions formed a mythology which separates God from everything, submits all to His command. Humans or anything else in the world can't be divine because that quality is exclusively owned by God and those whom God may bestow it upon, usually after they die. People are prohibited from even conceiving of themselves or any aspect of the world as naturally divine, for the divine means the supernatural in our tradition of the word.

Because terms like "divine," "holy," "sacred" imply the supernatural, such words aren't commonly used by people who don't believe in a separate, supernatural entity and domain, namely God, heaven and His blessed followers, or something like that. Not only are those terms off-limits to non-believers, monotheists deny to them possibilities of experiences of the sacred, divine, holy. Opening to a dogma-free, Adult perspective, moved by freely played music of emotion, individuals can realize those experiences and claim those words.

Here's what the sacred has meant to some people who don't use the term as prescribed in those religious traditions dependent on supernaturalism:

- [T]he sacredness of nature is primordial, not derivative. It does not stem from some sacred being, presence or principle outside of nature, but is inherent in nature itself. ... Nature as a whole and in its every particular aspect is sacred and can be judged to be miraculous in the sense of arousing—when rightly reverenced and responded to—a persistent sense of awe and amazement. ~Donald A. Crosby[3]

- [The word "sacred"] refers to those inexplicable relationships and processes that govern existence. There is no reason sacredness cannot be manifested in any circumstances, even if some are more numinous than others. ... Reference to the ineffable aspect of the universe becomes a possibility. ... [W]e utilize the first twelve years gaining the substance, the referents, which can then be used as an allegorical basis for representing

---

[3] Donald A. Crosby, *More than Discourse: Symbolic Expressions of Naturalistic Faith* (Albany: SUNY Press, 2014) p. 86

in speech—and art—that which is not literal, tangible or visible. ~Paul Shepherd[4]

We need not idolize words and names in religious, psychiatric or other ideologies. I mean such words as "sacred," "holy," or "divine" to serve as poetic symbols to orient attention beyond perceiving and treating reality as something for human use, parts of a nature machine. Words of divinity can represent experiencing of the world and ourselves as beyond the usual human-centric, objectifying, reifying way of perceiving and acting in the world, to consciously connect with the symphonic complexity, aliveness and joy of all that is here.

Experience of the divine isn't mentioned in any contemporary psychology textbook I've seen, with the notable exception of the psychology of Carl Jung and his theoretical heirs. The subject was seriously investigated by William James in lectures he gave in 1901 – 1902, published as *The Varieties of Religious Experience.* He noticed that the mystical aspects of the experience exceed the adequacy of words: "no adequate report of its contents can be given in words. ... mystical states are more like states of feeling than like states of intellect."

Rudolph Otto explored the "state of mind" given by the presence of the "holy" or "sacred" in *The Idea of the Holy: An Inquiry into the Non-Rational Factor in the Idea of the Divine and its Relation to the Rational* originally published in 1923. He called experiences of the holy, related by mystics of Western and Asian religious traditions, "numinous." He said that numinous experiences are available through *Mysterium tremendum et*

---

[4]   Interviewed by Derrick Jensen in *Listening to the Land: Conversations about Nature, Culture and Eros* (San Francisco: Sierra Club Books, 1995), pp. 257-258

fascinans—an overpowering awe, viscerally felt, as in the state of terror, in the presence of the "entirely other"—feeling the wonder and vastness of what's outside of human control, which could potentially devastate the human. Awe is accompanied or followed by fascination with the majesty and power of the presence that you've communed with. The experience would leave you with non-objectifiable, deeply felt reverence for the universe, which may inspire reflections and insights.

Otto conceives of the Holy as the experience of overpowering awe, more akin to terror or dread than a nice feeling of unity. The experience could be of nature, such as an overpowering storm, or of the reality of one's own death. The ultimate, non-pacifying quality may explain why contemporary clinical psychology refuses to come near the subject. What I've seen in workshops and current books on spirituality promise a more peaceful and, let's face it, happy experience, which fits in with the function of lifting people's mood above ungrounded, meaningless or depressing ways of living. Otto's concept of the holy (*das Heilige*) would blow away the protections of Technology in the comfortable settings of climate-controlled homes with electronically powered entertainment. The Mythology of 21st century capitalism would make it safe to ignore older meanings of life, like the Holy, and rely on products of Silicon Valley and Hollywood for meaning, or at least obsession. But the Holy can't be transmitted by Technology, can't be adequately represented by words, much less cinematic special effects.

It can be hard to take deities seriously when they can be portrayed in animated videos and their names can be used in commercial brands. Otto's *Idea of the Holy* can't be used or have meaning for the values of our dominant Mythology, for the Holy doesn't make us feel safe, productive or fulfilled; it isn't even for us. The Holy is essential to a full grounding of humility—feeling what vibrantly, actively transcends us and our Mythologies and overpowers our power or control. Such humility is a threshold to experiencing unique realizations beyond words, beyond what our culture offers as entertaining and worthy of financial investment.

One can arrive at reverence for the divine through many kinds of experience, not necessarily terror, trauma or psychedelia. The transcendent experience of sacrifice for love may overwhelm, bring a realization of human vulnerability and one's decentered, dependent place in the cosmos. On this tiny, tenuous place in the universe, a person may be filled with awe and reverence at the marvel and majesty of being a living process, living for love and beauty. The music of the Holy, the numinous, isn't useful or productive. It is a participation in Being.

While our culture offers many ways to do without reverence, I found a few different sources in Positive Psychology literature and podcasts promoting "awe" for mental health, e.g.: "Feeling awe can boost your mood and make you feel more connected with others." "Need a mood boost or a stress slayer? Some studies suggest that experiencing awe may help." Certain exercises to feel awe are prescribed. Giving up divinity for stress management may seem a fair trade.

It's up to the individual to cross the threshold into genuine humility, entailing a realization that life is more than the beliefs and practices of any Mythology, that beauty, love and creativity can be more overwhelming than comforting, that one can play in the ever-present Holiness of all that one lives within. There is no reward or profit to it. But if the primacy of rewards (like Heaven or bliss) doesn't govern, how can the individual maintain a sense of the sacred? Words evoking the sacred— read, spoken or sung—can be part of the structure of one's Personal Myth.

Revering the natural world and oneself as embodying the divine, opens one to playing what James Carse calls an infinite game: "A finite game is played for the purpose of winning. An infinite game for the purpose of continuing the play."[5] The infinite game of life would then parallel the play of nature naturing, its patterns of continually self-creating. One of the ways we play is with words. We can use words for the purpose of winning or for the purpose of continuing the play of self-creativity. In our culture's Mythology, individuals use others as resources to gain rewards and advantages, obviously a finite game. Words that don't serve that game, like literature, aren't taken seriously.

Poetry

Literature can be understood as gifts of words that may or may not move the reader. When allowed the full range of metaphor, irony, imaginative and witty designs and rhythms, words have possibilities as described by the poet Octavio Paz:

> Words constantly collide and throw out metallic sparks or form phosphorescent pairs. New stars continually populate the verbal sky. Each day words and phrases appear at the surface of language, still dripping moisture and silence from their cold scales. At the same moment

---

[5]   James P. Carse, *Finite and Infinite Games: A Vision of Life as Play and Possibility* (New York: Free Press, 1986), p. 1

others disappear. Suddenly the wasteland of a worn-out language is covered with unexpected verbal flowers. Luminous creatures inhabit the thickets of speech.[6]
This way of using words is a way of playing an infinite game. Words themselves have become a process of self-creativity.

In the tradition of literature, writers have tried to play to win. They can win prestigious awards, some handsomely compensated, or the praise of critics or the monetary rewards of being a bestseller. Those finite games of writing never result in the kind of creative art that comes from literature as an infinite game. Many of those writers, like Kafka, got hardly any reward in their lifetime. Others, like Faulkner and Beckett, wrote books that were abject failures in the market until the French brought them to the attention of the Nobel Prize committee.

Poetry in our time has become valued for self-expression, clever effects and political messages. A lot of biographies of poets are more voyeuristic than examples of how beauty can arise from messy lives. So, again, it's up to each person to find words—written, read or sung—from past or current artists, that give a sense of the divinity of reality, that play an infinite game. Symbols and metaphors in this poetry wouldn't be overtly religious, but true to the subtle, gritty, sensual, and convulsive qualities of a sublime music of emotion.

Limits and potential of words

Despite our perceptual and conceptual instincts to categorize, music isn't received in chopped up designations like words. Music is an aesthetic process reaching the senses, imagination

---

[6] *The Bow and the Lyre* (Austin: University of Texas Press, 1956/1973) pp. 24-25.

and body, moving through a continual flow of feelings and meanings. Unlike the limited set of words to match to feelings, the tones and textures of music have an almost infinite range of expression. Susanne Langer pointed out how "music articulates forms which language cannot set forth. The classifications which language makes automatically preclude many relations, and many of those resting-points of thought which we call 'terms'."[7]

Using words alone for feelings can create "resting-points" that can easily get us stuck. We can ruminate upon words and messages to create music that is constricting or demoralizing. Understanding that we play, through the mind-body, qualities of a flow of experience can open up our abilities to alter or create those qualities. How I feel can be understood as active notes and chords of a music I'm creating, with lyrics and motifs affecting and affected by the music. I can be imaginative and creative with complex mixes and shifts of feeling and thoughts, without clinging to the particular lyrics of thought. Again, Langer's insights are helpful:

> The real power of music lies in the fact that it can be 'true' to the life of feeling in a way that language cannot; for its significant forms have that ambivalence of content which words cannot have. This is, I think, what Hans Mersmann meant, when he wrote: 'The possibility of expressing opposites simultaneously gives the most intricate reaches of expressiveness to music as such, and carries it, in this respect, far beyond the limits of the other arts.' Music is revealing, where words are

---

[7] *Philosophy in a New Key*, p. 189

obscuring, because it can have not only a content, but a transient play of contents.[8]

Words may be expressed with awareness of their rhythm and imagery and their multiple meanings in metaphor. Speaking, writing and reading with a musical sense can overcome the limitations and distortions which come from reifying effects of words. In a poem that's to be verbally played as "The Four Quartets," T. S. Eliot showed how words can convey emotion in far more depth than the categorical terms we commonly use:

> The trilling wire in the blood
> Sings below inveterate scars
> Appeasing long forgotten wars.
> The dance along the artery
> The circulation of the lymph
> Are figured in the drift of stars

But, you may say, that's poetry, it's unreasonable to think that I can ordinarily use language like that, the poetic is a category separate from ordinary experience. Our culture's dominant Mythology doesn't validate the aesthetic as a dimension of each person's psychology. (I'll explore this dimension further in a later chapter.) Instead, we're taught to simplify language, resulting in simplifying people and the world for a model of functioning parts in our economic and social systems. We can explore aesthetic aspects of ourselves in the cosmos that can allow our Personal Myth to break out of the culture's Mythological model. We can compose our lives in actions, ideas and words that revere the human and non-human beings of the world, with soundtracks of emotion that have vital effects on ourselves and others.

---

[8]   *Philosophy in a New Key*, pgs. 197-8

Do we need new words for emotion? Especially if most of those words have become too familiar, especially if those recycled by mental healthians are smothering? That would be an example of attempting a quick technical fix rather than a qualitative transformation. Rather than plucking words here and there, imagine those who've created wholly original realms of emotion by the impact of their words. Imagine the human artists devoted to the beauty of words, the passion that moved ancient reciters of epics, chanters of sacred hymns, the troubadours. Imagine Shakespeare, Mallarme, Celan, poets and writers who didn't write for a mass market, who plunged audiences into wholly other realms of emotion by the impact of their words.

While skills for the dominant Mythology use words as blunt instruments chopping up experience for mechanical purposes, for bureaucratic files, fantasy and virtual reality, skills for purely human, uncommodified potential may be rediscovered. No one knows how the first music was played. However, songs or chants are as ancient as any human music discovered. Words are and always have been part of emotion's Creative Energy.

Words can be flexible, evocative and interpretive signs of emotion. They can be more or less helpful to understand emotion's notes and melodies flowing in continuity with what's already happened and what's desired. It's usually less obvious how "positive" and "negative" themes can shift and even blend together in sometimes rapid, unique and weird ways. Words and categories for emotion usually imply distinct, sometimes opposite, states. Common emotion words can give the illusion that a feeling or mood is a solid, distinct whole, one that we may be stuck in. Feelings aren't static or solid, but are always transforming beyond the names and categories, playing complex and subtle rhythms and tones within movements of situations. Emotion's notes aren't categorically separated from each other, but are always related, always producing sensations, images and thoughts, connected to memories and the body's wordless flows. Different traces and uprisings of emotional tones can overlap, can contain their polar opposites. Commenting on a poem by Stefan George, Heidegger reflected how "the more joyful the joy, the more pure the sadness slumbering within it. Sadness and joy play into each other."[9]

We may desire excitement, care, hope and other positive feeling states, and try not to think how they can rapidly shift to fears, confusion, frustration, resentment. But notice how the words in the prior sentence imply distinct, even opposite, states and solid wholes. Instead, what if we think of our experience as dynamically moving with mixed effects naturally arising from the live music of mind-body. The qualities of the music flow and shift in accents, tones, rhythms, melodies, atonalities, not in solid blocks under labels, but in mysterious energies from many sources, structured by multiple tracks from the past, continually forming meanings and values, played with various textures and styles. The multitude of overlapping variables include (i) memories, interpretations and judgments arising in the mind, telling how reality is or should be, (ii) the shifting flows of heart rate, stress, cellular energy reserves, muscular tension, hormones, (iii) the body's physical spectrum of pain-to-relaxation, (iv) the role and norms by which the person is acting, (v) the anticipated or feared consequences of choosing how to

---

[9] Quoted in Robert Avens, *The New Gnosis: Heidegger, Hillman and Angels* (Putnam, Connecticut: Spring Publications Inc., 1984/2003), p. 83

respond, (vi) vulnerabilities triggered, (vii) protective reactions to the vulnerabilities. Words or phrases for "an" emotion cannot do justice to the dynamic multiplicity of variables that go into any encounter with reality, which I've called the Wild, as an evocative, multivalenced term.

The feeling of what happens seems closely akin to music's dynamic multiplicities of notes, chords, intensities and qualities of harmony or dissonance. Feelings arise from what happens, influenced by what happened and what might happen. Some feelings may be unsayable.

Styles of the words

There is always a feeling to words that are spoken, read or sung. We can attune to the music of words. If the words come from a calculating, controlling source, the feeling may be of cold, dominant or forceful tones. And, if the calculator is good at it, the words can be smooth, socially charming, getting a laugh every other sentence, as good salesmen have shown.

Neutral cadences are used to relate to reality analytically. Scientific studies and reporting are usually narrated in sober tones and rhythms. Words can be technologized, delivered in inflections and meanings tamed into "objective" modes, attempting to filter out effects of bias and persuasion. Analytic narratives are articulated in measured, even boring notes. But science can also be sold. I've seen attempts to dissect and label emotions in pictures of fMRI'd brains to convince us of the mechanics of emotion and how to commodify its repairs. With the names of these brain parts, the expert or clinician can speak or write as if truth is in technical jargon, authoritatively given for submissive belief. We can question such "truths" by critiquing the tricks and tones of dominance or control. Science doesn't need to convince or persuade anyone. On the contrary, rigorous science includes the language of math that shuts out most of us and requires experts. Even if we're unable to comprehend that symbolic system, we can appreciate the wonders revealed either by learning more math or skipping it and appreciating the complexities as one can appreciate Bach fugues without understanding notes of the score or the frequencies of the sound. We can open to scientific discoveries as further depths of the mystery of Being, approached with the humility and intelligence needed to perceive what was thought of as mere matter in a human-centered universe. We can appreciate the continually developing knowledge brought by neuroscientists to better perform our music of emotion.

Words can be markers pointing to commonalities in experience, such as sadness, panic, aggression. Yet they should always be taken as no more than indicators rather than certainties. Words have tonalities, rhythms, harmonic relationships that are always infusing the concepts conveyed. Meanings of and from one's Personal Myth come in words, narratives, poems, songs and abstract theories. Even some of the most fundamental words we use such as "self", "I", "will", "mind", could be understood as notes of useful fictions, images and metaphors to play the music of emotion in the Wild in our unique, genuine styles.

You may speak or write not just for the content, accuracy or the truth of your words, but for the quality and style of how you express, the evocative images and metaphors you use. You can gain awareness of the tones, pauses, rhythms and elegance of your words. You can act and express from the imaginative vision and dignity by which you choose to live. You can express, not with the aim to be perfect, accepted or impressive, but with the spontaneity of an improviser on an instrument well cared for. You can dare to speak and move beyond your own ego, embracing the mystery of the Wild, in the concert of processes of neural firings, social, cultural and biological systems, surpassing the music of popularity, disconnection, kitsch and fear.

Styles of emotion

Just as music we listen to has different qualities, structures and genres, we can analyze aspects of emotion in terms of styles. Emotion, like life itself, isn't something we own; it is human process miraculously present. A style isn't to be imposed on emotion, but is compelled by the process. Categories such as positive v. negative may begin to describe styles, but categories are too broad. Even commonly used words like excitement, care, hope and other words for so-called positive feeling states, and their negative counterparts—e.g., fear, confusion, frustration, resentment—can be deceptive in implying that the words fully describe or explain.

The inner sources of responses to the Wild aren't really within our control. We can get thrown out of balance. Once we attune to our vulnerabilities and protective forces, we can become better aware of how and why we feel compelled to respond to situations. We can learn methods to center ourselves with curiosity, self-acceptance and care as we join with the flow of the Wild. The more we improve our patterns of perceiving and responding to situations and the more we realize the possible pain and cost of taking a stand for what's meaningful and good, the more we can trust ourselves and free up our Creative Energy into what emerges in the Wild. Humility and reverence can infuse the soundtrack of our lives, allowing perceptions and values that give us a shot at creating beauty, justice, joy. We can develop a style which allows us to naturally turn on Creative Energy in our music of emotion.

Confusion or uncertainty are realistic responses to situations. Knowing I can practice centering, it can be good to get into situations where I'm not sure what's happening or what to do. I want a style of improvising that isn't about looking cool or being in control but allows my body and mind to play. My Personal Myth is to be shared and performed, not defended. I go for a style like that of a Fellini movie: I try to play a soundtrack that welcomes acrobats, angels and animals into the scene, attunes to their lyrics of love and cosmic relevance; I want to meet my protective forces with smiling appreciation, realizing their protection isn't needed, I'll be fine; I'll ask for caring and creative flourishes from my realistic Adult and buoyant Child Minds. Challenges can seem like a threat until I realize the challenge is to improvise in creative response—not to win or save face, but to play for the possibility of joy.

Let's say there's a leader of a work team in an organization—either for- or non-profit. The leader's ideas, directions, and inspiration can be played to the team in styles that are dry and boring or in crisis mode or as gleaming optimism for the music of the employees. The leader's conducting of the ensemble can make it clear that their dignity is more important than any rigid measures, their committed purpose and creativity can inspire their personal growth as well as innovations for the project. The leader can have a style that reaches people's hearts and values, that emphasizes Creative Energy rather than an obsession with profits.

Instead of following a prescription or recipe of how to think or behave, consider allowing yourself the creativity of a poet or composer who welcomes the mystery of the Wild. Living and acting in your chosen roles and contexts can be understood as creating works of art. In the aesthetic mode, you can allow the mind-body to enter situations in a natural, generative chaos, letting words, sounds, and images arise from the Soul to improvise in situations. There can be opportunities to open to the transcendent Holy in the Wild. As an artist, each day can be here to learn the most interesting, rich and vibrant forms of emotion's music to create in living.

The style of my soundtrack of emotion will affect what I do and what my life means. If it plays a mostly egocentric score, my life will follow a composition of narrow range, often defensive. Each day, decisions, actions and effects can seem to be of minuscule meanings, played and replayed in familiar, comfortable tunes. If my music is open to the aliveness of the natural processes of the world, if I aspire to play vital movements within those processes, I'll allow a greater range of sensitivity and inspiration for my mind-body. I may then trust how I play my instrument. I can allow curious explorations and discoveries of rhythms and themes of others. Understanding emotion as music playing in a personal style of living means tossing out the mechanistic model of the mind from mainstream psychology and psychiatry. Composing and performing music from the generative processes of my mind-body can allow loving improvisations to emerge. Rather than a machine, I am a potential for emergent processes that harmonize with those of nature, with responsibilities to uphold beauty and goodness. The best sciences, arts and philosophies help me attune to those natural processes of living.

Personal Myths can arise from the individual's commitments to living meaningfully for all beings, not from blindly conforming to the Mythology of the culture. Heroic epics, such as the Iliad, tell stories of violent men triumphing, ignoring their effects on others, conforming to a patriarchal mythology of domination. Deities like Zeus inspire and enforce such a mythology. Love stories can be told in the style of pornography or kitsch or they can go for more complex narratives of the messiness, sexiness, rash acts, devotion and sacrifices of love. The stories are told and understood from particular perspectives within cultural Mythologies. We can expand or alter perspectives to reject interpretations of the world as resources for maximizing ownership, profits, comfort or other personal gain. Rather than styles of egocentric mastery, dominance by nations, companies or families, we can choose styles of reverence and humility, acknowledging the sacredness of the universe and our part in the dance of Being.

Durée as a quality of style

Henri Bergson wrote of how we can open to experience without trying to capture or hold on to it in words, categories or measurements. Suzanne Guerlac usefully summarizes:

> Bergson is asking us to consider a level of experience that is immediate in that it is not mediated through language or quantitative notation, an experience of the "real," we could say, that resists symbolization. Bergson examines inner states as such; he considers feelings,

sensations, passions, etc. as pure quality, or in terms of the experience of qualitative difference.[10]

Bergson's philosophy of a direct relation to reality, as earlier pointed out, is in terms of the music of reality, with striking parallels to new revelations in physics. Under Bergson's model, reality involves vibratory fields of processes flowing around and through us, bearing the influences of the body's physiology, the mind's interpretations, memories, and values influenced by development within a family and culture. These elements go into experience, though we can't adequately express in words the whole of experiencing reality. Bergson told of how language can shape our possibilities of awareness of and relation to reality:

> This influence of language on sensation is deeper than is usually thought. Not only does language make us believe in the unchangeableness of our sensations, but it will sometimes deceive us as to the nature of the sensation felt. ... In short, the word with well-defined outlines, the rough and ready word, which stores up the stable, common, and consequently impersonal element in the impressions of mankind, overwhelms or at least covers over the delicate and fugitive impressions of our individual consciousness.[11]

Playing the instrument of mind-body can be with attunement to reality as dynamically interactive presence, in what

---

10 *Thinking in Time: An Introduction to Henri Bergson,* (Ithaca, NY: Cornell University Press, 2017), p. 43

11 Henri Bergson, *Time and Free Will: An Essay on the Immediate Data of Consciousness,* trans. F. L. Pogson (1910 rpt. New York: Harper and Row, 1960), pp. 131-32

Bergson called "durée"—direct experience before naming, conceptualizing and measuring get their chance to put wrappers on the moment. Opening to what I call the Wild is essentially the same as "durée." G. William Barnard gives an excellent overview that's worth quoting at length:

> From Bergson's perspective, durée is an indivisible fusion of manyness and oneness; it is the ongoing, dynamic, temporal flux of awareness; it is a flowing that is ever new and always unpredictable; it is the continual, seamless, interconnected, immeasurable movement of our awareness, manifesting, simultaneously, as both the knower and what is known. In English texts, durée is often translated as "duration," which is a rather problematic translation in that "duration" is often associated with notions of "endurance" and has connotations of grimly and stoically "enduring" something painful or difficult (which is why I prefer to leave the French word durée untranslated). Durée is not something that we have to endure, it is not necessarily painful or difficult. Instead, it is the natural manifestation of our inner being; it surges forth, in reality, with complete ease—it is the most natural occurrence in the world. (Bergson also claims that durée actually is very difficult to experience in its purity...) Durée is accessed through a subtle intuitive introspective awareness, not simply as the contents of our consciousness, but rather as the dynamic essence of who we really are, both the inner knower and what that inner knower knows. As such, durée is not something that exists separate from us; instead, "it" is the temporal flux of our consciousness— it is our own awareness as

it persists (while always changing), that is always present (and always moving), that endures, in time, as time.[12] We can allow curious, creative, playful, and courageous styles for joining in the flow of reality. The more we learn to care for and unconditionally accept our vulnerabilities, the more we practice ways of letting go of defensive reactions, we open the way to improvising creatively in the flow. We play our music of emotion with certain qualities. Durée can be incorporated as a quality of our style.

Bergson's insights allow a conscious experience of reality as uninterrupted flow and flux, not tied to words representing a static set of objects sequentially lined up. Suzanne Guerlac clarifies how this involves feeling reality:

> This is why Bergson constantly reminds us to consider lived experience in all its concrete specificity, instead of through abstract ideas. It is very simple. Abstraction evacuates the force of time. We cannot know flowing time cognitively. We can only know it concretely through the way different qualities feel to us at different times. That is why the appeal to the concrete—to lived experience—is fundamental. And, once again, this is why language is a problem, for, as we have seen, it is inadequate to the task of conveying quality in all its singularity.[13]

We may feel closed in by beliefs or the past or future, but this is an interruption of awareness of the flow. We aren't the center

---

[12]   Barnard, G. William. *Living Consciousness: The Metaphysical Vision of Henri Bergson*, (Albany, NY: State University of New York Press, 2011) pp. 7-8

[13]   *Thinking In Time*, p. 80

of existence. There are processes outside my awareness, from the ecological and neurobiological to the quantum, from which each moment arises. Experiences are continually transforming each other and having effects outside ourselves. A style incorporating durée would recognize situations as moments of processes of change. I can interpret particular situations of those processes as threatening or as potential transformations. Rather than considering reality as objects or phenomena there to master, I can embrace my lack of control, while attuning and improvising in the flow. I can meet the Wild with the skills as well as spontaneity that allow me to play in this continually changing music of many different rhythms, tones, harmonies and dissonances in the untranslatable openness of durée.

Understanding emotion as musically attuning to reality, we may play at deeper, more adventurous levels of meanings from a style that incorporates durée. We can open our potentials for discoveries and enjoyments felt in continually flowing, unquantifiable experiences. The feelings of acting in the world can help tell us, sometimes much later, what our actions mean, what our choices could bring to ourselves and the world. As we continue to expand our experiences and learn from them, new forms of thinking, acting and understanding can unfold.

Accepting and embracing reality as continuously changing and outside my control can be difficult because the forces of fear instinctively try to keep me as safe as possible from possible threats. From a Survivalist style, I'd assume that what and whom I encounter are some version of a threatening opponent or obstacle and react to maximize my safety and control. Paradoxically, fear is an important force for life. Its music can be intense and overwhelming, but it's just trying to protect me. Sometimes its force results in overprotection by backing down when I should take a stand, exaggerating the dangers of a situation I can manage. If I can lose my fear of being afraid, I can accept it, invite it to transform into Creative Energy with which I can play. I can develop a style of taking on risks to play an infinite game. If I realize each moment is being created, though under the influence of my memory, genetics, vulnerabilities and defenses, as well as energies of the whole of nature, I can realistically play Centered Improvisations and Transcendent Flows from a centered space of awareness.

Durée means that we ourselves are part of the continually changing flow of reality, though it seems like the situation or incident that occurs is outside me as a discrete, graspable unit of what happens. Bergson explains this seeming contradiction:

> Our attention fixes on them [the particular incidents] because they interest it more, but each of them is borne by the fluid mass of our whole psychical existence. Each is only the best illuminated point of a moving zone which comprises all that we feel or think or will—all, in short, that we are at any given moment. It is this entire zone which in reality makes up our state. Now, states thus defined cannot be regarded as distinct elements. They continue each other in an endless flow.[14]

Not only is it illusory to consider what I encounter as units defined by words and definitions, but the "self" itself is an illusion of a stable Me, whom I don't realize is continually changing. There is something new about Me, as part of the whole, each moment. This can allow a very different perspective

---

[14] Henri Bergson, *Creative Evolution*, translated by Arthur Mitchell (Duke Classics, 1911/2012), p. 14

on each moment of the Wild. Actions that I and others take awakens new notes in the erotic concert of the nervous system. I can allow Me to be disrupted and transformed by the music of emotion. I can imagine, form ideas and create interactions with others in playing my instrument in an infinite game. When we try to treat emotions as objects, with words to box them into categories, we can feel stuck, we can play compositions that others dictate, we can miss the experience of improvising our music attuned to the Wild.

Playing with words

We usually don't think about what words we use unless trying to stumble through a foreign language or write something well. We also usually don't pay much attention to how we say them—unless trying to sell, impress or seduce. We often don't even know what'll come out of our mouths. When we do pay attention, it may be to try to use words to manipulate and gain, to play a finite game to win.

Words can be thought of as notes being played by the instrument of mind-body. What pitch do they have? What volume, tone and rhythm? What do they mean? Rather than using words for calculating, manipulating, or winning, they can be played as gifts of beauty and grace. They can be conveyed with a style and message that create something new in the Wild.

I don't mean to imply that we can completely control the quality of what's expressed. My words are produced from physical, psychological and environmental influences I can't be anywhere close to knowing from moment to moment. I do mean that we can become more aware of the quality and effects of the words we use through sensitive attunement to others, reflection and the feedback of others. I can become aware of my style and purposes in using the words. I can know the words are part of a music of emotion I'm playing with another person, with non-human and even non-living others, with the infinite forces of the universe supporting my life and its continual changes. I can play with words to play in what happens each moment in the Wild.

The more words, images and metaphors I have available, the more imagination can experiment with and blend concepts, allowing greater creativity. When delivered and received like lyrics of a love song, words may allow a co-creation of the highest qualities of living. Words flowing from the shock and awe of the Holy can lead me into unknown territories where I may find beauty, conflict, danger, delight. Words can blast away or procreate perceptions and ideas. But words can also be part of limiting and deceiving my perceptions. They could be turned into slaves to try to shove reality into boundaried conceptual objects that are substituted for durée. Words can attempt to give an illusion of stable, controlled fact. They can be propaganda to distort perceptions of reality.

Being labelled v. Choosing styles

The crude and clunky labeling of emotions serves various special interests, pharmaceutical companies to psychiatrists and psychotherapists who claim to "treat" diagnoses rather than people. Reducing oneself to labels also serves the prevailing cultural models of people. Labels are like brands—people become simple units for marketing, for profits. It can pay to flatten a person into a definition, a statistic or a diagnosis.

A conventional mental health practice is to give people some institutionally approved questionnaire (such as the Beck Depression Inventory, "BDI"), have them rate how strongly they agree with certain sentences. Then the clinician simply adds up the points from the answers, sees if the score qualifies the person for the diagnosis. This pretty much gives the professional power to define a person's emotion as a part to be fixed. If you buy into this, you won't look at the more detailed variables that might clarify what hidden vulnerabilities may have developed in your history to trigger particular protective patterns. Nor would you better understand how the concert of your neural network is affected by the surrounding music of your culture and ecosystem. A highly paid psychiatrist gave the BDI to a person who was seeing me for counseling. Because that particular day, this person was playing self-critical music and his BDI score was high, his psychiatrist doubled the dosage of a prescribed anti-depressant. My client didn't like the effects of that dosage. We worked together to clarify that the BDI didn't represent his continued state of mind and to allow him to have a voice about this. He regained control from the doc over how his mind-body was influenced.

I've witnessed how psychiatrists and other mental healthians comply with the DSM's language of symptoms and ignore the notes, tones and rhythms of emotion from their clients, the themes being continually created and creating in the music. Rather than symptoms, I believe emotion can be better described with such terms as cacophonous, dissonant, a monotone blah, a droning single lyric, or by how harmonious it may be played with others in felt meanings and possibilities. Melancholy melodies may be telling someone about a relation to her or his environment and history that's keeping the music and lyrics limited or dangerous. Getting to the sources and possibilities of the music of emotion, daring to play more freely and responsibly, can be the beginning of changes in one's style of living.

Chapter 8: Songs of Self-deception

—◦◦mmʃmmˌ◦—

T HERE are many ways we can deceive ourselves. Of course, there are also countless tricks of deceiving others. Usually, we deceive ourselves about the deception to feel better about it. It should be surprising how people can ignore or twist facts so easily—bad habits justified, conspiracy theories more attractive than truth, the killings in wars, gulags, pogroms, domestic violence that are too soon forgotten or ignored. Is it deception if we don't realize we're forgetting or embellishing what happens? Why do people accept, promote and cling to lies about themselves, their families, countries and lovers? Are we innocently brainwashed by our childhood conditioning, by social media, by our own brains?

The music of emotion we play for self-deception is usually meant to help us feel good. It is music to feed us comfort, pride, self-satisfaction, superiority, relief from a bad choice or a conscience. It's music to distort or alter beliefs about oneself, one's situation, and other aspects of reality. One can make self-deception essential to self-esteem and esteem from others.

Cognitive scientists let us know we have many biases, instinctive tools to confabulate. We tell ourselves stories and beliefs to satisfy ourselves. For example, my natural confirmation bias can lead me from (a) my belief that my counseling is helping people improve their lives, to (b) showing evidence of real improvement from what people tell me and/or objective measures, while (c) ignoring or downplaying independent factors that affect their improvement. It can be very hard to detect our own self-deceptions. A whole life can amount to compositions of deception, in sweet or attractive melodies, warm and passionate songs, as well as screeches, honks and poundings of anxiety, guilt, resentment, disillusion when the deception is exposed.

Some argue that self-deception at times can be good: illusions can give us motivation, hope, endurance, perhaps even courage. It helps to think your cause is for the good and against evil if you're part of a war and killing people, putting yourself at risk to be killed, or laying waste to everything in your path and beyond. The music of war can create all kinds of self-deception for a fighter and a country. The music of machismo can feel ecstatic in its lies. In lots of arenas, the music of my ego's self-glorification can blind me to my effect on others.

When we fall in love with someone, the romantic music idealizing the lover motivates us to overlook aspects of the loved one that are less than ideal, or at least to convince ourselves that it won't be that bad or that we'll lead them to reform. Similarly, we can deceive ourselves and others to promote or protect family members and allies or to manipulate someone for our benefit.

We can also deceive ourselves and others out of an instinctive need to be right, to create justification of ourselves or to create meaning. In each case, we'll play the music of emotion appropriate to the purpose of the deception. Who can blame you for any of that? Look around you: doesn't the view place you at the center of the universe, a universe whose vastness you can't even imagine? My mind can make up stories about how important and wonderful I am. I can even believe a politician really cares about me.

Songs of Narcissism

A pattern of thinking, feeling and behavior known as narcissism is a particular amplification of our common tendency to deceive ourselves, a music that's often played with glitz and ferocity. Aspects of American culture foster narcissism as an effect of social status and financial "success." The successful entrepreneur or professional athlete or movie star is given slack for being brash, s/he's admired for successes, for winning personal rewards (especially wealth and power) at any cost. The renowned expert on narcissism and other personality defects, James Masterson, describes this ideal:

> The successful narcissist ... must be creative and imaginative, and often quite talented, to develop a lifestyle that will resonate to his grandiose projections of himself and fuel his narcissistic needs. ... As he basks in the comfortable habitat that he has constructed, an airtight cocoon of narcissistic enjoyment, life can seem pretty good. In fact, he does feel good; he feels secure,

and as long as nothing punctures the closed circle, he will not be aware of any serious personality problems. He thinks he has it all, and those who know him would agree, since he has carefully selected and enlisted them to be part of his world and thereby buttress his view of himself.[1]

Narcissists feel exhilaration at being looked up to, adored, envied. They rely on such feelings for self-esteem. Their highly charged willpower results in forceful convictions that they're right and they require that others fervently believe they're right, even despite clear facts. Donald Trump seems to be our greatest recent public case.

Sure, Trump's vulgar music of narcissism is highly charged. His aggression and lack of empathy, flouting the law for the sake of power, connecting only to people who support his power or ego show him to be also an example of the manipulative songs of a sociopath, who shows: disregard for laws and social mores; disregard for the rights of others; failure to feel remorse or guilt; a tendency to display violent or aggressive behavior.[2] Trump goes beyond the line from those who may be no less grandiose than him, but who aren't as aggressive and potentially violent toward others.

Narcissism can be understood as one of the protective forces of our emotional system. I go for inflating my importance, I attempt to stoke my seductive appeal to others, I try to prove

[1]   *The Search for the Real Self,* James F. Masterson, M.D., (New York: Free Press, 1988) p. 93

[2]   See "The Differences Between Psychopaths and Sociopaths," Scott A. Bonn Ph.D blog "Wicked Deeds" in *Psychology Today* Posted Jan. 9, 2018

how excellent, heroic, hardworking I am, to be protected from feeling vulnerable or incompetent, to try not to be unliked. I can seek admiration to avoid feeling abandoned, unworthy or ashamed. Any of us could fall into this pattern. Full-time narcissists should be helped, in the unlikely event they're wanting and willing to change. We shouldn't stigmatize or shame people, including ourselves, for falling into this defensive trap, unless they're politicians or cult leaders or heartbreakers who should be accountable for harming others.

If I fall into a narcissistic pattern, I can be helped by understanding the purpose it's serving for me: the highly charged motive of protecting myself from the fear or pain of my vulnerability. I could learn alternatives. Realizing that the fears come from the Primitive level, I can pause in acting upon the Primitive motive, allow whatever time I need to take an Adult perspective that can allow me to be realistic and compassionate about myself and others. I can learn how to invoke my Centered Harmonies to lead me into a mature, responsible, compassionate pattern of freedom, acceptance and care for my vulnerabilities and a natural, loving connection to myself and others. My emotional music then would come from a deeper, stronger source than glitzy, sensational, dominating or superpotent self-promotion.

Feelings of exhilaration from going for fulfillment of my potential, striving for my personal standard of excellence can be distinguished from the exhilaration of inflating my ego. The passion of personal excellence is a music played within myself rather than for public display. The music is composed from the emotional integrity of living for meanings beyond myself, for transcendent experiences of what is beautiful, good and compassionate. The music of this exhilaration feels different from that which is used to protect me from feeling vulnerable.

I believe it's unrealistic, silly and yes, narcissistic, to think one can be immune from narcissistic feelings and episodes. They are a part of the egocentric orientation of our selves. They are always lurking in the Pre-Adult level of mind. They seem to come out easily in certain social dynamics and after drinking a certain amount of alcohol. But usually narcissism isn't a pathology, it's a potential inherent to any mammal who needs the regard, connection and, in the accepted mechanical term of psychology, "attachment", of relationship(s) with others. Yes, I mean mammals: see if your dog or cat doesn't often act like a narcissist. Narcissism may arise in part from a natural rhythm of our need for others to value and love us. For various reasons, usually in one's childhood development, this need becomes an excessive hunger, even perceived as essential to survival. In its moderate form, it's called self-esteem. It can flood any of us.

Like all other aspects of our egos, our melodies of narcissistic need can be accepted as part of our natural self-centeredness, which arises out of our bodily and mental orientation that plants each person at the center of the universe. Because narcissism comes from the Pre-Adult, Primitive level of mind, it won't ever be completely extinguished. We can acknowledge these melodies and songs of the self with humor, among our repertoire of less than perfect tendencies. It's a matter of degree. Where narcissism pervades thinking, feeling and behavior and the emotional music is played obsessively for self-gratification and power over others, it becomes a problem so deeply entrenched that one's greed for gratification and power completely overcomes the person's ability to love and be loved. The only effective remedy I've heard of for this distortion is long term individual counseling, with a counselor who's discerning, compassionate and tough, to help transform the music. Especially when one achieves social or financial success from the lifestyle fueled from narcissism, he or she is unlikely to seek such help.

For those of us not fully taken over by narcissistic patterns of thinking, feeling and behaving, we need to bring our Adult Minds in to play. The Adult Mind realizes our narcissism is always potential. I can grudgingly admit that my Personal Myth has a certain amount of b.s. to it and that it can be much greater if I can't be radically honest with myself. My Adult Mind can help me become aware of self-deceit, why it's triggered, how easily it can get out of control to the extent of damaging or destroying valued relationships or at least to make a fool of myself. There are times when narcissism can add music to an overly critical judgment of myself, assert some strength or hutzpah when I need it. But from my Adult Mind's perspective, I should tell myself when I'm acting like a big baby before anyone else does. I can take myself less seriously, realize I am enough just as I am, the best imperfect self I can be. With doses of good humor, I can accept my Pre-Adult Mind, know the temptations of narcissism, lead myself to more mature perspectives and actions.

In a consumer culture such as the current American, narcissism can easily become a style of an unnatural way of living. There are certainly plenty of well-paid public examples of glamour glorified, rewards of ego gratification. Feeling self-worth from impressing others is an easy hook for the emotional system. It's okay in certain doses, but let's recognize how its music plays. Self-esteem from being impressive can lead to a Personal Myth of superficiality, a soundtrack to life that's about gratifying the ego's need for self-satisfaction or power. It plays the comfortable music of the consumer culture in the mind-body, submitting to artificial ways of living, gratifying oneself from cheap thrills of the internet, status, being right. The guiding value that still predominates in our business and economic system is what's-in-it-for-me. Self-esteem has become a necessary reward, an important psychological goal.

Just as our choices aren't determined by our childhood upbringing, neither are they dictated by cultural influences. What's important is to be aware of the influence of both and to find different sources of guidance and inspiration for a mature perspective about ourselves and reality. We can choose the Adult Mind's capacity for self-improvement, humility, reverence, humor, wisdom and self-respect, leaving the ego-centered motivations behind for values that transcend what's-in-it-for-me, a style that's noble, music of emotion that inspires.

As with other patterns of self-deception, the narcissist doesn't realize that what is most craved—a desperate grasping for control, power, approval and security—is a trap. Realizing that you don't need any of those protective states, and that, on the contrary, letting go of wanting any of them, is the way to liberation. Releasing ourselves from the self-deception of control, approval, security or anything else opens us to our potential Creative Energy. To release the desperate conviction that we lack power or perfection or security is usually a process. Our Adult reasoning and responsibility can recognize the music of inadequacy, insecurity, abandonment and victimhood when it plays. Those songs can be deeply ingrained. Allowing the world to be as it is, allowing yourself to discover yourself as a vital and essential part of existence, not the center of everything, you can flow into the music of life, playing your instrument of mind-body, creating a Personal Myth of imperfectly striving for goodness, freedom and beauty, trusting the music of emotion played from the Adult you and from the Soul.

Sentimentality

Related to the sources and effects of narcissism, and almost as poisonous to the potential for one's Personal Myth is sentimentality. It is music that's played to honor the unacknowledged gods, Comfort and Convenience.

I should clarify what I mean by the sentimental. The music of emotion flowing through us can include a compassionate sentimentality as a tone that fits into our whole experience. For example, a great movie, that is quite moving and meaningful, may artfully have scenes that are sappy. Such experiences can be a natural relief of comfort that at times can be necessary to receive and give love. What I'll target here as sentimentality is music of emotion that's meant to make me comfortable at the expense of the truth of an encounter with people, events, and the history I live. A sentimental attitude to American history would include beliefs that America has been exceptionally virtuous, ignoring or rationalizing the brutal violence of what's occurred in the history. When going out with someone, a partner can finally one day say "I love you" and even believe it, while it's no more than a deceptive move (conscious or not) to feel good or gain some advantage or, at most, a sentimental desire.

Sentimentality can be part of a deception—of myself or others—which I may or may not be aware of as deception. Deceiving myself with sentimentality is usually to feel good, especially about myself. I lie to myself or to others, or I put a spin on something in the world, that avoids a difficult truth in order to indulge my comfort. I'm sure all of us have done this. There are times when the comforting is appropriate and healthy for myself or others. As with narcissism, it's a matter of degree. When I sentimentalize compulsively, when I avoid truths so much I deform my quality of life or harm that of others, sentimentality needs to be curtailed. I need to face truths.

Though I may be self-indulgent or sappy in how I interpret myself or the world at times, this becomes a degenerated, mediocre style of living if it dominates how I perceive the world and myself. I would give up so much of my potential for experiencing and creating love and beauty in the world because I don't want to endure costs to my comfort, risks to my security, I don't want to taste the pain and fear that growth requires, I don't want to know the vulnerability of failing, hurting, needing. I want the easy way almost every time. Giving up a sentimental orientation can result in a certain quality of felt experience called emotional integrity.[3]

Fears

It seems like we're naturally afraid of being afraid. We also can be ashamed of being afraid, especially if we could be called

---

[3]   In the next chapter, I'll explore emotional integrity. It's been written about by such writers as the Stoics, La Rochefoucauld, and contemporary philosophers such as Rick Anthony Furtak and David Pugmire.

cowards. Therefore, we could feel better by lying to ourselves or others about times we were afraid or failed to face threats courageously.

The music of fear is usually played from the forces of survival in the mind and body: a perceived threat (to safety, status, self-esteem, other's esteem, etc.) triggers neurons, hormones and neurochemistry to blare music warning of danger, the potential of serious harm, the need to get away or get protection. The smart science used to bet on the amygdala region of the brain as the source of fear. But more careful research, summarized by Lisa Feldman Barrett showed "the emotion category 'Fear' cannot be necessarily localized to a specific region."[4] The music of fear and aroused reactions shoots through the body and mind and usually is so disruptive that it gives rise to false thoughts, ideas and beliefs about ourselves and others.

Rather than denying fear, trying to banish it at its first twitch, I've found it more useful to acknowledge its presence, open to it, get to know it and befriend its sources within me. When I allow it to be with me, care for the many tones of fear and their sources, I can more easily thank my nervous system for the warning, let myself feel and use the energy of fear to transmute it into a different music. This of course isn't always easy; it requires practice. I've also found it useful to portray my fear as an image, such as an inner ferocious beast, know that the beast needs empathy, acceptance and respect. If I truly accept and approach the beast, allow its energy to have a part in playing my music, I may be able to make friends with it to help me think and act effectively with notes from both my Adult and Primitive Minds.

---

[4]   *How Emotions are Made,* op. cit., p. 18

The potential for false thoughts and beliefs from my fear is infinite. I can believe people, places and situations are dangerous because I really don't know them and have developed false stories and beliefs about them. The false stories can come from my childhood history, my culture or my interpretations of past experiences; usually, all these factors contribute. I can have the misfortune of having delusions that range from exaggerations of how great I am at certain things to how the government is listening in to my house through a particular light outlet. There is a whole category of phobias that are distortions of the possible threats of situations. From the most hallucinated to the most life-saving, fears come from the deep pool of vulnerabilities that lies within each of us. Getting to intimately know and care for the vulnerabilities can allow me to practice and learn a different genre, to be inspired by the music of love of myself and others, accepting my neurotic fears, letting them arise with the assurance that I'll care for them. Accepting and caring for my vulnerabilities can allow me to expand my repertoire into areas I don't know and may have stayed away from.

Relating to fears and to situations that feel threatening is a matter of skill and experience rather than of some distinguished status called courage or heroism which one hopes to attain. The term "courage" can be useful as a shorthand signal of certain skills of facing threats and discomfort and the development of confidence. I can patiently understand the inner beast of the particular fear, approach it with a music of compassion rather than going for the status of courage. The term "courage" can be a term to label people, to judge them as being superior, as a winner, as fearless, to be admired. Judging someone as courageous or cowardly is often according to norms developed in masculine culture. Such norms are fundamentally based in violence. Will I fight a violent attacker, bully or predator or will I cower away? The body's feeling of intense excitement when risking physical safety is usually from the energetic flow of adrenaline and/or testosterone. Taking risks to feel that charge can be labeled courage, but that music is primarily from the Primitive Mind. It can be necessary to survive or protect myself when physically attacked. It can be a pleasure so intense as to be valued far above those of less intensity and more complexity. It can become addictive.

Courage could be understood as visceral, primitive risk-taking for the sake of proving I can face physical threat or it can be a virtue informed by the Adult Mind. I've defined the virtue of courage as willingness to face fear to take a stand and act for the sake of the good in a situation, when doing so subjects you to some risk. When courage is lived from the Adult Mind, I don't act to prove how brave I am, nor merely to win nor to get the adrenaline fueled high of risk-taking. Courage doesn't even depend on outcome. It is a form of mature excellence. It is for a good greater than myself. It is to play the instrument of my mind-body as well as I can to produce music that transcends myself. It is to take risks of failing from my human flaws and weakness or not playing as well as the music requires, while giving my full effort, striving for my potential, in solidarity with other players of the music of the good.

Illusions

Illusions, similar to sentimentality, have their place in the music of excellence. Well below the extreme edge of delusion, illusions are part of ordinary thinking and feeling. They can be needed at times to exceed the ordinary, to energize or clarify our hopes, goals and desires. Without illusions, life would be too limited, boring or miserable. When aiding a perspective that's beaten down or dull, illusions can make us think there's something beyond what's perceived—some greater sense of justice, beauty or joy in what is happening.

The trouble with illusions is they can allow me to avoid truths and lead me toward acts that are limiting or harmful to myself or others, or at least they can tempt me into a style of foolish or ineffective thinking and behaving. Illusions can be self-deceptions. An illusion may be an escape or an inspiration. For Don Quixote, illusions were inspirations from ideals, and also a way to escape a less than noble path in life. It can be hard to tell when illusions are helpful or a detour away from great music of emotion.

Between me and what I perceive there are various perspectives, associations, memories, and fantasies that affect what I believe to be reality. What's real is veiled in a unique blend of interpretations, desires, vulnerabilities and self-protection. We can accept that no one can purely see or interpret reality. This isn't a crisis or absurdity of life; it is a play of encountering reality, like a veiled dancer on the stage of reality.

Like magic shows and fictions, illusions can bring pleasure, inspiration or laughs. How I perceive, feel and think about an experience will be affected by how I'm attracted, needing, greeding, desiring. Desires seem to have a life of their own and can lead to some of the greatest ecstasies and frustrations. A lot of religious and philosophical teachings are about the potential trouble from illusions arising from pleasures and appetites that lay in wait within. As individuals, we can accept illusions as part of perception and desire, tempered by the Adult Mind's care and willingness to assess how helpful or harmful the illusion may be. We can be amused, intrigued and lightened by the illusions of magic, movies, jokes and art. We can be aware of how illusions may be affecting perception and how we'd better be careful about what we assume. We can assess how our illusions can interfere with or aid in making decisions. We can discriminate among the illusions that arise from desires and pleasures and practice the difficult art of choosing which to allow as influences and part of a style, just as a composer chooses notes, chords and qualities of the melodies and intensities of the music to create illusions of grandeur.

Self-deceptions as supports or cop-outs

I could easily make a case that self-deceptions can serve some very positive purposes. Fooling myself that I can do something a lot better than I'm currently able to do could lead me to try harder to get good at it, to even in fact get better at it. I can fool myself into exaggerations of the great qualities of a lover or friend to bring out a more loving and devotional music from within myself, to give the lover or friend greater respect and affection. Religious and secular stories and art may use symbolic deceptions to open my imagination, to increase my commitment to doing good. Congregations, political parties, schools and armies, all require their members to practice various kinds of self-deception to make their systems function really well, to allow greater cohesion. It's even been argued that any thought I have requires me to deceive myself into believing it before or while or even after expressing the thought. Self-deceptions can make my effort easier, give me a boost in energy or confidence, give my commitments greater strength, encourage me to practice more interesting styles of playing the music of emotion. Perhaps self-deception can allow me to influence (or is it deceive?) other people, to bring me wealth (by deceiving myself about how great is whatever I'm selling).

Even if I make the case for the benefits, if not the inevitability, of self-deceptions, the music of emotion I play will be of a more profound quality and meaning if I can be aware of my tendency to self-deceive, if I try to challenge my deceptions, and if I realize when they serve purposes or people that are contrary to the greatest potential and excellence of my Personal Myth. If that is a self-deceptive illusion, I embrace it.

These days, it's almost the most natural question to ask, So what? Who cares if you're deceiving yourself, if your felt meaning is shallow or profound? Since self-deception seems so natural, why make it a big deal? In fact, it can be part of making deals. We live in a society that is everywhere quantitatively measured, particularly in monetary units. Am I contributing to the Gross Domestic Product or taking from it? Am I selling enough units of product or art or online views and likes? Whether one acts for morality or integrity is irrelevant to the bottom line. Marketing seems more important than truth: technologies of deception can give you a highly paid job or lucrative business. The means of enriching a company or individual isn't cared about unless someone's victimized and they sue for monetary damages. Money seems much more definite than morality or justice. Making money doesn't require morality. Surely, we have freedom to choose against the amorality, to not be part of it. Or can we?

Higher illusions

There are various ways people describe to go for a "higher state of consciousness." Could dissolving the self in meditations or psychedelic trips be no more than really wonderful self-deceptions? If I could attain the higher state of consciousness, maybe I could do without dogmas or any beliefs. This could leave me feeling not simply blissful, but also ungrounded, directionless, afraid, despairing. Relief from the latter conditions have been the bread-and-butter work for religions and psychotherapy. In Zen Buddhism, the experience of successful meditation, through which I exhaust the grasping for answers or meanings, is the experience of "no-thing-ness," as explained by David Loy:

> According to Buddhism, letting go of myself into that no-thing-ness leads to something else: when consciousness stops trying to catch its own tail, I become no-thing, and discover that I am everything—or, more precisely, that I can be anything. With that conflation, the no-thing at my core is transformed from a sense-of-lack into a serenity that is imperturbable because there is nothing to be perturbed.[5]

At one point, I questioned why it's necessary to get rid of my self. Is it mostly to avoid being "perturbed" or unhappy? Even if Zen enlightenment doesn't depend on beliefs or concepts, but on a special experience, I'm not sure we free ourselves of beliefs or the self. It seems even those Zen masters who lived in monasteries or caves had to keep up a belief in what they're doing and the troublesome self could invade even a sealed-off,

---

[5]   David Loy, *A Buddhist History of the West : Studies in Lack,* State University of New York Press, 2002, p. 8

ascetic way of living. But I've realized there is a music of the No-self or no-thing-ness. It's a way to allow Centering as music that can liberate me from the daily triggering of the Primitive Mind in automatic replays of the music of self-protection. I don't feel much help from the monotone chants of Buddhist monks I've heard. But from nothingness, there can arise the music of love.

A different answer comes from the extreme opposite corner: the music of the hedonist who accepts the selfishness and exploitative exploits that come so easily to humans, who wants to get better at deceiving others and oneself, which is the philosophy of sales. The hedonist believes, as truth, that humans are by nature greedy, therefore we should utilize the greed for all we can get by way of material pleasures, security and comforts. There seems to be ample evidence that the mass of modern humanity has been converted to the religion of money, with its gods Comfort and Convenience dictating the culture, economics and Mythology of consumerism. Nothingness is badly needed.

The meanings and music of human pleasures become confused and infected by the faith and rule of money in our culture. I happen to think Lewis Lapham was right in his thesis that money is the secular religion of America, as pithily expressed by a newspaper gossip columnist, Suzy Knickerbocker, whom he quotes: "'Perhaps it's dreadful that money is God, but that's the story.'"[6] In its landmark *Citizens United* decision, the United States Supreme Court christened cash as a protected power in the American form of democracy. Pleasure has become

---

[6] Lewis H. Lapham, *Money and Class in America: Notes and Observations on the Civil Religion* (New York: Ballantine Books, 1988), p. 246

commodified in products mass marketed by advertising and media. As earlier discussed, however, we can choose to depart from the culture's Mythology of living for pleasures offered by Comfort and Convenience. One can choose to develop patterns for styles of behaving and thinking for a Personal Myth with qualities that thrive on feeling the depth, intensity and consistency of acting for love, beauty and justice. This involves allowing the Adult Mind to draw upon and guide the Primitive Mind through openness, curiosity and exploration of how people have formed their most profound meanings and values in past and present times. Illusions and deceptions can be accepted for how the mind naturally moves. But for a Personal Myth that forms from actions of integrity, with a sense of the sacred and the comic, illusions will be faced with rigorous, caring, and imperfect honesty, as well as responsible pleasure.

Guiding themes of Truth, Beauty and the Good have become old-fashioned or rejected as "grand narratives." They certainly aren't mentioned in most trainings and graduate schools of clinical psychology, psychiatry or social work. What if we took seriously the ideal of Truth for individual norms of thinking and acting? What if I focused less on what's wrong with me, why I have symptoms of a mood disorder and focused instead on being radically honest about the meaning of what I'm doing now and in the past, the truth of what I should be doing? What kinds of music would I make?

I close with lyrics of aphorisms from a master of the form, La Rochefoucald:

> It is easy to deceive ourselves without noticing it, as it is hard to deceive other people without their noticing it. (No. 115)

We are so accustomed to disguise ourselves from other people, that in the end we disguise ourselves from ourselves. (No. 119)

We could have few pleasures if we never flattered ourselves. (No. 123)

The qualities we have never make us as absurd as those we pretend to have. (No. 134)[7]

---

[7] All quotes are from the translation in *Collected Maxims and other Reflections* translation by Blackmore & Giguère (Oxford: Oxford University Press: 2007)

CHAPTER 9: THE PASSIONATE MUSIC OF INTEGRITY

—◁◁◁◁◁◁◁◁▷▷▷▷▷▷▷—

W HAT does it mean to act with integrity? Do I have to
prove it? To whom? What music does the mind-body
play while acting with integrity? What does it mean to be
cynical, content, corrupt, never having enough? What music
plays when I act without integrity?

To get her take on the music of integrity, I asked Angie to
come back and share some of her thoughts. She's settled down
a bit more, sometimes a bit less. She just moved in with the
piano player and she's been working as a counselor to college
kids at a nearby university.

Angie's take on integrity

It's a word I use with care, with the right people. Very few
students who see me ever use the word or have any idea what it
means. Of course, it's not cool, probably not politically correct.

Mostly, I think it's scary to truly consider it for themselves. But it's more profound than ever. I really try to act and feel integrity in my work and my life each day. And I use the word "integrity" because it's essential.

The meaning of integrity can be elusive in a land that puts everything up for sale. It's not something that you get from following rules or from a therapist or guru. It's not even something you earn. Integrity is completely personal and private. I don't even know exactly when and if it's happening. I know it happens when I catch myself in my own lies, when I finally accept my failures and flaws, those endearing quirks, those less than charming outbreaks of what they call in my business "maladaptive behaviors." The emotional chords of integrity can give me a vague pull, they can freeze me in place, they can liberate me from the self-deceptions, the fears, the inertia that always invade my Personal Myth like a virus. When it gets nice and clear, integrity can stop me from wallowing or making excuses. And it can modulate the music of self-protection I'm playing to transition into centering, maybe even transcending, my self. I can play beyond the self's fearful notes. How do I know any of what I tell myself about integrity is true? How do I know I'm not just trying to prove I'm more than an embarrassing, needy, greedy self, that I'm beyond all that, I'm better, I should be approved?

My integrity isn't anyone else's standard. It's how I've practiced and played a music of meaning in my Personal Myth. It's not composed from my will alone. Integrity has its own energy and direction. It's played comic operas of my self. It's tried to incorporate all kinds of good advice, but those tunes can get too familiar. "Integrity" can even be a song of self-deception.

It can be performed in costumes and masks of heroism, suave lyrics, self-assured silence. It's when those pretensions are given up, even if they promise feelings of esteem, that I can dare to try to play the music of integrity.

The music of integrity calls for stepping through all the self's unflattering, uncharitable and unintelligent tunes and segue into the Wild. Sometimes, ancient hymns arise when I open to the air breathed by the trees, lit by the sun. I've felt inhuman voices and silences that have been singing all this time to me and everyone. The music of the Wild no longer feels scary then. I'm invited into the harmonies of birds and animals hunting and mating, friends and other musicians of emotion sharing their tunes. I attune to the music of streams, stones, houses and roads. I want to move to the steps of integrity's dance, following my own Myth's music.

The Mythology of this culture has to be discerned for what can inspire integrity and what's offered for bait to everyone's appetites for being approved, taken care of, fed, housed, happy. My Personal Myth has been developed within that Mythology of modern American ways of living. I have to practice different notes and songs to find more natural harmonies, to live true to the joy of the world that's been here since before the Mythology, even before human beings. The music of integrity is a commitment to be true to reality, to be responsible to natural ways of living, with the help of responsible guides and artistic offerings not created for a market.

Integrity is the skill and virtue of knowing when I'm fooling myself or being fooled to fall for pitches made to my self. Integrity reveals how my Personal Myth is constructed, whether there are cheap frames of self-deception holding parts of the Myth together. Integrity gives me sensitivity and taste for music I can play beyond self-protection and approval. I have no guarantees of holding on to integrity. But by realizing how its music is always accessible in me, to inspire with beauty and excellence, I can let it play when I should take stands for the good, for beauty and love. Integrity can warn that I can be fooled, especially by my self, by how well I think I'll act, how I can say words about standing for the good that are said only to feel good. Integrity can tell me my motivations are serving a shameful Myth, an artificial set of ideas about security, superiority or rewards. Integrity can play a music that's noble.

When people do talk about integrity, it's usually something like being true to one's word, honest, trustworthy, reliable. Those are traits and outcomes of integrity. Integrity means all the ways those and other qualities can be generated from one's Personal Myth. It's not an accomplishment to be proud of, to be praised by others. I think acting nobly isn't known by others most of the time. It's the set of practices that ensure qualities of excellence and goodness are played in the music of my Personal Myth. I want integrity to be more that an honorific. The integrity I want to live up to is about being true to all that sustains me, that calls to me every moment. It starts with respect and reverence for others and for the life-giving wonders and forces of my body and the natural world. I believe integrity requires that:

- as much as I can, I monitor and adjust my perspective beyond its egocentric bearings, which tends to inflate what I want or need, to always see what's in it for me;
- I take responsibility for my choices, risks and acts, based on living for the good, fallibly;

- I'm honest with myself and others about being flawed and sometimes foolish;
- I own the results of my action or non-action, as affecting and affected by a larger whole;
- I regularly reflect on my actions, values, interests, virtues and vices, sometimes discussing them with others to see how well I'm doing;
- I modify or expand my goals, values and interests for the sake of personal development, vitality and excellence, as well as bringing what is good and beautiful into the world;
- I make and keep commitments to others and myself.

Training for the music of integrity is, like almost everything, very individual. I think it starts with being clear about what it means to me, as I've tried to do above. Then it takes focus on how integrity is called for and applied in day-to-day living, always being aware that my thoughts and words about myself can be fooling myself about how well I act in situations, how I believe I'll stand for the good. What's most important is how well I train myself before arriving at the choice of action and taking a stand, for at that moment, my attention and choice can be suddenly swiped by selfish, self-protective motivations.

So many of my interpretations and stories about myself consist of fantasies and illusions biased to favor myself. This makes it hard to be sure my Personal Myth can be guided by integrity. I know Socrates said "Know thyself." But what I may wind up with is self-deception. A psychotherapy that aims at self-esteem may wind up building esteem on a foundation of fantasies about oneself and one's potential that crumbles when tested by challenges in the world.

It doesn't help when, as a blogger for *Psychology Today* puts it, "The United States is the most narcissistic nation in the world and everyone knows it. We are a nation of narcissists."[1] There are plenty of studies to support this and there have been plenty of warnings since Christopher Lasch's 1979 book, *The Culture of Narcissism*. What's more than a cultural diagnosis is clarity about the actual values of the culture's Mythology—the ocean we swim in—which I believe are mostly based on Adolescent, Pre-Adult or Primitive motivations that inspire superficial and aggressive music of emotion. The culture's values seem to me to be steered by power, money, and passively consumerist styles of politics, economics and art. Every culture's Mythology should be questioned for its values, especially those trumpeted for patriotism.

It's useful for me to assume that my thinking is almost always tuned to illusions and fantasies. It's cut through a lot of psychological theorizing. It helps me get past the simplistic categories of good and bad people and allows me to focus on the quality of actions rather than labelling people. Acts that produce the good and the beautiful don't occur because certain people have become geniuses or saints. Evaluating my Personal Myth is not the same as evaluating me as a person. I try to evaluate my Myth by my patterns of behavior over time and every day. The values of my Personal Myth are shown in what I do, including what I choose to focus on, how accountable I am for what I do and say, what good or evil effects result—for myself and others—from the way I live.

---

[1]   Gordon C. Nagayama Hall, Ph.D., "Is Narcissism the Cost of Being an American?" posted April 24, 2018 in his *Psychology Today* blog, "Life in the Intersection."

If I want to assess if someone is dangerous or safe, irresponsible or trustworthy, capable of love, it usually takes time and testing in situations to get a feel for the other's Myth. If I think someone is heroic or pure or perfect, I'm fantasizing. My Personal Myth always includes flaws, imperfections, vulnerabilities. Because the Myth is of a human being, we should all know we're going to be unheroic, fail others, screw up. Perfection is a fantasy. While we all will fail and make mistakes, we can also learn ways to consistently act with integrity in the pattern of our actions. Sure, my actions will sometimes be motivated by fear, vanity and self-protection. I hope they'll be motivated by integrity more times.

Instead of labeling, in counseling I try to help people be aware of and improve actions and norms, using language that's both more traditional and scientific. We're all animals, with certain mental capacities for evil and narcissistic behaviors that can result in destruction, stupidity and violence, but also in love and creativity. If Mythologies of all cultures recognized those capacities and prioritized values developed from the Adult Mind, especially responsibility, sacrifice, humility and love, there could be tremendous progress. The progress could maybe flow from individuals to governments, though I know next to nothing about that.

I can play at all of this with a sense of humor about my flaws and egocentricities. I can kindly support myself to correct problems and take responsibility for what and how I play. As I try things and fail at many of them, I may feel dissatisfaction, frustration, demoralization, despair or other variations over how life is going because someone or something else is causing problems and it's unfair, their fault, or I'm the problem because

I'm not good enough or I'm inferior and deserve to feel bad. All of us can get stuck in mindsets of victimhood, self-centeredness, and self-judgment. To go beyond the repertoire of self-absorption in my needs, wants and blaming, there are principles to reorient beyond the limited self, to go for transcending those old songs to aspire to create beauty, love and goodness in the world.

I believe that integrity, as well as a human's full potential, comes from the dimension of Soul. Soul isn't about anything super-human or supernatural. It's about our ever-present potential to transcend our self-centered perspectives and desires. It's the dimension in which we sacrifice for others, live for meanings beyond our wants, needs and urges. Soul can open me to diverse structures and styles of the music of transcendence—a music lived with the passion of courage and love, played in muscles, veins, neurons, neurochemistry, hormones, the networks of body and mind, played for meanings that matter beyond myself. It's a dimension which has been obscured or devalued in our time because of many factors, like disillusionment with religions that compel or coerce beliefs and an economic system which promotes social values and meanings around making money. Lots of scholars with integrity have told how consumer capitalism shapes culture, belief systems and institutions. Ultimately, I believe we can transform the culture and institutions that limit people's understanding and realization of their potential. We can strive to alter a culture's Mythology, and our own, by critical thinking and integrity.

Love's passionate values

I ask students, "What is there to live for? Right now, this moment? Security? Comfort? Pleasure? Money? For your whole life? No? For what then?" Most of them have no answers. Some say they just want to have fun. They say they've never had such questions in counseling. It'll probably get me fired again.

They talk about how their parents live for family, for their standard of living, recreation, a time to kick back. I tell them surely they'll work and get as much as they can for their future, for their kids, for retirement. I say, surely there's something else, something secret in people's lives no one wants to talk about. Maybe nothing? I tell them that's what I've heard. We talk about how, in America, nothing matters more than increasing a standard of living, in dollars, nothing better than that status quo. Some tell me how the increased standard of living has brought good things. I talk about how their talents could fit well with a culture of narcissism, a Mythology of selves competing with other selves. We wonder together whether that's all there is, nothing except to live for the kids, to work and save for retirement or to get rich, make a killing in business or investments, giving some money to politicians who assure we'll have progress in the standard of living, in terms of money of course, and ... nothing else. They ask me what I live for.

I try to be honest. I say that for me, there's a different sort of nothing. It's an opening all the way down my mind and body, clearing thought and thoughtless routine. There can be a different meaning for nothingness. When there's nothing to acknowledge, nothing in one's self as a source, I can center my focus. Quieting the mind, refining its neural firings is a different kind of thrill. I tell them I want the thrill of joy from the sunlight, the clouds, that bug crawling in the corner. There's nothing but what's continually created outside the open nothingness of me. After I tell them some of this, it usually gets quiet, awkward, they change the subject or ask me for a letter of accommodation for a test.

Whether I realize my potential to be more than as an "I", there will always be a nothing that's more than to be dead. I try to get my mind to clear its debris to feel the nothingness— in the Buddhist sense of Sunyata, the emptiness or void of a primordial awareness of living when the ego is forsaken. This can liberate the mind-body for a music of connection without an object separate from a me, without reward of any kind, without signs or directions in the Wild, just the music playing from this instrument in a flow of love.

I know there are a lot of ancient teachings of Sunyata. I don't claim to completely understand it, but I've felt something of the sense of emptying my mind to be receptive to reality. It allows the mysterious music of love, a sensitive improvisation. Rather than analyzing others, if I can let go of most of my security by voiding the calculating, defending and hiding ploys of the ego, I can open to the rhythms of others, then respond with whatever my instrument plays in a shared emotional field. Sometimes, I'll try to shift my notes to bring out something beautiful from whatever I'm playing with others. Sometimes it goes nowhere and I like it there too.

I play this track of an album of a live performance by the original extraordinary group Shakti. John McLaughlin tells the audience, "This is a piece that's very simply called 'What need have I for this, what need have I for that, I am dancing at the feet of my Lord, all is bliss, all is bliss.'" Then he begins playing tender, exploratory notes on his acoustic guitar against a background resonance of, I think sitar strings, until the guitar calls out in notes that are plaintive, then quick, playful riffs, then response comes first from a violin, which calls out in its own tender, plaintive flights, then tablas join in and the rhythm picks up more and more, the audience responds with applause, the band begins a melody that will launch the players into a series of improvisations and ensembles that drive the rhythms and measures into passionate intensities the audience responds to, at one point clapping in rhythm with the music as a communal percussive instrument, all with vigor, reverence and joy. For me, the performance shows what freedom, discipline, generosity and challenge emotion's music is capable of, moving performers and audience with indescribable love. The range of emotion's music in this piece always inspires me.

Love's passion isn't necessarily expressed in overt intensity. It may seem very moderate. Self-restraint may be an excellent move. Although I once took passionate stands for political causes, I see how self-restraint and listening to opposing views is important, not to agree or disagree, but to create a music between us that comes from love. There can be a kind of passion in moderation. Passionate love doesn't mean opening your heart to anyone anywhere. Just as in the Shakti piece, the initial notes can be exploratory. Once you know others will be receptive, may even join in with their caring notes, love can be more freely improvised. How great we can play this music depends on much discipline, learning, and practicing with the mind-body.

We can continue to use human and non-human others for security, pleasure, profit, various rewards and satisfactions. It's easy and even natural, based on the fact that we live through a body, with its many needs and wants, looking at the world literally from the center of the universe. There's hardly any public discourse about values beyond self-sustenance, going for advantages and of course improving our standard of living. There's so much bad stuff happening in the world and anywhere in this country—gun killings of innocent children, weapons of the superpowers building up, global warming wiping out innocent species. Without big moral stands by most people, I can't have much hope. Only pitiful anger. People ignore the need to take a stand for the good every day. They want their stupid ... Alright. Enough. Listen to me—judging! There are students who do take stands and want to do something about all that. I really try to help them. And I do. I need to do whatever I can.

I talk with some students about how and why people lived passionately for purposes beyond themselves, for qualities of character like honor and nobility. I've learned so much from the philosopher and novelist Iris Murdoch. She'd be so helpful for these problems now. I share in counseling what she wrote about how to orient by "moral vision" "in which the concept of love, so rarely mentioned now by philosophers, can once again be made central."[2]

To begin with, Iris examines the self or ego: "Our minds are continually active, fabricating an anxious, usually self-preoccupied, often falsifying veil which partially conceals the world. ... The psyche is a historically determined individual relentlessly looking after itself. ... It is reluctant to face unpleasant

---

[2]   *The Sovereignty of Good* (London: Routledge Classics, 2001). p. 45

realities. … It constantly seeks consolation. …"[3] Without
even trying, the mind creates a "proliferation of blinding self-
centered aims and images."[4] The "self is such a dazzling object
that if one looks there one may see nothing else."[5] Oh yeah,
that's right. All of that's part of the protective forces I wrote
about before. There are different patterns in each person, with
different intensities. So much depends on what happens in the
family and home we were born and raised into, friends and
events we moved through as kids. There's a repertoire of the
ego's music of emotion played in each of us. In counseling and
in myself, I try to be alert to that music's self-centered energies
and manipulations. We may not want to admit to others or
ourselves how selfish we are. Not so attractive.

To live for greater qualities in my actions, to act for love,
involves more than any set of techniques. A fundamental step
is "the extremely difficult realization that something other than
oneself is real. … Love, and so art and morals, is the discovery of
reality."[6] This isn't nearly as easy as it sounds. She doesn't mean
that we can discover reality from some superhuman stance. We
only perceive through the limits of the mind-body. She means
I can recognize what's independent of my mind-body. I can get
there by letting this thing called the self drain to nothingness.
Along with it disappears priorities like survival and winning.
To recognize another person, an animal, plants and stones as
miraculous Being, wholly separate from my needs and wants

---

[3]   "The Sovereignty of the Good Over Other Concepts," in *Existentialists and Mystics* (New York: Penguin Books, 1999) pp. 369, 364

[4]   "On 'God' and 'Good'," Id. p. 354

[5]   "The Idea of Perfection," Id. p. 324

[6]   "The Sublime and the Good," Id. p. 215

takes not only the emptying to nothing, but a clearing for the mature Adult Mind. When I fall in love, like everyone else, I put my lover on a pedestal. But maybe not. I'm not putting my lover above me, what I'm really drawn to is what would most turn me on. I've gradually realized I shouldn't try to know the reality of my lover—mysteries that aren't there for my grasping—I just let us be present to each other.

Discovering what is real can be through a profound experience that moves us out of ourselves. For me, this was being with a lover who died beside me. In my apartment afterward, the walls and objects that were so familiar suddenly felt illuminated. It wasn't like a ghost, but a light from the loss of this beautiful person gave me a realization of what Rudolph Otto called the Holy, suddenly feeling the world brilliantly alive. Everything every day has ultimate worth. I realized that giving up my life for someone or for the Good can be the clearest choice, without difficulty, when the full force of love fills me. I try to keep that alive in my Personal Myth. It doesn't matter that I'm still naturally self-centered, that vanities and insecurities are also part of my Myth, that I'm part of a human comedy and I'll be apologizing and learning from my ego's less than noble noodling.

Murdoch tells us that love involves engagement with others and the world, as well as a monitoring of our self-orientation and a continually lived education about limits of the self and the potential for a magnetic relation to the moral Good:

> Good is the magnetic centre towards which love naturally moves. False love moves to false good. False love embraces false death. When true good is loved, even impurely or by accident, the quality of the love

is automatically refined, and when the soul is turned toward Good the highest part of the soul is enlivened. Love is the tension between the imperfect soul and the magnetic perfection which is conceived of as lying beyond it. ... And when we try perfectly to love what is imperfect our love goes to its object via the Good to be thus purified and made unselfish and just. ... Love is ... capable of infinite degradation and is the source of our greatest errors; but when it is even partially refined it is the energy and passion of the soul in its search for Good, the force that joins us to Good and joins us to the world through Good. Its existence is the unmistakable sign that we are spiritual creatures, attracted by excellence and made for the Good. It is a reflection of the warmth and light of the sun.[7]

This love can shine in the workplace, in all kinds of relations with others, in serious studies and the wonders of nature present right now.

Getting beyond the habits and limits of the ego to discover reality isn't just a condition for love. It also can allow me to experience and create beauty. Murdoch clarifies: "Fantasy, the enemy of art, is the enemy of true imagination: Love, an exercise of the imagination. ... The exercise of overcoming one's self, of the expulsion of fantasy and convention ... is indeed exhilarating. It is also, if we perform it properly which we hardly ever do, painful."[8] Fantasy isn't just escapism; it's an immersion in the solipsistic self. Fantasy takes the place of reality. Imagination is the effort to go outside the self, to

[7] "The Sovereignty of the Good Over Other Concepts," Id. p. 384
[8] "The Sublime and the Good," Id. p. 216

discover the reality of other persons and of all that is in the world in itself rather than for me. Beauty is the form of what's independent of me, resonating, taking me beyond myself, in loving, in beauty's inspiration. Beauty can cause me to lose consciousness of my self.

Yet I'll fall back into the needy, greedy ego's ways every day. The music of love isn't perfect. I can allow fantasies and illusions to naturally arise. I can allow my lover and I to fail each other, to veer into detours, to forgive. Love is a tragi-comic concerto rather than a heroic fanfare. To overcome the forces of my ego and self-deceptions, to orient and go for the Good I guide actions and roles from my Adult Mind, without taking myself too seriously, with Primitive energy kicking in the passion.

Emotional integrity

In psychology textbooks and trainings for mental health professions, you'll see none of the concepts or words like those of Iris Murdoch or, for that matter, of the humanistic psychologists from a few decades ago. Certainly, you won't hear much about love or the American Mythology that stokes the ruthlessly egocentric minds of all of us. They medicalize the mind, explain anguish and despair by brain chemistry. The mental health industry presents itself as science and medical practices to get rid of people like me who talk about love and the high paid technicians who want to make prior knowledge obsolete. As I said before, there's plenty of reasons why the practices of clinical psychology have nowhere near the kinds of rigorous standards of real sciences, like physics and biology. Nor should it. Nor could it. Life's variables can't really be quantified. The professional measures and jargon about emotion don't represent the textures and meanings of what's felt. Psychiatric assessments are simple games of fitting people into the disorders of the DSM. In that Manual, there are no assessments of cynicism, corruption or greed. I've worked as a counselor to people who've killed others, who've failed others and made moral mistakes with the rest of us. But nowhere in any therapeutic training or manual is there the word "conscience." So much of the anguish and struggle of people in counseling is over the morality of what they do and what's done to them. The professional assessments will say nothing about morality or meanings. They flatten emotion into labels which won't include integrity and the potential for passionately lived values of love.

Most people in the profession blindly follow the Mythology of psychiatry. They don't realize they've become technocrats following orders, like Eichmann claimed. I've gone off their grid, finding older concepts and newer metaphors like the notes, songs and melodies of emotion. I've experienced how this can open up possibilities beyond the dominant jargon. People need more meaningful ways to relate to emotion. Integrity can lead people to allow passion its mature role in life, to living responsibly and decently on earth.

The quality of people's soundtrack of emotion will determine what meanings they seek, what they're bringing into the world. The music of my soundtrack moves me to whatever dance of actions I choose and how I choose to dance affects my Myth. The dance may be only following steps of what I'm told. It can be a habit. The dance may be focused on particular patterns planned for this day. Different meanings are danced according to different rhythms, riffs and melodies. The music can be composed just according to what the culture tells people to do for their needs, urges, appetites, protection and rewards. People may not ever learn about music that can move them to act for the Good that transcends the self. I can learn elaborate dances of nonsense with others. I can dance in steps of laziness or self-absorption. The culture gives the population music and dance that makes waste and destruction of the natural world comfortable. If I can realize the limitations or harm of my dance, if I can learn to compose and play emotion's music of integrity, so can others.

Living with integrity comes down to taking a stand. Each day is filled with choices I make about what I do. My choices are based on my living Myth. What Iris Murdoch calls the Good can be seen in my choices, which reveal my Myth. Do they result mainly in self-protection, going along with whoever is exploiting, violating the dignity of human and non-human others? Or does my Personal Myth inspire me to passionately stand for beauty, love, and the moral Good of living in organic relation to the earth's natural systems? My choices affect all those issues in the particular circumstances and potential of each day. It's not a drama that anyone else may ever notice. It's not the music of a fanatic. I can choose to follow a soundtrack of comfort, conformism, greed or cheap thrills. I could try to avoid taking stands. I could blame others for what results from my decisions. Or I could take radical responsibility for how my life is lived. I could take a risk to try to play the greatest of life's music according to my particular abilities and tastes, or I could play it safe and limit my playing to trivial, mediocre tunes. Unless I set standards for the music of emotion I create, I may let life happen without knowing what it's like to play noble movements of the Soul.

To take a stand with the high standards of integrity is to risk losing, failing, even being wrong. When it gets tough or unthrilling, I may lose my bearings on integrity because ... well, at that point, I'll make something up. If I base my actions on gaining approval from others, the actions will have no integrity, for I'll need to be willing to risk rejection or disfavor by taking certain stands. If I base my choices just on increasing my wealth, I'm not living with integrity, for the standards of beauty and the most morally justifiable positions for the Good can't be secondary to making more money. The stakes for integrity aren't measured by money, prestige, approval or security. Acting on integrity is no sure thing. I'm sure I'll fail at times. When I fail, I can do so with integrity by admitting my failure and trying to learn from it.

Integrity comes not only from being radically responsible, but from making commitments. By commitment, I don't mean a pledge or promise, but a choice to gather my best thinking and energy for my highest purposes, with the soundtrack of emotion playing themes of moral and aesthetic excellence, curiosity, self-acceptance, playfulness, vibrancy. I need to be clear about what exactly should be my commitments. I need to get guidance about those to which I may best aspire, which commitments I need to develop or alter.

I know I can deceive myself about having integrity. I've learned to suspect my estimation of myself. Because the music of emotion isn't heard, it's not always easy to know how my feelings are serving the Good or my ego. It takes practice at playing with the music of others and playing for noble effects to know and feel how my actions are part of a greater whole, how at times that means taking a stand against a group, organization or culture I'm part of. It can be important to listen to the feedback of others just as good musicians check their playing with trusted listeners. But others may not always be available, or they may be mistaken. So, it's important to develop good patterns of action to get the feeling of music that inspires acts of integrity. I can test the effects of my actions in the world through responsible self-examination and the feedback from my body, my conscience and others in the world.

The demands of integrity can result in some confusing, anguished notes of emotion. Rather than relieve the anguished tones with psychiatric meds or camaraderie or "evidence-based therapy," the confusion or anguish may be part of assessing the meanings and qualities of how I'm living. Somehow, struggle, a sleepless night, the cacophony of hungry birds who care nothing about me, can allow hard realizations of illusions and self-deceptions and openings to integrity. Questioning how I'm living, how my desires may be shallow, impossible or foolish, how false my illusions may be, can be part of an essential process of honesty. When I have "the extremely difficult realization that something other than oneself is real," that I have no say in the ordering of the universe and I genuinely consent to this, I can be more clear about committing to what's greater than me in what I create with my time. I can tune my instrument to play, in my unique way, the music of integrity. I can feel exhilarated by taking a stand for the Good. There's a transcendent lightness and humor available on the other side of dark or heavy times.

In a society based on making and spending money, meanings beyond getting paid don't matter nearly as much. In this value system, integrity is a foreign or distorted word. Its absence is evident in the waste, destruction and self-destruction that goes on. It's easy to live a Personal Myth made of shallow meanings. The comforts, conveniences and cheap thrills of a high-tech living environment, the freedom and enticements of private pleasures, the virtual (un)realities of social media—all that and more can create a soundtrack of happiness and esteem of the self based on material satisfactions, easy entertainments, which can go on indefinitely without thinking of bigger questions, much less quests.

Making choices to live with integrity will involve mistakes and more than a little hardship. Shortcuts can be escape routes—whether the shortcut is a happiness formula or suicide. Taking life seriously takes humility as well as realistic idealism. It takes bravery to seek joy and depth of meaning. The bravery isn't macho bravado, another false shortcut. The bravery is with myself—allowing myself to sing despite clutzy attempts, going for what's more than catchy, cautious lyrics that can be popular with others. Bravery is really about gaining confidence to face fear and take risks for the good. It can involve Primitive energy, like anger. Courage with integrity involves the Adult Mind's expansive thinking and imagination, consideration of others, strategies for higher life purposes. Once the serious themes begin to develop, I try to give the music a rhythm that fits, I let the movements take me into sequences that lead to more than self-satisfaction, a music that isn't self-contained, that takes me and maybe others into noble realms of experience. I try out soundtracks of integrity. Others may let me know I'm being insensitive or pompous or kind, and I then may make adjustments to the music. Others may be wrong too. I continue to practice on my instrument to play the music of integrity as well as I possibly can.

I can open to the wonders of my living presence, the powers of my body and mind, my miraculous senses and imagination, the unconditional love I can give to others and myself. If I don't take account of and care for my vulnerabilities and flaws, if I don't trust my ability to play, I'll stop short of the transcendent music of giving love, of creating beauty and virtuous action. When I get good at playing this music honestly and well, it can form my Personal Myth in ways that allow integrity as a natural response to what happens. Playing this music of integrity requires wise guidance and a good gut, reflections, admitting mistakes, continual discoveries. It requires learning and practicing patterns to allow me to choose to act beyond myself while being myself. The music may have missed notes or be played self-indulgently. I don't have to play it perfectly.

Emotional integrity calls me to feel the amazing forces that connect me to the world, that give me life and the gifts of my body and mind. I open to those forces by engaging in loving ways with others, with works of art and works of the earth. I try to keep attuned to all those generous forces and gifts, even when I'm dealt a bad hand. Emotional integrity also means recognizing the limits of my natural instrument, valuing the skills and knowledge I've acquired, while practicing harder, going for the highest inspirations. The music gets better as I play it in what I do with and for others, the wider society and the natural world, in how I care for my body, in how I expand my knowledge and implement it.

Emotional integrity doesn't always prevent stupid, inadequate or narcissistic choices, but it can ground, influence and correct music I play in my expressions, feelings and behaviors. No one plays perfectly. I get better at responding well to situations by taking stands carefully, learning from my mistakes and flaws as part of aspiring to excellence.

My Personal Myth is formed by what I do, not what I say. It's not just a story or collection of behaviors. Music of emotional integrity plays in patterns from the virtue I enact and the virtue I enact is inspired by the music. It's my responsibility to choose what to learn to play to my highest potential. The vibrancy and resonance of the greatest music comes from experiencing and enacting love, a love that leads to upholding and sacrificing for the Good, relating to myself as a friend and to the other as "Thou"—autonomous and worthy, as another participant in the creative process. Emotional integrity resounds from the Soul's infusing the self with beauty, Creative Energy, confidence, inspiration and good judgment. The soundtrack comes from developing good qualities of character through patterns of virtuous actions.

Character and virtue

I gradually realized how a long-time friend of mine was a big-time deceiver. I couldn't believe how well it was hidden. It was shocking. What should I have done? Drop him quickly as a friend? Because it was revealed to a lot of people, it felt embarrassing to be associated with him. I was angry that he could do the deceptive things I discovered. How could I not have caught on? Was I deceiving myself?

It wasn't even clear at first that I had all these choices I could make. My first instinct was self-protection. I wanted a clean break. It seemed black and white. What he was doing was wrong and could harm others, even if he didn't realize it. I of course considered myself on the righteous, good side. At the same time, I was realizing my emotion was being driven by my vulnerability. I wanted to get away from him, to judge, no, really to condemn him, to protect myself from being associated with him. Because I knew that the music of self-protection was compelling me, I centered myself in solitude to reflect on my friend and myself. I knew I've been guilty of deceit to get some advantage or avoid what was fearful. I knew it was an automatic move and I deceived myself about it. I knew all of us fail morally more than we like to admit. Therefore, I could and should relate to my friend. I gave it some time and started to approach him in a low key. I knew there were vulnerabilities in him that I couldn't know. So we met. He felt my unconditional acceptance of him as a person. He dropped to the floor in front of me, folded himself as if in a womb. It kind of scared me. I didn't know what to do with his freaking out and I wanted to get away. But then I realized he was being himself, he was being completely vulnerable with me and I held him. I realized my role there was to go to a higher level of compassion. Eventually, we were able to talk about it. He didn't understand himself. He did understand how he needed me as a friend. I said I could if we'd talk openly about values.

I think any of us can relate ourselves to others' moral failings, unless we think we're perfect or that moral choices are always black and white, simply about categorizing someone as good or bad. Whether to flee from someone who's done wrong for the sake of joining with others' judgments or to not get your hands dirty, is itself a choice, a choice that's moral. Abandoning, rescuing, pitying, condemning would all be signs of failure to act with integrity. To meet moral challenges, to make wise choices we'd best train for them by developing skills of responding to challenging situations with what's traditionally called good character.

A Personal Myth includes good, bad and indifferent qualities, especially those unattractive features we don't like to think of. The qualities (or, if you will, traits) of a Personal Myth continually, even if minutely, change every day. My Personal Myth is porous, not isolated from reality, not impervious to change, but open to interchanging energies, influences, feelings. I am not a settled frame of a character with "enduring traits." I am in a process, participating in the real, material reality, trying to act according to moral standards, through my living Myth.

Virtue and good character don't get a lot of mainstream attention these days. The words themselves may sound old fashioned, outdated, conservative, elitist, unscientific. I never saw or heard the words in teachings and practices of contemporary psychology, in either academic or professional mental health settings. Fashionable or not, virtues make a huge difference in my Personal Myth and, therefore, in the quality of my life.

I've learned how the meanings and language of virtue have varied over the centuries. Many may be surprised how universal virtues have been in the world's religions and cultures. This has been documented by various scholars, including work from Positive Psychology researchers, Christopher Peterson and Martin Seligman, in *Character Strengths and Virtues: A Handbook of Classifications*. This work was a massive effort at surveying virtues across the world, across centuries, to identify 24 "character strengths" for the modern world. Unfortunately, the subsequent implementation of their work in Positive Psychology amounts to a formulaic approach that departs from the traditional meanings and teachings. Positive Psychology, through the Values In Action website and trainings, offers a test of your 24 Character Strengths, which yields your top five "signature strengths" and a standard profile of you based on those 5, which you should focus on to get ahead in life. Whether or not this was the original intent of the *Character Strengths and Virtues book*, I've personally seen the approach carried out online and in trainings, where people take the test, focus on their top 5 "signature strengths," and forget the rest. This substantially departs from philosophical works on virtue and character, which emphasize virtues as guides to live with excellence, not a determination of your top 5. Traditionally, virtues are means, not to get ahead socially or economically, but toward a participation in beauty and the good, a realm of experience transcending individual satisfaction, involving personal commitment. Living a virtuous life could result in losing status, material security or even one's life. The ultimate meaning for one's life was stated well by Iris Murdoch, who said virtue is "the austere consolation of a beauty which teaches that nothing in life is of any value except the attempt to be virtuous."[9]

One reason virtue isn't popular in America is that it's not about being sensational, powerful, popular or publicized. It's not like a movie showing a heroic achievement of a Hollywood handsome star. It doesn't go viral. Virtue is about holding oneself to particular standards and styles of behaving for the moral good in ordinary day to day life. It is about practicing and aspiring to embody particular dispositions to be sensitive to and recognize a situation that calls for a moral response or

---

[9]   "The Sovereignty of Good over Other Concepts," in *Existentialists and Mystics*, pg. 371

intervention, then doing one's best to act virtuously. To develop my Personal Myth to allow me to be sensitive to choices to make for action, involves many attempts to learn, to practice, to make mistakes and to commit to "nothing ... except the attempt to be virtuous." This calls for loving the virtue for its own sake, not for some reward or admiration. This requires educating myself about what the virtues are.[10]

Committing to the standards of excellence of the virtues is not about remembering rules or principles to follow. So, I must learn about virtuous action from exemplars and texts, focusing on the meaning of my action, whether I feel the music of integrity in acting and in the consequences of my action. I enact virtue by going for integrity in everyday choices, learning from mistakes, acknowledging my flaws, getting help for creating a pattern of virtuous perception and action.

None of this is easy. I can have exaggerated ideas of what is virtuous, then reject them as unrealistic. I can vainly presume that I'm virtuous (the test I took proves my top 5 "signature strengths"). I can fool myself in ways recognized by La Rochefoucauld in the 17th century, who wrote: "The name 'virtue' is as useful to self-interest as the vices themselves. (Maxim V: 187)[11] ... Virtues lose themselves in self-interest, as rivers do in the sea." (V: 171) La Rochefoucauld was far more pessimistic than I that people can inculcate the quality of good character through acting virtuously. He thought talking

---

[10]   I have adapted a summary of particular virtues from Peterson & Seligman's above-mentioned book, listed them in an appendix to *Discovering Soul*.

[11]   All quotes are from the translation in *Collected Maxims and other Reflections* translation by Blackmore & Giguère (Oxford: Oxford University Press: 2007)

about virtue was mostly pretense and deception to cover over our flaws, mediocre and immoral acts. He wrote beautifully and boldly about how we naturally believe we think and act better than is the case. His maxims are useful in helping us to acknowledge the power of the ego in deceiving ourselves about our motivations and actions. They are aids to practice the virtue of humility. He believed narcissism (which he names as vanity and self-love) can take on the disguise of virtue, a caution relevant for a culture of status-seeking and celebrity.

So, in these times and this culture, how does one cultivate good character and embody genuine virtues? I believe the first step is to get rid of any ideas that one can do so perfectly or purely. We act from alloys of the Adult and Primitive/Pre-Adult levels at all times. We are egocentric by default. We'll fail and be less than virtuous every day. Virtue is relevant as an aspirational ideal and standard to allow a meaningful quality of life, what Aristotle called eudaimonia, or flourishing. The music of living for and loving virtue ranges through the most important motifs of life and death. Each person can find the music that serves her or him to take stands for the highest moral meanings, for tough moral decisions, for a beautiful way of life, which includes pain, defeat and death.

Another fundamental step is Murdoch's invitation to "the extremely difficult realization that something other than oneself is real." Being able to overcome egocentrism isn't a matter of learning how and achieving it. It is an ongoing process. We can easily fool ourselves into believing we've got it down. Sometimes it takes "hitting bottom" as they say in Alcoholics Anonymous, to really confront the ego. I'm inspired by Rudolph Otto's description of experiencing the *Mysterium*

Tremedum of the Holy. What I think it means is humility from an experience of awe, resulting in treating yourself, others and the world with reverence and love, participating in the beauty and mystery of the universe. It isn't a sense of unworthiness. What's important is honest self-assessment, recognition of limitations, keeping accomplishments in perspective. A sense of humor, taking myself less seriously, helps a lot. Humility is even compatible with a sense of greatness of myself, not as status, but as respect and appreciation for the natural gifts and potential of my natural, human being, participating in something greater than myself. This can fill me with passionate music.

To live from and express the passionate music of the Soul requires actions that will form virtues as structures of behavior. To live only for the self, we can play music that's pretentious, that's meant to get the approval of others. The self's music may find a market, may even produce some hit songs. Allowing the music of emotion to flow from the Soul leads to noble forms of behavior. People have tried, tested and discovered these structures known as virtues.

Some traditions of virtue count anger as a vice. Tones of anger can be appropriate, even necessary, in responding to a wrong. Instead of mad dog instinct, the anger can be part of effective courage or justice while also informed by virtues of self-control and humility, which should stop the anger from becoming hatred, resentment, or revenge. I try to channel anger for the good with a style that's dignified and respectful. I may have to correct my behavior or apologize, especially if it's an outburst or inappropriate in tone or effect. It's tricky. I think I've eliminated from my repertoire anger that can denigrate people or violate their dignity. It helps to activate respect, prudence and effective decision-making which I have to practice. That's what a committed relationship is for, right? Anger may or may not allow quick, strategic responses without the crudeness of flailing, reactive noise.

The human dimension of Soul calls for actions that transcend our naturally self-centered appetites, needs, and instincts for power over others for me and what's mine. Virtuous action is a participation in the creation of beauty, goodness and excellence as part of the ongoing creative process of the whole of nature. To experience and orient life in this dimension of transcendence engages Creative Energy, which I'm calling passion.

The passion of emotional integrity is less about intensity than depth and commitment. The passion isn't necessarily loud or operatic, but can be fairly quiet and private. It's more about allowing and trusting emotion to flow from deeply felt, meaningful values. Training myself to form habits, actions and reactions aligned with virtue (such as courage, gratitude, humility) gives me greater skill and confidence to live a well lived life of excellence, especially when I lose in outcomes. Losing and learning from it is essential. Learning and practicing virtuous actions can expand capacities for tough decisions and creative responses to obstacles, setbacks and evil, as well as for enjoyment. Like my lover, who's become a virtuoso piano player, I can cultivate my capacity to play virtuously from committed learning and practice, testing my capacity in decisions and actions, playing for noble stakes passionately, win or lose.

A passionate life of integrity

Okay, I think I should summarize what I think of developing the music of emotional integrity. For me, it involves:

- Understanding how the soundtrack to my Personal Myth, playing in the background on my instrument of mind-body, is composed of what I'm bringing into the world, what meanings I seek, whether and for what I take a stand.

- Finding, practicing and cultivating music for my soundtrack that's aligned with an organic relation to the human and non-human occupants of earth.

- Learning from wise traditions, from all parts of the world, to understand and implement standards from tested examples of enacting character and virtue.

- Taking a stand for integrity means I have to be willing to risk losing at some ventured action or project, for stakes beyond outcomes. I have to even risk losing my bearings on integrity because of my flaws.

- Integrity isn't a solo playing of my music. How I play affects and is affected by others, in contexts of my social environment, relationships and the natural world. This can mean breaking from other people's standards supported by the culture and economic system.

- Decisions involve radical responsibility, making commitments for myself and others, finding how songs of self-deception infiltrate my efforts. There's certain to be mistakes, anguish, even suffering because of being human among other humans. What's essential is to be aware of how the music can be conducted by the Adult

Mind, while allowing the Primitive level and the kid in
me to improvise in the passionate spirit of the music.

- When I've developed consistent patterns of behavior
and self-correction, I can be counted on, relied upon by
others for playing with integrity. I'll still make mistakes,
but because of my effort to recognize my fallibility,
egocentrism and imperfection, I'll learn from and
correct my playing as I act, with humility and a sense
of humor.

A life of emotional integrity requires serious practice and
discipline to play the instrument of body, mind and Soul. When
I get good at playing, I make daily choices that are meaningful
moral responses, as distinct from mere reactions to situations.
The meanings enact what I've been learning and practicing. I
play from my Myth with the energies, intensities, harmonies,
dissonance and rhythms I've learned for a way of life. The
morality of my choices can come at first from rules, like a
musician learning chords and scales from rules.

Living with integrity also means learning how culture, our
Mythology, influences choices affecting the non-human world.
Though I play within a network of relations to other people and
institutions, I have to learn how the Mythology influencing us
has followed a trajectory of destructiveness and arrogance in
relations to nature.

Though passion can spontaneously arise, emotional
integrity means I continually hold myself accountable for how
I affect others, the world and myself. A passionate, fulfilling life
isn't necessarily filled with drama and certainly isn't reckless
or grandiose. Passion can quietly underlie an ordinary looking
life of generous care and giving, with commitments to the long

game in such activities as parenting, innovating responsible service and products, study and scholarship, stewardship of the natural world and its beings.

Playing and improvising well at this music is distinct from crude, impulsive, immediate reactions. Just as a good improvisor makes quality choices in notes and pauses, my choices in acting are with attention to effects on others (human or not, present or future) as well as on myself, but not for praise or approval of me. At times, I consciously follow explicit principles, but more and more these choices become intuitive. Continually cultivating integrity allows me to trust in my emotion and add my part to the many styles of emotion played in the world.

To play my instrument at my best, cultivating physical health, strength and vitality are important to allow vibrant responses to the flow of life's circumstances and demands. Situations can call for optimal physical fitness and freshness for the playing of a score that lends beauty and depth to my music and to what's playing around me. When suffering or a disabling condition occurs, I have a much better chance of asking for help I need if I've gotten good at the virtues of self-compassion and humility. Love, hope and resilience can give great tunes of recovery.

Though we all falter when facing challenges at times, we have a much better chance of responding with integrity if we can turn on the music of love that allows us the courage and energy to transcend needs and desires for security or comfort. A life dominated by self-protection can block or pretend at passionate playing with integrity. Fears can trigger the excesses of protective music of escapism, comfort, sentimentality, narcissism or a brutality that can be blustery, cruel or conniving.

For a lot of my life, I didn't realize how I was structuring my Myth to protect me from taking the risks needed to stand for integrity. In my relationship, as we become closer, vulnerabilities get triggered and revealed, which can trigger protective forces of avoidance or narcissistic moves, maybe to hide or try to be attractive. These are self-limiting moves. I need to be able to access centered harmonies and the Soul to correct those mistakes.

Cultivating a style of integrity involves practicing with and learning from others who play with quality, in environments that give me time and space to play. Each day, I try to reflect and feel how my choices and actions have moved me toward or away from creating a life that's fulfilling, beautiful, and loving. I know we all can create some really great Myths.

Another epilogue

I brought all this out of Angie despite her concern that she'll sound like a know-it-all who's got it down like some hero. I told her to play it from her heart, not worry about how she sounds. She says that writing about it helps her better understand integrity.

CHAPTER 10: PLAYING BEAUTIFUL MUSIC

W HEN FULLY engaging with a work of art (i.e., literature, music, visual arts, dance), attention is focused, the imagination is freed from assumed rules and roles so that we're able to be surprised and moved, we're able to experience beauty. The experience can inspire new possibilities, meanings and intuitions freed from the normal.

The implications range beyond the established arts. *The aesthetic dimension is the mind-body's delving and creating imaginative qualities of human experience*, not just in art, but in how we live each day.

An aesthetic orientation to emotion can allow freedom, awareness and care for style and quality. The philosopher Mark Johnson tells how aesthetics is a more fundamental approach to experience than labeling ourselves with abstract terms: "Aesthetics is not just about art, but is rather about all of our processes of meaning-making and is therefore the best starting point for any adequate account of human experience and understanding."[1] He contrasts the depth of aesthetics to the linear, categorizing manner of perceiving by abstract, stand-alone concepts:

> ... meaning is not just a matter of concepts and propositions, but also reaches into the images, sensorimotor schemas, feelings, qualities, and emotions that constitute our meaningful encounter with our world. Any adequate account of meaning must be built around the aesthetic dimensions that give our experience its distinctive character and significance.[2]

Living as an art

What kind of art is living? An art of qualities of how one engages reality, each uncompromising moment. An art that calls upon me to give up expectations and allow possibilities in the Wild. The art of living involves scenes of ordinary life, my imperfections and foolishness, the wild innocence of animals and plants, the metamorphosis of each day, meaning in multiplicities, an art of sensuous forms transcending the self.

How I move, speak, think or feel may be graceful, crude, imaginative or compliant. There is a certain form to me. It's ever changing in an art that defies critics. Like a sculptor with marble, clay or alabaster, I have this body, this attention, this imagination to work with. I look to how others have created beauty, grace, integrity and originality in the art of living. I may learn from them. When I was young, they saved me. I

---

[1] Mark Johnson, "Identity, Bodily Meaning and Art," in *Art and Identity: Essays on the Aesthetic Creation of Mind*, ed. Tone Roald and Johannes Lang (New York: Rodopi, 2013) p. 23

[2] Mark Johnson, *The Meaning of The Body: Aesthetics of Human Understanding* (Chicago: University of Chicago Press, 2007), pp. xi-xii

know what virtues are humanly possible. And, ready or not, I have to act.

No one, not even me, can judge my art, for it's gone after this moment. The art comes from my Personal Myth every moment and it changes, as my body and mind change. I don't need to impress anyone (unless the style of my Myth is narcissism) or prove I'm conforming to some standard. I know this ego of me is always there, I won't pretend it's not. I will allow it into the company of Soul, to be true to the divine human animal of me in a divine world. The art of my Myth will be allowed its originality in an unimaginative cultural Mythology. I can be certain and can be fooled in my Myth about what I stand for.

Creating qualities in the artwork of a Personal Myth is the destiny of each person. The instrument of mind-body has potential to produce grace, beauty, and love, as well as ugliness, brutality and kitsch as natural processes. No one can fully exhaust this potential of one's human gifts, to be enacted in the forms of one's Personal Myth. If I take on the role of a brave person, I just go for it on the stage of this moment. Art as noble as that of Michelangelo doesn't come about from haphazard dabbling or certainty. As Michelangelo showed, creating beauty requires focus, reverence and freely given effort to allow what may come from the material without playing it safe and compromising one's potential.

How I care for my health and body, how I cultivate concepts, intuitions and sensitivities, how I utilize the gifts of life, all will determine the aesthetic qualities of how I live. Unless I'm lost in fantasies and illusions, I can become aware of the aesthetic quality of how much I go for, the effects I create. If I help someone, do the right thing, without someone's regard or reward, if I create something that can inspire, if I fight for the protection and dignity of human and non-human beings, the quality of my art can be excellent. Ugly, egotistic, superficial and harmful qualities of living are usually from lack of cultivation of the mind-body and from excesses of the Primitive or Pre-Adult Mind which can form habits of making flashy, foolish or mediocre art. It helps to know what kind of art I want to create of myself.

There are no art critics of my life. There is no exam to pass. It's a matter of what level I go for. To create art that's fashionable or popular is like someone who seeks praise and flattery for nothing but self-esteem or, in the old parlance, vanity. Where art is produced for a culture like ours, in which the standards are based on appeal to a mass audience or a high investment value, it's hard to learn the art of the sacred. These days, beauty usually means being attractive on the surface. Experiencing all that we live in, including ourselves, as luminous, beyond human use, participating in ineffable, though material, Being, we can gain a perspective that breaks through habitual patterns of familiarity and egocentric meaning. We may discipline ourselves for perceiving and behaving in ways worthy of the sacred life we have, seeking inspirations and skills to practice styles that are graceful, loving, creative and beautiful, allowing a sacred music of emotion to play in us and from us.

Joining in the perpetual creation

Each day you participate in creating a living work of art in which you are a figure in the painting or tableau of what is happening. You are a character in the drama of life and you follow, embellish and alter the script of your Personal Myth as part of the dynamic whole this day. At any moment, what is happening may seem within your control, but, despite your illusive self, the music of cosmic energies plays within and beyond you. The question is how you'll join in. Once you truly feel you're living your part of the perpetually creating artwork, you don't really need words to describe it. You can allow yourself to be taken into its immediacy, choose how to play your original music of emotion in it or comply with what's expected of you or you retreat.

There is no definition or universalizing of beauty. It's strictly individual in realization. When you hear a certain melody of voice or instrument, when you see a graceful gesture or feel the wind through mighty trees, the sensation may initiate a cascade of meanings, memories and intuitions, connecting you passionately to the experience, inspiring you to joy, to act for the good, caring for more than just your own life. Creating beauty in how you live doesn't depend on lucky encounters or scenes. It depends on learning the moral and aesthetic effects of how you act in the world, as a musician learns the effects of playing in an ensemble or orchestra.

You play beautiful music of emotion not by grasping for security or acceptance by others or by controlling everything, but by choosing to live in the dimension of transcendence, Soul, which I've defined, in the book, *Discovery of Soul*, as *a present, felt process of living beyond, yet through, the self, in the realization and creation of beauty and goodness in the world, inspired and guided by love, excellence and the freedom of play.* You create beauty, with much practice, by the effects your actions create, which inspires you to continue to learn and practice playing music of the heart. Beauty is realized in the nobility of what you attempt. No one else may notice your music. You may creatively respond to circumstances that are ugly all around you, allow your music of emotion to move you to enact your highest potential.

When you enter a loving relationship, the two of you will play a kind of music to and with each other. What is the quality of the music? Is it in the genre of superficial sensation? Is it the whiny melody of dependence? Is it the same old tunes, same old playlist, familiar and boring? Is it the creative, complex passion of noble giving to each other, an art of intimacy?

Your instrument of mind-body may be practiced, the quality of your playing can be cultivated, to discern, attempt, learn and create beauty by living the art of everyday aesthetic excellence. You will know when you're going for it. You may not be aware that your playing is stuck in mediocrity, adolescence or crude power until you are shaken by the consequences of your actions or you realize how much of your potential has been wasted.

Beauty isn't a measure of winning, wealth or longevity. In other words, popular American measures of achievement or elation don't apply. This music is played passionately, even when it's light and sweet, for noble stakes. We would play this music not because we're supposed to but because it feels so much greater than the music of self-protection. Isaac Singer identified this feeling as aesthetic: "When we act morally, or when justice has been upheld, we experience an aesthetic rightness in ourselves. It is a feeling like the one we have in relishing a great work of art."[3]

---

[3]   Irving Singer, *Feeling and Imagination: The Vibrant Flux of Our Existence* (New York: Rowman & Littleton Publishers, Inc., 2001), p. 165

Composing and playing great music of emotion involves commitment to aesthetic quality in how you act, how you affect others and the world. Creating beautiful experience comes from experimenting with feeling the potential of life, for the joy that may be created for anyone at any time, even for those you'll never meet. Following precepts, gurus, formulas or gods can't give you this beauty. It must be given from your heart in your unique style of excellence. Your art must be created, not imitated, and must bring something new and good to the world.

Playing beautifully may or may not be playing happily. Getting high or drunk may serve happiness and pleasure, but it usually only takes you into your Primitive or Pre-Adult Mind, which is too immature to experience or create an original beautiful art. The happy state of mind-body could be like adolescent or narcissistic bliss, a craving for power over or gratification from others' responses. Living for beauty is to play your instrument of mind-body in tune with what is true and good even when it causes you pain, allowing the Child in you to become disillusioned and still bring out your fresh and vibrant innocence. How you cultivate, in your Personal Myth, values for what's greater than the self can allow you, like a virtuoso musician, to experience and create "aesthetic rightness," in Singer's words.

The values of violence

Beauty is fake if it's supported by values of violence. We live under the influences of our past and present relationships and the many forms of society and culture that are present no matter where we may be. A society's values, expressed in its Mythology, are influenced by the ongoing effects of shared beliefs and institutions. Every society I've ever heard of, including the one I'm part of, has a history and perhaps an economy and ideology of systemic violence in different forms, usually disguising its violence in appealing terms. In America, violence is glorified in entertainment to serve a soft propaganda, luring an audience to a sense of power, which connects to "the national interest," as well as the ego's interest. Guns and wars continue to entertain. Ideologies can be idealistic, authoritarian or pragmatic, but in almost every case, a belief system has the potential to turn its believers to violence as part of some solution—whether in actual war or denial of economic opportunity or destructive exploitation of the natural world. The mythology of Homeric Greece included the glory of invading and destroying a society, Troy, for the sake of possession of a woman, Helen, restoring her to her master, the Spartan king, Menelaus. Killing and enslaving the conquered society has been unquestioned in Mythologies, ancient and modern. The enslavement is less apparent when it's softly enforced in the kinds of "arts and entertainment" that simplify humans in their stories and images and in the dumbing down of language, psychology and ethics.

Systemic violence doesn't occur because of human nature. It's culturally created. Its primal form is male predatory behaviors in packs that hunt, kill and possess. Patriarchal authority usually flows from the establishment of predatory forms of power. Values, religious principles and personalities can be shaped by living metaphors and symbols of the power of a patriarchy. The violence of a country can be justified and accepted so easily, especially when given a patriarchal sheen of acting to protect citizens or at least maintaining their material standard of living. While every society must have some form of authority to be orderly and productive, the authority is to be judged by its "aesthetic rightness."

The art of patriarchal power can be fostered and enforced by heads of household, gang leaders, priests, preachers, bosses, politicians and other leaders. In any group or society, individuals must accept limits to individual freedom for the sake of others. The manner in which limits are set and enforced can be violent or peaceful, consensual or coercive. There can be an illusion of freedom from this art of power: the freedom to violate the safety and dignity of others, as in the abuse or neglect of children; the freedom to privately stockpile weapons, to destroy natural habitats, to cheat others out of their access to economic opportunities. The patriarchal style traditionally required submission by wives and children to the male head of household, enforced by violence or threats. Almost all gangs are male packs with violent rites of passage and means of cohesion, to maintain a spirit of manly fighting. Governments still do not have Departments of Peace or policies for the development of consensual acts of settling conflicts and sharing economic productivity and innovation. Trade wars, ruthless economic practices and real wars have been accepted as the status quo of international relations. Whether employed on behalf of the "ruling class" or the "revolutionary," the use of violence to achieve what claimants call justice usually goes unchallenged.

Violence can become a source of pleasure. Because it's from the Primitive level of a human mind-body, violence is oriented toward feeling power and victory over others, using others as a tool or object of self-pleasure. American culture encourages violence in such popular sporting events as Mixed Martial Arts (MMA) or football. In MMA, there are hardly any restrictions on violently attacking an opponent. At the end of a match, when a loser may be so bloodied, unconscious, even close to being killed, the perpetrator is ecstatic, as is the crowd. Any sense of guilt at the violence inflicted is unheard of. Anyone who'd show compassion for the damaged loser would be considered weak, laughable. Not only is MMA legal and tolerated all over the world, it's a huge money maker. The highest paid athlete in the world is the MMA fighter Connor McGregor, who was rewarded with $180 million in 2021.[4] The latest development has been for women in MMA to punch, crunch and choke each other into submission. The Roman Empire had its gladiators. Nazi Germany had its stormtroopers. Is something wrong with this picture of huge audiences whipped up by fighters demonstrating uninhibited violence in a cage? Extreme aggression has been mainstream in the Mythology of our contemporary culture and politics. This isn't new. Pogroms, lynchings, wife-beatings were overtly acceptable in societies not too long ago.

It's hard to find a sense of beauty in a culture that so blatantly promotes the Primitive and Adolescent psychology as cool, where public spectacles of violence are accepted in media attractions to bloodlust, force, counterforce, nationalism and wealth. The alternative is to cultivate norms to support learning and acting for imagination, beauty and goodness. This doesn't require wealth. I've worked on construction jobs where certain co-workers who didn't have great educations showed excellence in their work and doing the right thing when others got away with shoddy work or laziness. Their Personal Myths included "aesthetic rightness."

---

[4] https://www.visualcapitalist.com/highest-paid-athletes-2021/

Bad luck in family and economic backgrounds can limit exposure to the music of beauty. Each individual needs to find models and inspiration for one's own imaginative and beautiful style. No one plays great music without learning from a tradition of aesthetic excellence. When the culture and economy generate and support ugly and mediocre styles, traditions and exemplars from earlier times are available. Going for "aesthetic rightness" can require and inspire toughness to take a stand for what is true and good, while letting go of winning, or needing control, approval or security, for the source of beauty is in oneself.

Violence forever?

Most people I've talked to about this believe that violence inevitably breaks out because of human nature. Wars are assumed to be inevitable and, therefore, means for violent defense and enforcement of agreements are necessary. Preemptive military action, such as the US invasion of Iraq, is justified as necessary to prevent greater violence. The lie was easily accepted. Violence in one's culture and world calls upon each person to take a stand about violence.

As I write this, Ukraine is being bombed and invaded by Russia, which is committing horrible acts of killing and destruction. The only way to stop annihilation is for Ukraine to fight back with violence. This may be taken as evidence for the inevitability of wars and the need for violent self-defense. I heard an interview with a woman volunteer in Ukraine's army who said she was a pacifist before the invasion, but now has overcome those beliefs in her Personal Myth. Pacifism and non-violence may seem naïve in the real world of violent aggression. If I were in Ukraine now, I'm sure I'd follow this woman's example. But I don't agree with the conclusion that violence is inevitable because of human nature. It has been pervasive because of a failure of cultures to aspire to non-violence in their Mythologies and politics.

All wars have been caused by organized governments or tribes, not human nature. They aren't spontaneous outbreaks of men wanting to fight each other, as in barroom brawls. In certain societies, such as the Mongols and Spartans, war was a way of life. Male aggression and violence were glorified and mainstream. In most contemporary nation-states, the way of life of war is practiced by a minority of the population, a very small minority. The political and economic calculations for war are separated from the people called upon to fight in the military. In the US, a very small percentage of politicians or their families have enlisted in the military. To maintain the capacity and motivations for recruits to a military, governments must maintain a culture and Mythology legitimizing violence by the government. There is legitimacy for military self-defense for countries under attack, such as Ukraine, but this does not generalize into the necessity of institutional violence. The justification usually is that military violence is unfortunate though necessary "to defend our freedom." This justification was taken to absurd and bloody extremes in American wars such as in Vietnam and Iraq as well as covert operations in many parts of the globe. Usually, patriotic propaganda justifies false pretexts for military aggression, especially scare tactics about threats to the country to get the population to support or acquiesce in the wars. The same phenomena is occurring in Russia, where the majority of Russian people support the invasion of Ukraine based on Putin's propaganda. The warring government tries to influence its people to hate or be hostile to the targeted country as a threat. There's certainly no "aesthetic rightness" to any of this.

The world is a very dangerous place. The predatory capacities of humans, primarily males, continue to be encouraged. Despite the evil that is caused by warring governments, we are stuck with the need for protection by decent government. We can recognize how violence is a part of the Mythology of our culture and institutions, glorified in blatant violence in entertainment and sports. Aggression in politics and business is valued. Governments have an interest in maintaining values of violence, seen in extreme forms in the mass violence carried out by Putin's Russia, Hitler's Nazi Germany, Pol Pot's Cambodia, Rwanda's Hutus. All of those horrors should have been stopped. Unfortunately, the only way to stop their relentless violence was the use of violence against the predators. Recognizing the need for military defense does not mean blanket consent to a government's use of military force. On the contrary, each use of military violence must be assessed for its necessity and opposed if it's unjustifiable. Likewise, a Mythology of violence as the status quo should be opposed.

Beyond opposition to particular, unjustified uses of violence by nations, tribes or individuals, everyone can and should commit to developing a Mythology of non-violent processes of resolving conflicts. Economic and political norms of ruthless winning at all costs are connected to violence as a norm of the nation and its residents. The aggressive tendencies of the entire Mythology of a society should be continually addressed for ways to effectively value, develop and practice non-violence for the world. However, prospects for such a transformation are tenuous at best. In the meantime, predation, killing and conquering must be stopped, and violence may be the only effective means to do so at times. There is no beauty in it, only an attempt to stop or limit the ugliness of greater violence.

Aesthetic standards of style

Think about whether it's more helpful to be aware of your emotional energy as a live music from the instrument of your mind-body-Soul instead of as measurements of intensity or by symptom scales. Generally, to determine the quality of the music you're playing takes account of how your body and nervous system are engaged, what meanings you enact and aspire to, how you can choose to create different kinds of music by what you do and focus on each day. With unconditional acceptance of your humanity and trustworthy support and guidance, you can become aware of whether your actions are beautiful or ugly, vibrant or dispiriting, excellent or mediocre. Living each day as an art isn't aided by abstract labels.

Relating to emotion as live music means I can choose a style by which to live. I wouldn't choose to play a music that's kitsch or violent except when I deceive myself that I'm attaining comfort, self-protection or power. Knowing I can choose to create a style of enacting music from mind-body-Soul that can be beautiful, I can develop skills and creativity to cultivate the style. It requires that I attune my instrument for complex sensing, interpreting and intuiting what I experience and create in the Wild. It requires focusing, thinking and acting beyond only my self-satisfaction. Is this possible?

Beautiful compositions are enacted by a loving parent's valuing of her or his children in many frustrating, demanding, surprising and entertaining episodes. A worker plays beautifully by high standards of skills. Love songs can be coarsened away from love by hook-up culture. Romantic experiences may begin with rock and rolling sensations until tested by heartbreak or disillusionment. Being tested, the lovers show how far they'll go for integrity and depth in crossing the line into love. A person's style can be for financial performance or accumulation according to metrics of the Mythology our culture offers. A style can be limited to sentimental or sensational songs, or it may fall into the misfortunate restrictions of addiction. Or a style may be cultivated with radically liberated thinking and imagining as well as courageous sacrifice.

Self-transcendence is present as a dimension I may enter every moment. This doesn't mean stepping away from the natural world or the body. It means that a body is more than its needs and appetites for survival. Food, movement, sexuality and work can be aesthetic ventures. The ongoing self-creating processes of nature aren't just about me, though they offer gifts to me and the chance to participate in a creative process of Being. I can consciously participate in this process, feeling the experience of lived dignity, excellence and creativity, as well as the dissonance of fear, hurt and vulnerability. This would be a choice to live with a style of trusting in the divinity of myself and reality, to take risks for what is greater than myself.

Having an aesthetic perspective about each situation I'm in means finding all I sense to be real yet magical and new. It requires imagination and creativity in my Personal Myth. The emotional soundtrack played from my Myth isn't significant just for my own satisfaction. How I'm playing my part in the symphony of the whole, how I care for others who share this society and this earth are reflected in how my passions follow a libretto of giving and appreciating rather than possessing, overpowering or manipulating. My ego will always be a tricky obstacle to enacting great music, like a prima donna or untrained player. Rather than just knowing the right script or notes to play, I must get good at creating and improvising the transcendent music of courage, perseverance and love to respond to injustices, struggles, tragedies and greed. I must be curious and open-minded to continually learn to play well and join in harmonies of the good.

Let's say a good friend has treated me with neglect or unkindness. I may experience surges of hurt, anger, disappointment. But those words aren't enough. I'd want to attune to what music I'm filled with, what style is best to understand and express my complex feelings. Would I just go off on my friend? Stuff my feelings? Stay stuck in themes of self-righteous anger? Are those the styles in which I want to keep playing? How could I respond in a style that's graceful yet honors my integrity and self-respect? I could see my response to my friend as a hurt or belligerent movement of music followed by some bittersweet transition, then a movement that expresses care and dignity in attempting approaches or meaningful healing. The experience may teach or inspire me to compose new music for living with greater wisdom and depth in relationships. The experience may create a theme that I can play back, that helps me in responding to other painful situations, in expanding what I know of love.

There are aesthetic qualities to physical well-being. Like a serious musician caring for his instrument, I'm responsible for tuning and playing my body as well as I can, including practices for vitality, fitness, pleasures and strength. To practice the style I aspire to, I must learn from my body's receptivity to experience, its indivisibility from mind, its process in developing intuition and meanings, its ways of moving, touching and interacting with what's encountered. How I express my body's qualities will be felt as a dancer may experience and strive for grace, balance and beauty for the audience, the other dancers and for my own sake.

An aesthetic style for emotion allows a sensitivity and creativity in responding to life experiences and possibilities, not just techniques or rules of behavior. I can become skilled and talented in daring for noble stakes. I can learn from experiencing music of shame or guilt, from moral failures and mistakes. I can experiment and play with avant garde responses, subverting conventional expressions, reinterpreting and refreshing the familiar and routine. The aesthetic dimension calls for more than experiencing great art and more than mind-altering drugs. I remember hearing, as a kid, an interview with Salvador Dali who was asked if he took psychedelic drugs to achieve the surrealistic visions he painted. He responded, "Drugs? Dali does not take drugs. Dali is the drug!"

Pleasures, desires, delighting

Who doesn't want pleasure? But who can define what they mean by the word? Here is an attempt by Olivier Massin:

> There is a broad range of positive hedonic affects, such as joy, gladness, contentment, merriment, glee, ecstasy,

euphoria, exhilaration, elation, jubilation, happiness, felicity, bliss, enjoyment, amusement, fun, rejoicing, delectation, enchantment, delight, rapture, relish, thrill, satisfaction, gratification, jollity, gaiety, cheerfulness, relief, etc. Here I shall use the term "pleasure" in this most generic, encompassing sense, subsuming all of the items in the list above as well as other similar mental episodes. That is, pleasure, in the sense used here, covers the whole range of hedonically-positive affects.[5]

Certainly, these words (a whole string of adjectives) are all attractive, but they are really just more words. We seem to be sure what we mean by pleasure. Maybe it's like pornography, only instead of, as the US Supreme Court Justice said, "I know it when I see it," it's more "I know it when I feel it." We're sure or we convince ourselves it's a state, one we really like. Many people, many claiming to be experts, use neuroscience language to define pleasure as surges of the neurochemicals dopamine and serotonin. But the truth is, like so much else in our mind-bodies, there's such a multiplicity of things going on within and around me when I'm feeling good or thrilled that the words and chemicals do not begin to adequately address.

Words are what we have to communicate with each other about how good we're feeling, but there's probably no term more crudely degraded in our culture than pleasure. It seems simple: pleasure means, in these times, gratification of a need, an appetite, an itch. From a need to an urge to an entitlement, pleasure becomes a term of value that is sanctified in the theology of the gods Comfort and Convenience. In a

---

[5]   "Pleasure and Its Contraries," Review of Philosophy and Psychology volume 5, pages15–40 (2014)

very different culture (ancient Greece), pleasure was divine, sanctified by Eros and Aphrodite. In American Mythology, pleasure serves the economic system of consumer capitalism. People seek more ways to find, increase and buy what can gratify and produce expected sensations.

Beauty isn't secluded from pleasure. Its music can be sultry and sexy. It can play as rock and roll. It can play as the blues. But the pleasure isn't fleeting or used for relieving stress or a sexual itch. In his excellent book, *Beauty*, James Kirwan tells us "that our pleasure in the beautiful is not simply one pleasure among others. ...beauty is a yearning without object. ... Yearning differs from simple desire in that it posits a degree of desirability in the object which it would seem no object could ever satisfy."[6]

We think we understand desire. Usually, it's meant as what someone wants, and can be satisfied by shopping or by taking or otherwise possessing. But this is nothing more than a simple appetite from the Pre-Adult and Primitive levels. Whether from natural human urges for survival, for relief from hunger or other threats, or from the urge to reproduce or possess, the meaning of desire has been reduced to what ranges from the scratching of an itch to wasteful consumption. But there's a different kind of desire—without an object to satisfy some need, a desire for what is beyond possession or use, that can inspire one to seek and create beauty and joy.

There's really nothing beautiful in an object. Beauty arises in a process of responding to phenomena with the mind-body's play and delight. Whether I respond to certain architecture as

---

[6] James Kirwan, *Beauty* (Manchester: Manchester University Press, 1999) pp. 37 -38

beautiful or not doesn't depend on the architecture, but on my mind-body's settings for the perception of physical features of a building, the purpose and effect of the building relating to the world around it, and my tastes. Because I'm not moved by the architecture doesn't mean the building itself is or isn't beautiful. Another person may experience its beauty in ways that reflect differences in our mind-bodies.

Wouldn't anyone desire beauty? The term has been cheapened. Cosmetics, airbrushed photos, decorated cityscapes are what the consumer culture offers to beautify. Beauty that moves one beyond the self doesn't fit in that culture. Beauty's process is beyond satisfying appetites, needs or wants of the self. Desire can be a participation in reality, which requires adjusting one's perspective beyond the self for, in Iris Murdoch's words, "the discovery of reality." Desire for beauty involves the mind-body's music of participating in the embodied, pleasurable divine.

Erotic aesthetics

Playing the music of the body and mind for beauty involves, but isn't limited by, Primitive appetites and urges. Beauty is enacted in exceeding the ego yet isn't disembodied, certainly includes carnal sensations and pleasures. Richard Shusterman has clarified how the aesthetic dimension includes "aims to appreciate the artistry, beauty, and meaning, that sexual experience can offer, and through such appreciation also to enhance these appreciated qualities themselves and the sexual practices that generate them."[7]

---

[7] "Aesthetic Experiences: From Analysis to Eros," *The Journal of Aesthetics and Art Criticism* 64:2 Spring 2006, p. 221, republished in Aesthetic Experience, ed. Richard Shusterman and Adele Tomlin (New York: Routledge, 2008)

What especially complicates this subject are histories of religious and cultural pathologizing of sexuality, with the inevitable backlashes ranging from libertinism to sneaking peeks and paid sex. It's difficult to imagine how sexuality can be completely accepted as natural, beautiful, magic, even divine. But this has been the case in other cultures. For example, Greek religion deified beauty, sexuality and love in the goddess Aphrodite. Each individual has to find a way toward the creative art of the erotic. Shusterman provides useful considerations:

> A cognitive experience providing knowledge of one's own body and mind and also those of one's sexual partners, the sexual act typically displays a distinctive unity both of coherence and completion, a sense of something developing consistently and powerfully toward a fulfilling consummation. It also stands out distinctively from the flow of ordinary humdrum experience. Sexual experience involves a wide range of affect, some of which is unrivalled in its intensity, and it displays both moments of active self-assertive grasping and self-surrendering absorption.[8]

There are many styles, genres, and tastes of sexuality, as there are of music. The erotic can be beautiful if its carnal pleasure isn't enacted by degrading the dignity of the other. Divine pleasures can flow from interpersonal experiences of sensuality in the Wild.

Beauty as passionate, with practical adjustments

The soundtrack of beauty is played passionately. This doesn't mean it should be played with high intensity or drama.

---

[8] Id. p. 236

Passion can be very quiet and look ordinary. It's the devotion and meaning which we put into the playing that matters. An innkeeper I once met was so conscientious and caring in how he prepared the lodging each day, in how he'd built it by himself and supported his family from the revenue, he was certainly living passionately, though was modest as could be. I could feel his soundtrack of beauty and excellence.

When you share pleasures with a partner, inevitably there will be conflicts. The conflicts may be from sharing space or resources, differences in wanting pleasure, differences in taste. You inevitably will play and want music of emotion that your partner doesn't want to join or receive. Interpersonal mistakes always happen, people get frustrated, probably even in monasteries. The conflicts and anger need not result in violence. The conflicts can last a while, but the Adult Mind can recognize when you slide and sink into trying to win or protect the self in a conflict. The Adult Mind doesn't get you out of it by conceding or otherwise losing, but by having dialogues about the conflict, by going beyond the conflict to connect with one another. Connecting and communicating with others, including others who have completely different beliefs, ideas or desires than yours requires a set of skills that are continually practiced, allowing mistakes and failures as part of the ongoing experiments, while explicitly letting go of winning, being right, dominating, expecting.

Beauty may be experienced with ecstasy, meditative calm, awe. However, it isn't lived in complete isolation or impenetrable serenity. Because we're embodied, biological selves, we each have self-oriented needs for survival and protection. These needs are going to get out of whack, be excessive or stupid at times.

We can accept this as part of life, learn to practice the virtues of humility and self-control, committing to responsibility and self-correction in one's music. An individual's bliss or pleasure isn't sufficient for a beautiful life because we share life with other people and the non-human world. Playing beautifully on our instruments of mind-body requires playing with care for others, taking account of the whole, putting all of ourselves into passionate, conscientious actions. Thoreau wrote of how the music is scored on principles of morality and virtue: "Our whole life is startlingly moral. There is never an instant's truce between virtue and vice. Goodness is the only investment that never fails. In the music of the harp which trembles round the world it is the insisting on this which thrills us."[9]

The whole can sometimes feel like a big mess. We're usually not aware of what we're feeling in it. And then sometimes, there is a "magic moment or moment of metamorphosis, bust thru from quotidian into 'divine or permanent world.'"[10] Such moments seem harder and harder to arise in America, at least for me. The popular, the fashionable and the powerful can feel cheap, smothering or boring. I have to retreat at times. I don't feed on what's beautiful, for the beautiful cannot be consumed. As soon as it seems to be grasped, it can vanish.

Living by the metaphor of power

By far, the most popular and unacknowledged style of American Mythology is power. It is the American principle for

---

[9]   Henry David Thoreau, *Walden, and On The Duty Of Civil Disobedience,* Kindle Locations 2676-2677

[10]   *The Selected Letters of Ezra Pound 1907-1941* (New York: New Diretions, 1950/1971), p. 210

how business, politics, entertainment, romance and technology should run without ever identifying power as the model of motivation. Why not examine this dominant metaphor for its foundation in the culture's Mythology and its aesthetic qualities?

Power is advocated in society in many ways. It's touted as a virtue: people should be empowered. It's become a tool for politics and culture, which boil down to the virtue of beating opponents in battles, requiring limitless flows of cash. But I have yet to find anyone who questions the assumption that there is such a phenomenon as power. I will. Rather than a pseudo-Darwinian fact of survival, power is no more than a metaphor in a Mythology. The metaphor blends physical force (like velocity of particles, propulsion of jets, cars, athletes, race cars) with motivation for the finite game of winning and dominating as life's purpose.

How could anyone question the reality of human power? My electricity comes from a power grid, which sometimes fails, and I lose power. Isn't this what happens to me when I lose at something? So many other people, corporations and governments seem to be exerting power over us at any given moment. There are so many ways the metaphor "Power" is easily used to imply human acts are like a physical force, unencumbered energy. I believe the metaphor can be seriously deceptive and should be replaced with more accurate portrayals.

In one sense, power can mean felt ability, such as how the poet May Sarton described the benefits of growing old: "This is the best time of my life. ... I am happier, more balanced, and (I heard myself to say rather aggressively) 'more powerful.' I felt it was rather an odd word, 'powerful,' but I think it is true. It might have been more accurate to say 'I am better able to use my powers.' I am sure about what my life is about, have less self-doubt to conquer."[11] Those are inspiring words. But doesn't she really mean confidence, ability, vitality? Aren't we fooling ourselves if we think we use the word "power" without its infusion of meanings of domination, aggression, ruthlessness?

I used to encourage similar ideas of the positive value of personal power as agency and even a source of creativity when, as a counselor, I tried to help people find their way out of feeling helpless or powerless. I've since gotten away from loosely using the term "power" because the sense of power as aggression and manipulation is far more meaningful in our culture. Robert Greene's book, *The 48 Laws of Power*[12], has sold over a million copies and is often quoted or referenced in business and motivation books. Greene became a "cult hero with the hip-hop set, Hollywood elite and prison inmates alike."[13] His book presents what's usually meant as power, with chapter headings like "Get Others to Do the Work For You But Always Take the Credit," "Learn to Keep People Dependent on You," "Discover Each Man's Thumbscrew." The book really seems to be an American bible for success by maximizing power over others.

Consider why power as a value is so valued in our culture. Consider how wanting to be powerful is a distortion of human potential. The development of the ambition and practices for being powerful, in the sense of power over others, likely began in the hidden details of human pre-history. Ancient works of literature promote psychological and political values of warrior power that have been carried forward through the ages. Epics,

11 May Sarton, *At Seventy: A Journal* (New York: Norton, 1984), p. 10
12 Robert Greene, *The 48 Laws of Power* (New York: Viking, 1998)
13 Wikipedia entry on the book, quoting the Los Angeles Times.

such as Homer's *Iliad* and *Odyssey* and the *Bhagavad Gita*, present heroes and stories that model war and other forms of masculine violence as virtues. From the Mythologies of cultures sustained by domination, deities have been feared and worshiped for their power over humans and over the earth. In our own time, the tradition is carried forward in enormously popular superhero movies and video games. Sports heroes and teams are idolized for how nearly perfectly the athletes perform and overpower their competition. While these may be categorized as entertainment, people live the Myth of power to inspire efficiency and high ratings of performances in business, politics, education and pretty much all social pursuits.

What does power, among humans rather than particles or equations, really mean? Mostly, power is understood as the ability to do or get what one wants by individual or collective action. It often means getting someone or something to do what one wants, whether by coercive force, charm or deceit, and not accounting for the continued effects on the other. These commonsense meanings assume we are selves, separated from other people and everything else, and we're originators of our own power. As a self, when I exert power, it's for a "me" without regard to whoever or whatever is the object of my power and the effects from my acts. The power to build and occupy a house ignores the earth cleared, what's covered, what habitat is native. Real estate is for the power of an autonomous self, an owner, who's entitled to what he or she wants and pays for. Power is the name of the psychological protective force of wanting to dominate, take, possess or destroy whatever I think I have to, in order to survive, to overcome, to thrive as a self.

Rather than assuming power is inescapable and inevitable and you'd better get good at exercising it to gain ever more advantages or else be miserable, I see power as just a possible style of action, thinking and emotion. Prophets for this style, such as Robert Greene with his 48 Laws, aggressively cling to the assumption that there is no alternative to getting good at gaining power over others. Greene says those who express no need for power are covertly employing a technique to gain power by their pretending. The ultraconfident advocates of power would never take seriously teachings of Jesus Christ in the New Testament, much less Asian religious and philosophical traditions, setting out alternatives to the model of people as powermongers. It seems so hard for people to believe there can be economic and technological stability and innovation without people seeking to gain power over competitors. People fail to recognize motivations of important innovators, such as Einstein and many other scientists and reformers, who've been driven by fierce curiosity and a desire to benefit the world. Heroic, dominant stories of entrepreneurs, sports and other celebrities exclude styles of passionate music of emotion that have nothing to do with enriching yourself or beating your competitors.

Power appeals to the Primitive Mind in all of us. There's no grace or beauty needed or wanted, except maybe to seduce. The aesthetic value is limited to that of winning or losing. Donald Trump loved to make fun of anyone who wouldn't support him as "losers," which he didn't call his followers who lost their attack on Congress January 6, 2021. I've heard first-hand accounts of how good it can feel to let the Primitive loose in military combat. Music has always been a part of military combat. When the combatant wants to be aroused for violence, emotion's music runs through body and mind. An article on the internet gives "5 warrior playlists to get you pumped before a live fire range." On a lower scale of force, you can learn techniques to develop your own means of power for getting what you want with the right emotional music to energize you. You may get so good at manipulating various reactions from others, you hardly need to think about it.

Aggression is most often power's music of emotion. The music may be played as an undercurrent of motivation or acted out in violence and other kinds of force to desperately attain security and advantage. The music is composed from adrenaline, greed and the perception that it's me against everyone else. This style of living has been cultivated for centuries, if not millennia. It's motivated people to get good at killing people or amassing wealth. The aggression may be channeled into sophisticated manipulations and strategies, as Robert Greene advises. Power players may try to be heroes, practice charisma or charm to influence or seduce for their conquests. The aggressive style of the music of power has had destructive consequences in wars, environmental degradation and enslavement, with the ever-present power game of nuclear war. Alternatives are given very little chance to be considered, much less practiced.

Like any other style of emotion and behavior, power is created and maintained by how a person orders, patterns and sequences experiences according to a mental model and belief system. The style is fostered by perspectives and values formed in one's family and social networks, and other arenas of the culture and economic system in which one lives. The cultural values of America, displayed from highly paid celebrities to highly priced real estate, emphasize power as success through maximum ambition and performance, rewarded by admiration and big financial payoffs. Power has been a dominant concept for American Mythology.

J. Krishnamurti, who warned against following leaders, including himself, once summarized the modern cultural shaping of individual psychology:

> All of us have been trained by education and environment to seek personal gain and security, and to fight for ourselves. Though we cover it over with pleasant phrases, we have been educated for various professions within a system based on exploitation and acquisitive fear. ...
>
> There is an efficiency inspired by love which goes far beyond and is much greater than the efficiency of ambition: and without love, which brings an integrated understanding of life, efficiency breeds ruthlessness.[14]

Our culture's Mythology considers power essential for fundamental goals and continued progress. It gives no option for very different values. Faith in individual and national power are theologically grounded in faith in man's dominance of nature with rewards from the gods, Comfort and Convenience, whose Mythology is protected by those who maintain power over us. Recognizing these gods may be the first step in opposing the metaphor and Mythology of power.

Doing good has been understood and expressed as a power to help or save others, and to convert them to a good cause. Love has been conceived as a power to capture others' hearts. Lovers, parents, and leaders, by virtue of the roles they think they're

---

[14]   J. Krishnamurti, *Total Freedom: The Essential Krishnamurti* (New York: Harper Collins, 1996) p. 90

playing can see emotions as energizing power. The mental health industry formulates most disorders as a disabled power of the self. There are many self-help books and gurus who offer to help you develop power, to become aware of how to create effects on those you're leading, loving or parenting, to influence moods, minds, and desires for success. But compassion can be understood very differently. True compassion is a natural manner of responding to others with a different style of music from that of power, which draws upon Primitive modes of fearing, distrusting and overpowering others.

Living involves continual interactions with others, which includes non-human animals, plants, elements, molecules, etc. How one interacts with others is according to certain styles. The style may be ruthlessly competitive and dominating, overpowering others with force, cleverness and strategy, with such maxims as "greed is good." The style of power of those controlling the economic system gives rise to complementary styles of compliance for their consumers. Our culture's Mythology is formed from commercial values. What sells most to a mass audience shapes the aesthetic quality of the culture's values. Those who maximize profits from the mass audience specialize in styles that cater to their consumers' protective forces, from passive compliance to macho aggression, devaluing intelligence and depth to critically question power. Mass culture provides social cohesion as well as profits to the producers of it. The less the consumer cares to critique or even question the dominant metaphor of power, the cheaper and easier it is to produce and sell. Power becomes a value people depend upon. Few care to question the elements of aggression, stimulation, dumbing down and comfort that become aesthetic values at Primitive and Pre-Adult levels.

Power or process?

Styles alternative to that of power could be based on creative, balanced and reverent relations to whom or what one interacts with. Qualities of life experience and meanings we commit to could be based on more intellectual and emotional depth than superficiality, more playfulness than compliance. We could strive to live for values that transcend the ego instead of the gusto of Me.

If I were to believe, as many do, that emotions are primarily instruments of the survival of the fittest, that they simply provide various forms of power to dominate or evade or reproduce, I could believe we should try to use these instruments in those ways. I call that perspective "Survivalist." With a Survivalist perspective, I'd structure my beliefs, interpretations and behaviors according to the principle of exercising power for me and those others I may choose in order to possess, use, consume or lay waste to what I encounter. Children are raised to go for victory and development of power in Survivalist games. The mind and body are assumed to be instruments for asserting power.

We each have a level of thinking, feeling and behaving that can enact Survivalist purposes every day—the Primitive or Pre-Adult Mind (so-called because it's our primary mode in our first couple of decades in life). This comes from our self-oriented forces for survival (aggression, escape, greed, reactions to fear) and primal appetites (food, sex, various pleasures and urges). The Primitive is contrasted with a different level—the

Adult Mind—so-called because it's more fully developed, for most of us, after our first couple of decades or so. This level is based on the individual's mental and emotional development of skills and maturity beyond the Primitive Mind. The Adult Mind involves our more complex thought functions, like reality-testing and creativity, assessing and organizing information and behaviors according to memories, learning and values. The Adult Mind's advanced capacity for creativity and love contrasts with imagination from the Pre-Adult/Primitive Mind, which generates alarms, urges, quick reactions, with forceful sensations, expressions and strategies. Of course, there are times when these Primitive sensations and inspirations are necessary. They can be called up with the guidance of creativity and compassion to produce and support interactions and considerations for the ethical good of the whole.

Power primarily from the Primitive level usually results in the music of Fighting rhythms or Ego tunes, to protect myself from vulnerability, especially the fear of being victimized by others. Again, sometimes notes and rhythms of this Primitive music is necessary to respond to dangers and injustices. The Adult Mind can control the potential for misuse of Primitive energy and inspiration. We may think power's necessary as protection from vulnerability, to cope with such background music as worry, anxiety and self-doubt that's playing to some degree in all of us. However, often "power" isn't the right word or interpretation of what we need. Instead, it may be more accurate to understand our need as confidence or the energetic response of the mind-body to protect from danger and assert the moral good.

With self-awareness, you can pierce the illusion of the autonomous self of power. You can recognize persons and the non-human world as participating in processes of continual co-creation. You can know and experience each person and non-person as meanings within the process of natural beauty and creativity. In the tough situations that life gives us, we can take stands for values of goodness, truth and beauty. Living by the passion of integrity isn't simply from my autonomous power. Whatever capability, vitality and strength I can feel and exert is and has been nourished and sustained by physical, developmental, social and aesthetic networks and processes. Whatever actions I take are part of those processes every moment. I am only a detail in the artwork of Being that is continually created. I can exert my mind-body for beauty, harmony and the good or to mar, deface and cheapen my detail of the artwork of nature. My actions are part of the process of the artwork. I can creatively contribute to its beauty by striving for aesthetic excellence or, alternatively, to retreat from my potential and play music of mediocrity, greed or violence in striving for power.

From the Adult Mind (indivisible from the body), we can utilize energies and pleasures of Primitive capacities with purpose. We can generate Creative Energy. When cultivated, the Adult level can allow you to center the body and mind, enabling equipoise and vitality in experiencing the moment of whoever and whatever may be happening with you there. You'd recognize you are part of the music of the world rather than served by it, you can form life purposes transcending your self, participating in the flow of natural processes and enacting an Adult role in the world.

It's probably hard to even imagine that your life is not owned by you. If you can, there is a different kind of freedom— not freedom from limits, but freedom of the music playing from you. What you do as part of the creative process of enacting meaning is your unique participation in the symphony of the whole. What's called "I" can be understood as always a metaphor of being interdependently, mutually entailed with other phenomena in a continual process of creation and co-creation within the whole of nature naturing. This process can be understood as the concrete yet mysterious music of beauty and love. It is a love that is non-possessive, yet passionate and fulfilling. To love in this way is to lose your grip, your hold on whom or what you love. To love your life is to let it go in giving to others even unto death, allowing the music you play to be free of copyright, attribution to you, labels, recognition. There is no return on an investment of love, for love is not possession of and profit from the other.

Understanding ourselves in this way can give a sense of how each of our acts can enrich the process of organic creativity. I can understand my obligations and loyalties, as well as my enjoyments of and repulsions from others in this process. I can play my part in a symphony of love and beauty being played even if it is beyond my ability to sense and understand the complete dynamic pattern of the whole. As the poet Stéphane Mallarmé once put it, "Every soul is a melody which needs to be readjusted; and for that are the flute or viol of each."

If I don't know how to play a musical instrument, I can't do much with it except bang on some piano keys or drum or create screeches on a violin. If I don't learn the ways emotion can be tuned, how to recognize its tones and registers, incorporate them into meaningful behaviors, words, thoughts and expressions, I will miss out on opportunities of playing emotion's music at my highest potential. To play this music requires the discipline and devotion of learning and practicing. I can play my instrument to manipulate others, or, in the words of Robert Greene, to "Pose as a Friend, Work as a Spy" and "Crush Your Enemy Totally." This might make me a rich rock or hip-hop star if I play what's most marketable. This is music played from the Survivalist, the ego-oriented self. Or I can go for more profound and joyous experiences. I can cultivate my instrument of mind-body and Soul, transcending the ego for what is greater than the self.

Our interactions and co-existence with others involve energies exchanged between the rich resources of mind-body and the phenomena encountered. Conflicting interactions can be interpreted as challenges for creating beautiful vibes and notes. The music of emotion involves one's whole history, the conditions of the body, vulnerabilities to feeling scared, hurt, ashamed, less-than, which in turn trigger defensive forces to guard against feeling the vulnerabilities. We can accept and transform the defensive music through centering in a space of awareness and a dimension of transcendence, allowing care for and acceptance of our vulnerabilities, as well as inspiration and practices to recover from inner wounds, to love, to creatively live.

The Survivalist perspective of power is not the truth. It's simply a metaphor creating a perspective that can blind or limit us from going beyond survival, manipulation, victimhood and immaturity. From the Adult Mind, with its flexibility, compassion, imagination and self-awareness, we can transform Primitive

Energy into Creative Energy, respond to the uncontrolled forces of reality with our excellence in enacting beauty, goodness and play, composing music of joy and noble pursuits. This would be living for truths more profound than power, with depths of emotion described by David Pugmire:

> ... in deep emotion life is lived close to one of its limits. For there is the sense that then people give of themselves unreservedly, that the person is engaged as a whole by this state of mind and by its subject, for better or for worse. For this reason it is an arresting moment when a person is genuinely transported by something. Fullness of emotion lifts the person from the half-lit drift and small concerns of ordinary life and gives a transfiguring importance to things (which reflects itself in action).[15]

The music plays in nature

The music of emotion isn't to be played for itself. It's a music that's part of the processes of nature in its continual creation of itself, present in the ancient dirt, rock and snow we walk upon, the shifting phenomena of weather, the inhuman wild green growth and decay, the flow of molecules, gases and rhythms within and around us.

The music playing from the natural world can be more deeply understood in its complexities through scientific knowledge. The revelations of a mystic can be limited by the individual's history, sensibilities and biases. When the keen observations of science are not reduced to reductionism, they

---

[15] David Pugmire, *Sound Sentiments: Integrity in the Emotions* (Oxford: Oxford University Press, 2005), p. 31

may reveal fascinating details for hardy seekers of truth. In a "conversation," David Fideler explores

> ... the idea that harmony, goodness and beauty coincide. ... For example, all living systems embody a proportional harmony between the extremes of stability and change. If a living system becomes too static, it dies; but if it changes too quickly, it falls apart. ... contemporary astrophysics has shown that the existence of the entire universe rests upon a host of delicately balanced harmonies. For example, the density parameter of the universe determines the rate of expansion. And if the density parameter was either one-trillionth of a percent weaker or stronger, the universe itself would not hold together. ... The universe, by achieving a finely-tuned proportional relationship between expansion and contraction, allows the beauty and goodness of life to blossom forth.[16]

The human body and mind are taking part in this harmony, every moment. We have choices as to how deeply to open to it. We may choose actions and styles of power over what's present, guided primarily by the Primitive levels of the mind-body. Instead of narrowing ourselves to that level, those Primitive beats and energies can be tapped into by the Adult for styles of music that can lead us to open with awe, reverence and inspiration to the world, allowing Creative Energy to infuse and pulsate the mind-body, to play the music of Soul.

---

[16]   David Fideler, "Cosmology, Ethics and Relatedness," in *Alexandria 4* (Grand Rapids, MI: Phanes Press 1997), pp. 123-124

Chapter 11: Soul's Music

—◆∼◆∼◆—

There is always a rush to know methods of reaching the transcendent, to learn to practice them. For what seems like most religions or spiritual teachings, some amount of denial of pleasure, up to the point of denial of the senses and body, has a place. This is supposed to elevate the adherent above human needs, desires, mortality. All the asceticism does is produce a different kind of music, a hymn of arrogant loftiness of detachment. The Soul, the divine and sacred generate a music that is possible every moment, but known only when living beyond grasping for it and accepting the wonder of being human.

Defining the Soul and the sacred is contrary to its experience, for it is entirely personal and ineffable. It's usually considered to be beyond "ordinary" experience. However, the symphony of human experience is composed throughout each day and night. Its themes and motifs include brilliant flourishes followed by dragging dullness, inspired notes and lyrics next to out of tune mistakes. Cloistered choirs are harder than ever to find. No matter. When we stop looking for something to transcend or save ourselves, the holy music can arise in the ordinary world. It must be experienced in your unique way.

In this ordinary world, I can open to a music that's mysterious, from the heart and Soul. The emotion of the sacred has been expressed in performed music through the ages—harmonies, chants, polyphonies, requiems—that take people beyond certainty and self-satisfaction, in solitude or in chorus, in echoes of the ineffable. It may not be possible to discover and engage this music in modern, technologized, overpopulated, commercialized cities without truly connecting to the natural world. The possibility of allowing sacred music to flow through and from the mind-body requires a perspective that decenters oneself from all that is, a perspective that isn't intellectual, but experienced in contact with the non-human world of the earth within the boundless sky. The experience and its potential for wisdom is very individual to each person. There's no mental healthian formula, no religious dogma that will get you there.

What makes it hard to conceive of this dimension is a narrow defining of the sacred only in terms of established religious beliefs and symbols, such as theologies promulgated in churches or temples. In modern culture, life is separated into work and leisure time, in neither of which does "sacred" come to mind, so that traditional religious places seem necessary as enclaves to experience the sacred. What so much of religious teachings imply is that there is a separate realm, beyond the human or the natural. Whether it be blessedness, enlightenment, heaven or the chosen people, the sacred realm has been conceived as a goal to attain or a place to be, and once you've attained it or been admitted there, you've got it made. But only fiction, fairy tales and dogma create such a realm. The sacred realm of reality is not to be located or captured. It's moving like an uncontrolled fire, throwing off images, laughter, metamorphic music. There is no fixed state or blessed haven. Because it is real, the sacred is dynamic, not an enclave of static peace, not a goal to be attained.

To posit a realm separate from the complex, sometimes confusing music of ordinary life is to offer a step back from reality, to seduce denizens of this ordinary world with the illusion of relief in some dimension cut off from this world, here where people can have a hard time getting through the day. The fictions of enclaves such as heaven, nirvana, utopia, etc. are for a finite game, the spoils of winning at some spiritual aspiration. As myths and poetic metaphors, such imaginary realms are intended to infuse ordinary life with a reenactment of sacred experience, to inspire and uplift people in powerful ways. People in the modern world seem no less in need of such inspirations than people in the past. They resort to vacations at Burning Man, revelations from hallucinatory experiences or born-again fundamentalism. Older evocations of the sacred are mostly considered outdated for a technologically dependent, materially comfortable society. Spiritual events are formed each new generation. Some of them are from chemicals to be ingested without even leaving your living room.

I believe the sacred can be experienced in this ordinary world. I believe it's from the same human capacity to experience and create beauty, our potential to receive and give inspiration, to be filled with a sense of dynamic purpose that exceeds the self's biological purposes. The sacred invites us to open to the mystery of the Wild, happening every moment, by opening to one's own vulnerabilities without the protective forces to guard us from reality, without dogmas telling us what it is, without an escape from some of the difficult and even demoralizing turns of reality.

Opening to the sacred isn't through following methods of some religion or cult, but through freeing oneself from chasing it and allowing the vibrant music of reality to flow through the mind-body. It has been accessed through rituals, chanted prayers, hymns, meditations, dances, songs, and the infinitely possible enactments of love. This dimension isn't for the spectator or passive experiencer waiting to be saved or entertained. When we allow ourselves into the uncontrolled freedom of the Wild, we allow the flame of who we are to illuminate and consecrate encounters with all in the world, each moment germinating ideas, efforts, skills, decisions, continually transforming with the tides of the world's music, with aesthetic complexity and depth. The transcendent dimension of Soul is entered without seeking some reward or a high or bliss or whatever; it's there in people's struggles and sacrifices for the good or in engaging with works of art, including ancient images, poetry and music, with humility gained from experiences of the natural world, realizing the limits of human effort, the tiny scale of humanity in the cosmos, the terror and glory of experiencing the *Mysterium tremendum et fascinans* of the Holy which Rudolph Otto tried to describe.

To find the sacred dimension of every moment involves filtering out the convenient noise and drifting of the surrounding superficial culture, together with practices for attuning the mind-body to beautiful and generous forces given to us in every moment. The forces can arise in love that is erotic, self-sacrificing, playing. Sacred experience isn't fixed in bliss or oneness with all, doesn't result in an attained, blessed state; it continues to creatively move. There is no endgame. The game is infinite: we play "for the purpose of continuing to play." Deeply moving music can lead us to continually renew our movement in this play. The music is the soundtrack of the miracles of reality, playing in noble, comic, ironic and sublime modes.

I can play the safe music of my self—limited to my own wants, to possess something or someone—and I can allow the transcendent music of what's beyond my self. Both genres of music exist in art forms of performed and recorded music and in the mind-body. The sacred music of Gregorian chant, Hindu Ragas, Bhajan songs, Native American or Renaissance chorales were each developed within religious practices of transcendence. Outside formal religions, sacred music can play in the song of a lover yearning from the Soul, opening oneself into vulnerability and intimacy. It may be played while feasting on sensuously delightful, nourishing food creatively prepared with skilled methods of cooking, discovered spices and flavors, combinations of dishes and drinks that can bring people together with each other and the fruits of the earth. Music of the self plays for the self's basic appetites, urges, comforts, and familiarity, not too hard, satisfying only myself, as in gobbling down food in hunger or addiction.

Sacred music may play simple melodies, but it calls for such excellence and, at times, high stakes, as may intimidate those of us unpracticed in playing it. It's a plunge of my self away from self's protection into the unknown Wild, not for my security or satisfaction but for the sake of what's more than me, a reality I can't ever fully grasp. It calls for my total trust and devotion, as well as practiced skills in playing my instrument in the key of Soul in ordinary situations. Soul's music calls for getting good at decisions in daily life, not for winning but to continue the play of the infinite game, recognizing the other as separate from my needs and wants, as someone to be discovered, cared for and supported in flourishing, as "Thou."

Play it with Soul

I've written of Soul as *"a present, felt process of living beyond, yet through, the self, in the realization and creation of beauty and goodness in the world, inspired and guided by love, excellence and the freedom of play."*[1] When we take life seriously, with integrity, without being ponderous, continually creating fresh rhythms and motifs, we can play our soundtrack passionately with Soul. This music is potential every moment from every human mind-body, infused with Soul. It's a choice to open to transcendence instead of music that's stays safely within the dimension of the self.

The music creates a dance of Soul with the self in what I do every day. With integrity, I could play the instrument of body, mind and Soul as part of the continual creative process of nature, from the trillions of cells in my body and the separate bodies of others, to the spectacular flow of energies evolving in lives, celestial formations, civilizations, systems that are wild and beautiful, and are a part of me. In the process, I change. My instrument can become better and better. I learn to freely play from my heart and mind with passion, to draw from Soul the energies and melodies that allow me to live at my highest level,

---

[1]   *Discovering Soul: Beauty, Virtue and Play in the Artwork of Being,* p. 7

true to reality, as a participant in the symphony of the universe, which continually invites me to enact meanings throughout life.

When the source of my music of emotion is Soul, I can be disciplined yet playful in my behavior, improvising daily choices toward a Personal Myth of my highest potential, even if I get into a few messes, mistakes and failures. Body and mind swing in sync. The music isn't played with perfect knowledge or skill. It's not about heroic outcomes or impressing anyone. It's allowing my body and mind to move me to enact a deeper level of meaning in my relationships with others, the world and myself, forming a Personal Myth of moving beyond the self through the self, within the *Mysterium tremendum et fascinans* of the Holy.

The music of Soul isn't played by superheroes. It isn't a soundtrack for sensational experiences. That's why Hollywood rarely gets it right. The music of Soul can be played badly until our practice and freedom allow us to play it very well, to be moved by its creative pulse and perhaps allow others to be moved from how we play it. Its sacred music has played through the ages. It is played in ordinary choices to act by ordinary people as well as extraordinary actions called for by extraordinary situations and callings.

The music of Soul is non-sectarian, non-dogmatic. It plays what's beyond the range of ego or self. It inspires songs of loving life and aspiring to give and receive love. One of the clearest examples of this music is given by Shirli Gilbert in a book about places where people were subjected to extreme degradation, torture and evil. From *Music in the Holocaust*, she gives this excerpt of an account by Elisabeth Lichtenstein, who "recalled the scenario that followed the shaving and tattooing of her newly arrived group" in Auschwitz:

> All the women were in a state of complete exhaustion and at the end of their nervous strength. Some were standing around apathetically, some were screaming and laughing hysterically, many squabbled and fought among themselves. There were also those that sang. A neighbour who had accompanied me from Szered and knew that I was a music-lover and that I had a good voice, said that I should sing something, so that we would not all go mad. I naturally did not have the courage to sing, but as the time dragged on and we had already been standing there waiting for hours, I began to sing the Ave Maria. I did not know the text, I sang only the melody. While I sang, it became quiet in the hall, those who were screaming fell silent, those who were fighting stopped.[2]

Notice how her song (even without words) was exactly right for the occasion, how she didn't know what to do, but was supported by her companion, who fortunately knew what to do. The music of Soul isn't a music of dominating power or of singular heroes. It is a music that comes from meanings forged, with others, in the highest stakes of humanity. It is a music that plays at times that may not be stable, that may be under the most trying circumstances, when one realizes this life isn't just for self-satisfaction and when we're called upon to give beyond what we think we're capable of giving.

---

[2]   Shirli Gilbert, *Music in the Holocaust: Confronting Life in the Nazi Ghettos and Camps* (Oxford: Oxford University Press, 2005), p. 149

But the music of Soul takes place also in less trying times and circumstances. It takes place every day in how a home may be created with meaning and love, how a couple's romance is tested and can go astray, then be recovered to go beyond what's in it for each partner, how love becomes a continually renewed dance of eros in the reality of transcendence, with a soundtrack playing from beyond the self.

Living by the music of Soul isn't overcoming the physical, the carnal, the pleasurable. To believe that transcendence is beyond the body would be to ignore the miraculous Being of matter, of bodies, of how we're called to engage our mind-bodies in reality, not in some imagined non-physical realm, nor in self-deception. To relate to others as "Thou" rather than objects to be used or manipulated does not mean to deny our bodies' biological requirements and pleasures. It's a matter of how deeply we want to enjoy the music of experience. To learn and practice the sacred music of Soul is to choose actions that transcend self through the self. Each day presents choices of how we affect others and ourselves, of the possibilities of creating life enhancing or life degrading effects, of creating the music of love, reverence, joy, including the exuberance of achievements, the fun of playing, the pleasure of orgasm, the pain of sacrifice and loss.

Life can be trying, even brutal. What level of music we cultivate in ourselves can allow commitment to excellence over mediocrity, being loving instead of narcissistic, taking on adversity v. staying a victim. It is the experience of Creative Energy flowing out in moral goodness and creativity. We don't learn to play such music on our own. We learn and unlearn from family and others during childhood. As we grow up, we become responsible for choosing our sources of learning. We aren't limited by the Mythology of our culture, but only by our selves. We form Personal Myths that bring our unique potential, meanings and energies into the world in certain styles. We can try to hide our true Myths from others and ourselves. But my Personal Myth is revealed in what I do, how I live this mystery of life.

The sacred music of Soul can be felt and played most deeply after long practice in daily choices, risks, confusion, mistakes and aspirations. You may create a soundtrack of integrity by decisions made and learned from in many situations. You may love at times without even fully knowing why you love. You will still be flawed and egocentric, but you'll acknowledge this and learn to overcome your self's harmful tendencies, to ask for and give forgiveness. Your soundtrack will be uniquely composed, not conforming to what you're told to play, in gradually expanding actions throughout life.

An uncanonized radical of the Soul

For many centuries, the human species was literally the center of the universe. Who knows for how long back? Since well before Aristotle said so in the 4th century BC, following centuries of Greek philosophers before him and what we can see with our own eyes.

This cosmology prevailed through the Middle Ages and beyond:

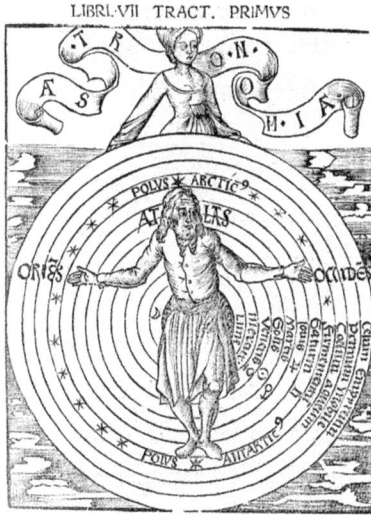

But somehow this common sense cosmology would be questioned well before modern science was born. A monk in a monastery in Naples in the late 1500's allowed his curiosity, love of learning and reverence to open his mind to the universe as being more marvelous and divine than the teachings of the philosophers, the Church and the powers that be. His name was Giordano Bruno.

Of course, we don't know exactly what was going on in his thinking. We only know from his writings and the recorded history of his actions. What's certain is that he refused to conform. Somehow, in a monastery in Naples, he latched onto books that were forbidden. He questioned the theology, philosophy and actual authority that prevailed, for the sake of rationality, infinity, and divinity. From books he found exploring the beginnings of science and his opening to the heavenly bodies blazing as stars, he allowed his mind to open to the universe, to explode the human centered model, studying and teaching the dynamism of the universe, concluding there must be innumerable planetary systems, made of matter like our bodies, dancing around their fiery suns. Other planets, other suns? This was directly contradicting the dominant religious beliefs and imagination of his time, which placed earth at the center of the universe. Bruno went beyond his teachers, his religion and his culture to decenter humanity and to consider a revolutionary realism of divinity. With his poetic imagination, his reverent intelligence, his intuition and courage, he passionately taught, not only that the stars in the sky were shining suns with worlds like earth, but that "divinity is identified with Being, which is matter itself, producer of all forms, as well as being recognizable in *interiore hominis* (inside man himself)."[3]

There was no organized institution or group that publicly supported Bruno. There was no gain in stature or survival for the stands he took against the status quo. Instead of reward, he faced the threat of being put to death as a heretic. So, he got out of the monastery and out of town. He eventually had to leave the country, wound up in Elizabethan England, where he would disrupt their status quo. England, France, Germany and Italy wouldn't tolerate expressions of truths he wouldn't keep quiet about. He would not conform to the lies of religion, he would not give up his integrity through eight years of trial and torture by the Roman Inquisition. For his passionately speaking, Bruno's tongue was split with an iron spike shoved through his lower jaw and he was burned alive on a public square in Rome on February 17, 1600.

---

[3]   *Giordano Bruno: Philosopher of the Renaissance*, edited by Hilary Gatti, Taylor & Francis Group, 2018 p 9

He had written a lot, often in Latin poetry. The pages were illustrated with images, often etched by himself in the woodcuttings. He allowed a passion for what would become science to be infused with images, rhythms and music of verse. While he was drawn to marvel at and understand the mathematical structures of existence, he found the source of numbers to be the divinity of Being. He used the word "God," as there was no other available to him, but relied on his experience of reality, prior teachers like Copernicus, and his realizations of the complex, living unity of nature as beyond human centered needs, fears or powers.

Bruno is an extraordinary manifestation of the human dimension of Soul. His heroic, passionate life of courage and integrity sets a standard that seems impossible to reach. The Catholic Church never allowed much recognition of him over the centuries. Few students, at least in America, are ever exposed to him in any classes. He dared to continue learning and living for noble stakes, enduring the cost of years of torture, imprisonment and being publicly burned alive. His dramatic journey is a noble music, that of the universe. His music played in his solitary study and writing, in his public sharing with many who loved his intelligent explorations, in the passionate stands he took, in his refusals to surrender to the Inquisition. The music played beyond his torture and horrible death by fire.

The meaning of Bruno's life for the ordinary person isn't that you must challenge or overturn an entire culture's belief system, that you must endure martyrdom. I believe his meaning is that each of us can examine beliefs and everyday actions instilled in us by our culture, family and history, and choose not to ever surrender truth, goodness and love in order to conform or to be protected by deceit. The music of Bruno's journey consists of noble movements of the costly grandeur of living for the highest life purposes, opening to the universe that calls to us, while accepting the imperfections and confusion of ourselves and others. Giordano Bruno was not perfect, he was no saint. He undoubtedly had doubts and made mistakes. His gift to us through the ages, especially his ultimate courage, was itself a gift to him by the divinity of Being.

Music continually created, revised, developed

It's worth exploring and learning different styles of the music of emotion—from operatic drama to pop to down home stomp. It's worth experimenting with the range of our emotional capacities. We can play a composed program of passion, in which we make plans that would generate different qualities (such as reflective, exciting, engaging, uplifting) that inspire and harmonize us into our highest life purposes and practices. We can use our energies and behaviors to create expressions and responses to life (ranging from the funky to the solemn) and to become interesting improvisors. We can allow ourselves to consciously create complex performances of our lives with tempos like allegro, scherzo, and adagio. We can join in playing blues with people who can connect with that experience. We can decide what kinds of energy and expressions of emotion we'll bring into the world. Or we can drift and conform to what we're told to think and do, to keep comfortable and self-satisfied.

The notes of our lives are played each moment. They absorb and contribute to what is around us, either by expressing or inhibiting the music of emotion we play. The notes flow into each other, affecting what is continually created. The notes can create a music through phases, either planned or spontaneously. Though there is tragic music being played right now somewhere in the world and we aren't aware of those suffering through it, their tragedy is part of all of our lives. There are individuals inspired now to play the music of emotion magnificently. Though we may not know them, they are contributing to the music of us and the whole. They need not think of their acts as magnificent or their emotion as music. What matters is the actions of each of us. Each of us is creating. We can be aware of and choose what we create and contribute.

If we open to emotion as music happening through us, we can learn how to transform emotional noise, jolts and numbing into notes of meaning that compose life purposes that guide us toward fulfilling our potential while participating in the transcendent symphony of the whole. We can learn how to compose for meanings beyond our biological selves though the music is played through our biology. There isn't a fixed sheet of notes to follow throughout life. We learn the music we most want to play from our lifetime of learning and experiences that can be, at various times, anguished, humbling and self-compassionate.

Emotion's music from within and around us affects our senses, our flesh and the network of flows within our flesh while cognitive operations are interpreting and imagining. The body and mind never stop playing this experience, like instruments playing a continual flow of shifting tones. We can learn to play in harmony or in opposition to the music continually playing around us. We can express our unique creativity and meanings through how we live and share our unique destinies.

We can become curious about how we pattern and organize our participation in the world. We can break through and free ourselves from patterns that seem locked in. We can learn from many sources: people who live meaningfully; artistic expressions; traditions and teachings that guide or inspire human excellence; the experiments and feedback of what we choose to do each day. The process can be liberating and joyful. It can also involve struggles, suffering and difficult commitments. We are tested by fear, loss, a sense of helplessness and doubt, and hopefully we find inspirations and practices to live for purposes beyond our need for protection and survival.

Soul's music isn't elevated above the limitations of the mind-body. It is played in the ordinary daily round of our lives, which at times can feel dull, achy, confused, fearful. It would be a big advantage if one could simply tune into the music of Soul from one true source, like a religion or other shared belief system. I suspect that Giordano Bruno originally became a monk because of how he responded to the devotional practices and structure, as well as the reverent, beautiful tones of the sacred. However, his life and tragic torture and death stand as a revelation that living from the Soul can be with great costs. A person has the capacity to go beyond the safe paths of following dogmas, authorities and social norms. Each individual can follow the light of the universe, the passion of the heart and play the music of truth, beauty, integrity and the thrilling goodness of connection to divine Being.

Why do the divine, the sacred and even Being have to be considered as some realm or entity or state beyond the human and beyond change? Deities are portrayed as invulnerable to the human or any limitations, beyond mortality and pain, with intimations of perfection and omnipotence. I say "Enough of that!" I want to unmask those pretentions. Let the divine or enlightened be as imperfect, continually changing, conflicting, mistaken and multiple as everyone and everything else. Let the gods come down to earth, share their hopes, fears, foolishness and joy. Let us learn from each other, dance to music that is unique to each of us, allowing each to strive toward fulfillment. Let us stay on earth, exploring scientifically and aesthetically, while leaping beyond trying to define or fully explain reality. Let us free our understanding of beings and Being from identities that would make them safely understood and controllable. We are indivisible from a divinity of ceaseless waves of dynamic change, interpenetrating multiplicities, a creative movement that's beautiful and mysterious. Rather than trying to pin down reality into definitions, we can step into the vibrant tones, harmonies and dissonances of what's sacred and Wild. We can do this with grace, spontaneity and skills, playing emotion's continuous music.

APPENDIX:
KEYS TO PRACTICE YOUR MUSIC

T HIS has not really been a self-help book. I don't intend to write one. However, I'll add on here some of the handouts I've used in my counseling practice to offer guides that may help. They aren't a complete set. They may not help you, for each individual plays her or his music of emotion in a unique style. I offer them for you to try out in practicing on your instrument and to help in the sometimes messy performances of life.

SOURCES OF MUSIC OF EMOTION, ACTION, WISDOM

HIDDEN VULNERABILITIES: emotional pains, wounds, fears, fearful or painful memories, often suppressed

- *Fears* – fortissimo shocks and strains of reacting to or anticipating threats
- Outcries of *inner wounds* from past trauma, abuse and hurt
- Undercurrents from *abandonment, rejection and early denial of love*
- The blues of *loneliness*
- Tones of *powerlessness or helplessness* fueled by beliefs and memories
- Recurrent themes of *guilt and shame*
- Dirges of *grief and loss*
- Self-defeating songs of *self-denigration or regrets*
- Recurrent themes of *inadequacy, inferiority*
- *Disorganized, out of control* noise

SELF-PROTECTIVE FORCES: can be automatically triggered, usually without intention, often without awareness, to protect me from experiencing those vulnerabilities by efforts to control, dominate, escape, be aggressive or admired:

ESCAPISM: Siren songs drawing me away or into fantasies:

- Avoiding experiences, people, responsibilities, risks, opportunities

- Addictions (substances, gaming, shopping, sex, gambling, eating, etc.)
- Obsessions and compulsions
- Suicide and self-injury
- Withdrawal (from others, the world)
- Pessimism
- Numbing or shutting down
- Paranoia
- Fantasy in place of reality

I MUST CONTROL: Tonalities of control, domination, criticism:
- Overly Controlling/Calculating/Managing
- Harsh mental pushing, criticizing, judging of myself or others

FIGHTING SONGS: played forcefully or intensely:
- Fierce blares of aggression, intimidation
- Angry, even abusive, acting out (verbal, physical, relational)
- Violence
- Hypervigilant, Survivalist reactions

EGO TUNES: attempts to compensate for, rise above or protect from vulnerability:
- Performing to be admired, #1, the hero, the smart one
- Perfectionism
- High-charged performance/Ruthless competition

- Overselling or proving how great I am/Undervaluing or finding fault with others
- Comic operas of blinding self-regard

CENTERED IMPROVISATIONS: I open to, recognize, accept and care for my vulnerabilities and protective forces. I can transform their energies by focused playing of:
- Curious, exploratory openings and overtures to what's within me
- Compassionate forgiveness of others and myself
- Creative, imaginative solos or polyphonies and jam sessions with others
- Embodied hymns of courage for the good
- Deep harmonies of love and connection (to myself & others)
- Rondos of enacting virtues, purposes, leadership
- Free, passionate playing of radical responsibility

SOUL'S TRANSCENDING FLOWS: music that arises from the boundless potential of my living Myth, which allows the living, embodied dimension of Soul to flow through and from me as:
- Luminous, felt presence and energy of love
- Soulful spirituals lifting me beyond self-interest
- Transcendent hymns of beauty and goodness in the world
- Devotional works of reverence, sacrifice and play beyond myself
- Rhythms of enacting my open potential in the now

Rising above Pre-Adult/Primitive levels

Emotion is the soundtrack of the body's energy and sensations playing a live music of mind-body according to how I interpret every moment—i.e., how I'm composing my music of emotion. I can compose this music from a higher level of my mind—the Adult Mind—but the music includes and may get stuck at a Pre-Adult or Primitive Level.

When my body and mind are dominated by the Pre-Adult or Primitive levels, I may play music of helplessness, defensiveness, blaming, escape, various melodies of misery. There are ways to lift the music to aspire to the music of love, beauty, and a flourishing life. To lift my music to this aspiration, I can play certain Keys to transform my energy and thinking, to participate in a continual loving symphony of life with others and the universe. When I fall from this level, I can fall into the belief (consciously or unconsciously) that life's happening to me as a victim, rather than by me and through me.

My Soundtrack Plays By and Through Me Participating in a Loving Symphony

-----

My Soundtrack is Pulled Down to Pre-Adult/Primitive Rhythms and Lyrics

The following 9 Keys can provide direction and energy to lift the music of my emotion to play soundtracks of meaningful, loving creativity and beauty.

9 Keys to Elevate My Music

RECAP LOVE
Radical Responsibility
Excellence
Curiosity
Accept yourself unconditionally
Play

Love
Optimism
Vibrancy
Every person and situation is an ally

1. Radical Responsibility

Adult Level:

I choose to take full **responsibility** for the choices of my life, and my physical, emotional and mental wellbeing, including **reaching out for help** in all these areas, **connecting with inspiration.**

Primitive/Pre-Adult Level:

I blame others and/or my past for my well-being. I can fall into the role of victim (blaming, powerless), villain (I'm no good or not good enough) or superhero (unreasonably rescue others).

2. Excellence

<u>Adult Level:</u>
I choose to aspire to my **highest potential,** using and balancing my time and energy to do everything well, inspired, at the level of my personal **excellence**, according to reasonable standards.

<u>Primitive/Pre-Adult Level:</u>
I give in to mediocrity and/or resentment about present or past circumstances, denying inspiration, with unreasonable standards (too high or low) for myself or others.

3. Curiosity

<u>Adult Level:</u>
I choose to grow in **self-awareness, open-mindedness and curiosity** as a path to effective living, every interaction as an opportunity to learn. I can question my thoughts, beliefs and stories, to learn.

<u>Primitive/Pre-Adult Level:</u>
I see things my way, insist on my way. I may be defensive especially because I am RIGHT, don't need to be open to views and interpretations that don't follow my own.

4. Accept yourself unconditionally

Adult Level:

I accept myself **unconditionally**. I choose **support and compassion to myself** in all my words, thoughts and acts, allowing flaws, imperfection, fear, etc., with humility and self-respect.

Primitive/Pre-Adult Level:

I withhold kindness, compassion and all that new age crap for myself. I'll give my inner drill sergeant free rein to be harsh and punishing.

5. Play

Adult Level:

I choose to create a life of **play, life as an adventure**, letting life **unfold in meanings I co-create**, detaching from external judgments or rewards, summoning **humor** to help.

Primitive/Pre-Adult Level:

I judge my life as win/loss, ratings of performance, in grueling competitions or measurements.

6. Love

Adult Level:

I choose to give unconditional love in close relationships, to help each other become the best version of ourselves. I appropriately give in family, friend and community relations. I'll interact with others **respectfully, positively, with patience and compassion for our mutual weaknesses.**

Primitive/Pre-Adult Level:
I can use people for what's in it for me, disregarding others' dignity and needs. I can also submit to unhealthy, inappropriate behaviors to keep relationships.

7. Optimism

Adult Level:
I choose to bring **positive emotional energy** to adversity, and to **realistic, energetic optimism** for the present and the future, based on the good.

Primitive/Pre-Adult Level:
I can give in to pessimism, assuming bad outcomes and bad people in most situations, excusing myself from giving positive energy.

8. Vibrancy

Adult Level:
I commit to **robust effort** for positive goals & practices for a **vibrant body and mind**, including optimal sleep, physical exercise, nutrition, learning.

Primitive/Pre-Adult Level:
I can disregard and let go of the efforts needed for a healthy, vibrant body and mind.

9. Every Person and Situation is an Ally

Adult Level:

I choose to see all people and circumstances as **allies** that are here to help me learn the most important things for my growth.

Primitive/Pre-Adult Level:

I see other people and circumstances as obstacles to getting what I most want.

ADULT MIND	PRIMITIVE or PRE-ADULT MIND
Mature, complex abilities for: self-control; long-term perspective; tolerate uncertainty & ambiguity; self-transcending experiences and values, esp. love, beauty, integrity, morality	Survival appetites & urges for food, sex, pleasure, without morality; aggression; escape; Me-centered; manipulative
Deeply imagining, playing at and pursuing meaningful goals	Little control: survival requires intense, fast reactions. Easily triggered when stressed.
Reality-testing: responsible judgments & perceptions; assess and organize information according to education, experience and values	Generates alarms, quick reactions, strong sensations and expressions; cf. smoke alarm
Honest awareness of biases, like confirmation bias, self-centered perspective, prejudices	Fear system: always scanning environment for threats, over-interprets these; negative judgments of everything to protect self, possessions & close relations
Interprets and improvises situations for beauty, vibrancy, morality & depth of meanings	Interferes w/ reality-testing, doesn't separate reality from beliefs, habitual patterns
Forms and develops values, meanings, life purpose beyond survival & self-centeredness	Fundamentally set in childhood patterns which Pre-Adult habits develop from, stay with us
Care for vulnerabilities of oneself & others	Childhood or primitive feelings, beliefs, behaviors can be triggered in similar circumstances or experiences later in life
Not "online" much 1st 20 years of life	
Can assess, override, limit and control Primitive and Pre-Adult thoughts, urges, actions, potential for immoral & destructive acts	Self-centered, self-satisfying, self-validating
Makes plans and strategies to care for oneself and others, self-improve	Behaviors: dominating; predatory; escapist/ avoidant; violent; reactaholic; try to control others; demand certainty; dependent; addictive
Living beyond just survival: engagement & commitment for the good, the beautiful, justice	Thinking & expressing: blame; denial; negative beliefs & interpretations; craves approval, superiority; can feel threatened easily; distrustful; preaching; victim mode; devaluing and demeaning others; resentment; helplessness
Creativity: from problem solving to artistic	
Mistakes, bad decisions are learned from rather than shamed, obsessed over	Intensity of pattern narrows perceptions & consideration of others, leading to insistent "need", sense of entitlement. Cooperating or contributing can feel like submitting.
Pain motivates correcting, healing, learning, repairing, improving	

Elevating My Music By:

Realistic, energetic optimism for set-backs & obstacles

Unconditionally accepting myself, including all vulnerabilities, flaws, self-protection

Play: life as adventure, unfolding in meanings I co-create

Curiosity, able to question my thoughts, beliefs, stories

Feeling life happen by me & through me

Radical responsibility—for my choices and well-being, let go of blaming myself & others

Something greater than me can happen through me: love, wonder, joy, beauty

Releasing myself into personal excellence

Pulled Down to Pre-Adult/Primitive Rhythms and Lyrics By:

Falling into patterns or addictions to self-protect or escape

Getting stuck or self-defeating by some old, familiar music, stories, identities

Reacting to triggered vulnerabilities by withdrawal, escape, or aggression

Victim consciousness: life happens to me, I just survive

Being right: my way or the highway

Denial, distortions of reality to defend myself

Assuming bad outcomes, bad people

Centering Lyrics

I can handle these sensations.

This feeling isn't comfortable or pleasant, but I can accept it.

This isn't an emergency. It's OK to think slowly about what I need to do.

This is an opportunity for me to learn to cope with my fears.

I deserve to feel OK now.

I can take all the time I need in order to let go and relax.

Fighting and resisting this isn't going to help—so I'll just let it pass.

I don't need these thoughts—I can choose to think differently.

Time to shake it off. I'm not going to be frightened off or lose control.

This is going to work out, even if not as originally planned.

What small act of goodness, beauty, or kindness can I make here?

Feeling the Music of Excellence

When you step into **meaning that's greater than getting by, security, self-satisfaction, into what's greater than yourself**, you step off the illusion of everything being for you. You summon your natural and trained gifts to give and receive from your highest potential. You may not know exactly what'll happen, but allow for many possibilities.

Emotion is going on continually—from the background of your body and mind to consciously creative energies. Rather than identify them with your usual words for emotions, I suggest you relate to the feelings as a music playing live in you, playing the soundtrack to the life you're living and aspiring to live.

Excellence is your personal experience of acting toward your full potential. It's neither a rating nor a rule. **It's a way to live the adventure of your life.** Taking stands and living for what's morally good and profoundly beautiful need not be dramatic, need not even be noticed by anyone else. It will be felt as the soundtrack of living, as music of your excellence.

Imagine what you'd be feeling, doing, accomplishing when living your highest potential:

1. Imagine you're achieving your highest potential of body and mind in what you're doing and experiencing—with your thinking, emotional and physical energy, and skills.

2. What is the purpose of your actions?

3. What effects may your action have on yourself, others around you, the world?

4. Are your purposes and effects trivial, selfish, even harmful, or are they taking part in creating beautiful experiences for yourself, others, and the world?

ABOUT THE AUTHOR

Ron Biela has practiced psychotherapy/counseling for 25 years as a licensed clinical social worker (LCSW), then as a life coach in Denver and Boulder, Colorado, developing and applying innovative approaches, such as: Post Traumatic Growth; Beyond Mental Toughness (resilience); Imagine-Play-Pursue (goals); Dare to Play for Noble Stakes (virtues). For much of his career, he clinically supervised and trained therapists and interns. Other education and experience has included assembly line work and fork lift driving in factories, practicing law, and studying literature and philosophy.

He is the author of *Discovering Soul: Beauty, Virtue and Play in the Artwork of Being*.

www.ingramcontent.com/pod-product-compliance
Lightning Source LLC
Chambersburg PA
CBHW060451030426
42337CB00015B/1549